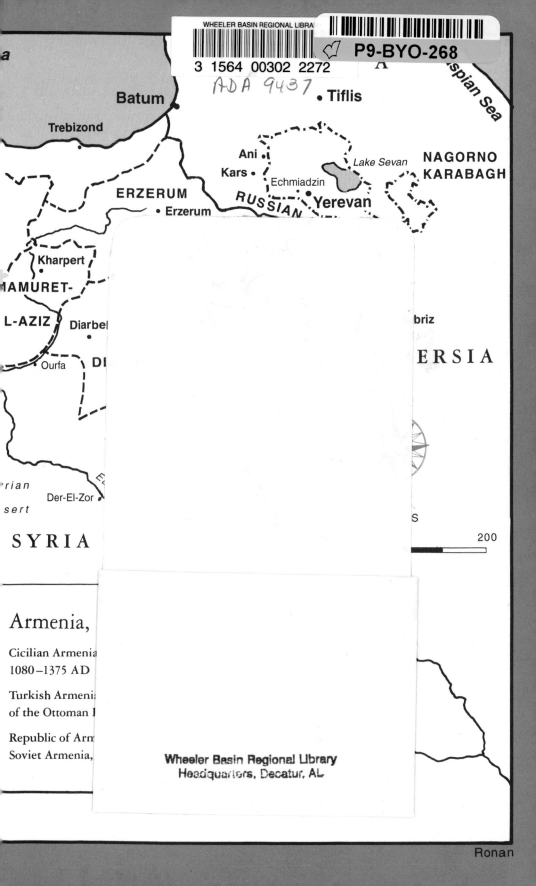

WHEELER BASIN REGIONAL LIBRA

P9-BYO-268

3 1564 00302 2272

ADA 9437

Batum

Trebizond

Ani

Kars

ERZERUM

Erzerum

RUSSIAN

Tiflis

Echmiadzin

Lake Sevan

Yerevan

spian Sea

NAGORNO
KARABAGH

Kharpert

MAMURET-

L-AZIZ   Diarbel

DI

Ourfa

rian

sert   Der-El-Zor

SYRIA

briz

ERSIA

200

Armenia,

Cicilian Armenia
1080–1375 AD

Turkish Armeni:
of the Ottoman I

Republic of Arm
Soviet Armenia,

Wheeler Basin Regional Library
Headquarters, Decatur, AL

Ronan

BLACK
DOG
OF
FATE

ALSO BY PETER BALAKIAN

Poetry

Father Fisheye

Sad Days of Light

Reply from Wilderness Island

Dyer's Thistle

*Bloody News from My Friend,
by Siamanto*
(Translated by Peter Balakian
and Nevart Yaghlian)

Prose

Theodore Roethke's Far Field

Balakian

BLACK DOG *of* FATE

A MEMOIR

PETER BALAKIAN

BasicBooks
A Division of HarperCollins*Publishers*

Wheeler Basin Regional Library
Headquarters, Decatur, Ala.

Copyright © 1997 by Peter Balakian.

Published by BasicBooks,
A Division of HarperCollins Publishers, Inc.

All rights reserved. Printed in the United States of America. No part of this book may be used in any manner whatsoever without written permission except in the case of brief quotations embodied in critical articles and reviews. For information, address BasicBooks, 10 East 53rd Street, New York, NY 10022-5299.

FIRST EDITION

Designed by Laura Lindgren

Library of Congress Cataloging-in-Publication Data
Balakian, Peter, 1951–
    Black dog of fate : a memoir / Peter Balakian. – 1st ed.
      p. cm.
    Includes index.
    ISBN 0-465-00704-X
    1. Balakian, Peter, 1951–   –Family. 2. Armenian massacres survivors–United States–Biography. 3. Poets, American–20th century–Family relationships. 4. Armenian Americans–New Jersey–Biography. 5. Armenian massacres, 1915–1923. I. Title.
PS3552.A443Z464   1997
811'.54–dc21
[B]   96-53351

97 98 99 00 01 XX/XX 10 9 8 7 6 5 4 3 2 1

To my children
Sophia Ann and James Gerard

CONTENTS

MY MOTHER'S FAMILY

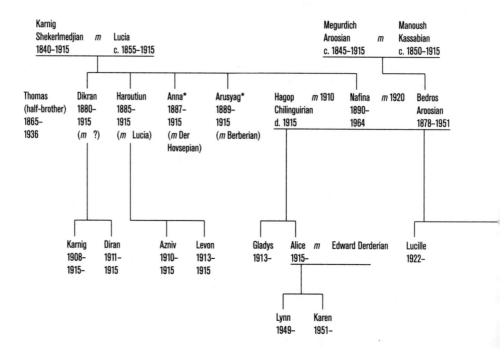

* The husbands and children of Anna and Arusyag (names and ages unknown) were also killed in 1915.

** Krikor and Narthui were two of five Balakian siblings.

*** Koharig Panosyan was the eldest of seven siblings. Diran Balakian (the eldest of four siblings) was her first cousin, once removed.

MY FATHER'S FAMILY

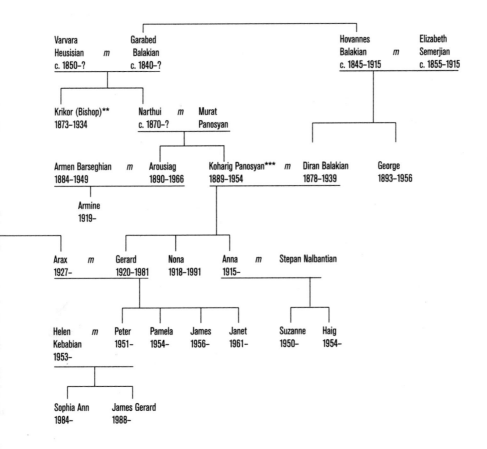

Varvara Heusisian c. 1850–? *m* Garabed Balakian c. 1840–?

Hovannes Balakian c. 1845–1915 *m* Elizabeth Semerjian c. 1855–1915

Krikor (Bishop)** 1873–1934

Narthui c. 1870–? *m* Murat Panosyan

Armen Barseghian 1884–1949 *m* Arousiag 1890–1966

Koharig Panosyan*** 1889–1954 *m* Diran Balakian 1878–1939

George 1893–1956

Armine 1919–

Arax 1927– *m* Gerard 1920–1981

Nona 1918–1991

Anna 1915– *m* Stepan Nalbantian

Helen Kebabian 1953– *m* Peter 1951–

Pamela 1954–

James 1956–

Janet 1961–

Suzanne 1950–

Haig 1954–

Sophia Ann 1984–

James Gerard 1988–

BLACK
DOG
OF
FATE

PART I

GRANDMOTHER

BLACK DOG OF FATE

I CARRY AN IMAGE WITH ME, LIKE A KODAK SNAPSHOT FROM 1960 WHEN the colors still looked gooey under the gloss. It's a picture of my maternal grandmother, Nafina (an Armenian version of Athena) Aroosian, and her daughters, Aunt Gladys and Aunt Lucille, walking up our flagstone path. Behind them, out of focus, a Chevy Biscayne, ice-cream white, with thick chrome tapering to the back fender. The tops of the turquoise-colored seats glare in the noon sun. It's Sunday, after church, and everyone is out. There's a hardball game going on in the cul-de-sac at the end of the block. Kids run through the spray of a sprinkler, darting between hedges of newly planted hemlocks.

My grandmother walks ahead of my aunts, with her aluminum cane, the one she brought home from the hospital after she broke her hip. She is dressed in navy or beige. A brooch or a jewel pinned near her collar. Pearls around her neck. A flowered scarf. She never grayed, so her hair is chestnut brown, braided in a bun studded with colored stones. My aunts follow behind. Their hair is coifed like Jackie Kennedy's. Every Saturday morning my aunts and my mother have their hair done. Every Sunday at dinner, conversation inevitably turns to the merits and flaws of Cilo, Rudy, Luigi, Alan. One hairdresser cut better. One styled better. One was more *avanti* or European. On Sunday their hair smelled of perfume. My aunts are dressed in white or pale-blue linen suits. Silk blouses, silk scarves. They wear pearls, gold earrings, and gold bracelets; the sun glints off them as they walk toward the house. Neighbors in tee shirts push power mowers, and everywhere machines are buzzing. Along the flagstone walk is a black Schwinn, a red Huffy, a go-cart made out of a milk crate, some bats and balls, scattered.

When my brother, sister, and I would see the white Biscayne pull into the driveway we knew our playing was over. We weren't happy about it, but we would walk dutifully to the house.

Every Sunday it's the same. Our extended Armenian family sitting around the dining room table in winter or out on the patio in summer for a full afternoon and more, and my grandmother quietly watching. Perhaps the crisscross of voices, the endless high-pitched exchange, and the chaos of conversation is too much for her. She seems detached, and because of her dentures, eats slowly. If we have corn on the cob, my mother slices the kernels off for her; if, God forbid, the kebab is not tender, my mother cuts her portion in small pieces. Through her thick lenses she looks serious. And sometimes I stare at the dark, wrinkled half-moons beneath her eyes.

After dinner she is always affectionate with me, often brushing my hair with her hand, which makes me slightly uncomfortable—especially if my friends are there—and then I try to ward her off with mental telepathy. But she hovers around me, forever asking how I am and what I want. She keeps repeating an Armenian word, *eench*. It means how or what, and is fraught with solicitousness, concern, anxiousness; and if you add all these things up in Armenian, it means love. *Eench. Eench. Eench-eh:* What's the matter, what is it, are you OK? *Eench gooz-es:* What do you want? *Eench gooz-es oud-es:* What do you want to eat? *Eench, eench, eench. Eench* is always followed up with *yavrey,* her vernacular for the Turkish word *yavros,* which means my little one or beloved, or *hokeet seerem,* which means let me love your soul. As she runs her hands along my shoulders, she tells me I'm as skinny as an unfed bird. Because I feel a bond of affection I can't explain, I let her continue, but if anyone else in the family begins *eench*-ing me I lip back sullenly, "Get outta here."

My grandmother's big brown eyes keep watching me intensely. I am Peter, *Bedros* in Armenian, named after her second husband, who went into a coma from a cerebral hemorrhage about the week I was conceived and who died without regaining consciousness about three months before I was born. I am the eldest grandchild east of Fresno, California, the first male of the next generation, a filial position that in our Near Eastern culture comes with patriarchal status. Although I did not understand then what the presence of a new generation meant for a culture that had been nearly expunged from the planet only forty-five years earlier, I felt the strange doting power of the word *eench*. It often unnerved me, making me feel as if something were wrong, or would be wrong. Was I sick? Was I dying of some secret disease my elders knew about and were keeping from me? Invariably, after I was *eench*-ed to death, my grandmother would lean over and kiss the fallen ski-jump of my crew cut where it spilled onto my forehead, say something even more elaborate in Armenian, compelling me to beat a track out of that stuffy room of oriental objects for the TV room and the Yankees on channel 11.

My sisters, Pam and Jan, my brother, Jim, and I never learned Armenian. In Tenafly, New Jersey, in 1960, who would want to know Armenian, a language spoken by an ancient Near Eastern people who lived half a globe away and were now part of the Soviet Union? My parents spoke Armenian when they wanted to communicate privately or when they were in public places and needed to discuss the price of veal or the amount to tip; confident that the waiter wouldn't know their language, once in a while they were wrong. Alarmed, my mother would turn to my father: "I think the waiter speaks Armenian." The little Armenian I knew was from church and from my grandmother, words and phrases mingled with English around the house: *ahno-tee-es? shad lav, khent, gatig, dok-ess? Khegj-uh, moog, paubig*: Are you hungry? very well, crazy, a little milk, are you hot? poor guy, mouse, barefoot.

I visited my grandmother in East Orange once a month. On Friday afternoons, my mother drove me south from Teaneck. The green signs on the new Garden State Parkway bright with white numbers, and the names – Irvington, Nutley, Bloomfield – exhilarating. East Orange in 1958 was another country to me. Wide boulevards divided by islands of maples and beeches, lined by old-fashioned street lamps and large Victorian houses that looked haunted with their turrets and gables and mansard roofs of gray and maroon slate.

My grandmother lived in an old brick garden apartment with Aunt Gladys and Aunt Lucille. The apartments were situated around a large courtyard of well-kept lawn and hedges of rhododendrons. The windows had leaded panes; the window boxes, red and white geraniums. It was mysterious and exotic after the suburban houses of Teaneck. When my mother closed the door at the bottom of the stairs of my grandmother's apartment, I felt free of my brother Jim and my sister Pam, who were back in the cluttered playroom in Teaneck. I sat at the big mahogany table in the dining room in front of a plate of hot dolma, a big dish of yogurt, some lemon wedges, a basket of Arnold dinner rolls, and a green bottle of 7-Up that stood by itself without a tumbler, because my grandmother knew I liked to drink from the bottle. Now we had the day to ourselves until my aunts came home from their jobs in the city.

On those Friday afternoons I would help my grandmother bake. Leaning over the counter in my Oxford button-down, white chinos, and scuffed bucks, it always flashed through my mind that if they saw me in the kitchen with my grandmother, let alone baking some Armenian thing called *choereg*, my Little League friends would think me a hopeless sissy – so I kept my maroon baseball cap on as a way of safeguarding my masculinity. Attentive to my baseball cap ritual, my grandmother would say, "Let's see your stance," and immediately I would go into a severe, Hector Lopez – like crouch, taking a couple of swings with my invisible bat until she nodded with approval, as if to say, See, you're OK; now let's bake.

It was a 1940s kitchen with long white cabinets, a white enameled sink, red speckled linoleum cracking at the seams, and a coiled, buzzing fluorescent light on the ceiling. The dingy light and bright sun streaming through the small rectangular window over the sink gave the room a strange hue. The cabinet I always opened by climbing the second step of the footstool released an earthy, sweet fragrance. Stacks of McCormick tins, brown bags tied off with rubber bands, squat jars. On the bottom shelf were bunches of dried herbs, clumps of twigs, tiny shrubs of gray-green leaves, flaking yellow flowers; some plants had dirt-covered roots. Things growing out of the shelf beckoned my fingers.

Allspice, coriander (powdered and whole), cayenne pepper, cumin in a square jar, fennel seed, cardamom, cinnamon (powdered and in sticks), sumac, black nigella seeds, zatar, saffron, paprika, oregano, basil. And *mahleb*, which my grandmother kept in a jar. The color of sand and fine as talcum, it was the pulverized pit of wild cherry, and its earthy sweetness seemed to carry the other fragrances with it like an invisible thread tying up a bouquet.

"The essence of a cherry pit," my grandmother said in her discernible accent, and then "*A garden enclosed is my sister, my spouse; a spring shut up, a fountain sealed. Thy plants are an orchard of pomegranates, with pleasant fruits; camphor, with spikenard. Spikenard and saffron; calamus and cinnamon, with all trees of frankincense; myrrh and aloes, with all the chief spices: A fountain of gardens, a well of living waters, and streams from Lebanon. Awake, O north wind; and come, thou south; blow upon my garden, that the spices thereof may flow out.* That's Song of Solomon."

My grandmother knew large pieces of the Bible by heart. At the missionary school she attended in Diarbekir, an ancient Armenian city in southeastern Turkey where she grew up, they drilled it into her. "If we failed our recitations," she said, "the missionaries made us clean the school that week." Then she flicked some flour on the bread board and rubbed it in.

She told me she recited verses of the Bible when things weren't going well. "Words are friends. In bad times they keep you company."

"I hate memorizing for school," I mumbled as I unrolled some wax paper.

"Just do it, you'll be thankful someday." Then she ordered me to get the *mahleb*, which meant we were going to make a sweet bread called *choereg*.

To make *choereg*, we mixed milk and melted butter into a ceramic bowl. I poured yeast into a glass measuring cup with red lines and watched it fizz. Eggs, sugar, salt, baking powder, and my grandmother poured in the *mahleb*. She sifted flour and we mixed it all with a large wooden spoon till it was dough. Then she scooped the dough out and put it on the flour-grazed bread board. We squeezed and pressed it with our hands. I liked how the wet dough stuck between my fingers. I liked how she took it to another bowl and turned it all over its oiled surface, then covered the bowl with a towel and put it in the unlit oven. It was warm there and free from drafts, and when we opened the oven two hours later the dough was an airy, saffron-colored mound.

I loved punching the dough down so that its porous insides collapsed. We pulled it into pieces and made ropes, braids, and rings while we listened to WMGM on the radio. "Rock 'n roll picks me up," my grandmother would say; Elvis, Fats Domino, Bill Haley and the Comets–"good stuff." And when the Shirelles came out in the early sixties with "Will You Still Love Me Tomorrow?" "Tonight's the Night," and "Mama Said There'll Be Days Like This," she said "They do good harmony," and followed them like a fan because they were girls from nearby Passaic. As we filled the silver baking trays with braids and rings and ropes and brushed them with a beaten egg yolk so that they would shine when they came out, we sang along with the radio, "Blueberry Hill" or "Jailhouse Rock."

While the *choereg* baked, my grandmother told me stories. They weren't like the ones my friends heard from their grandparents, about fishing trips on the Great Lakes, Babe Ruth and Lou Gehrig, sagas set at summer camps in the Adirondacks when Calvin Coolidge was president, or the stock market crash of '29, when good men jumped out of windows. My grandmother's stories didn't seem to belong to any time or place; she just started in like this: *Djamangeen gar oo chagar*, which means *A long time ago there was and there wasn't.*

"There was a rich woman who lived in a big house with her husband and was envied for her beauty, and when it came her time to meet Fate—because everyone must meet fate once in their life—she went to Fate's house to make an offering. And what an offering—the best spring lamb, stuffed with almonds and pilaf, apricots and pomegranates, quinces and walnuts, and to top it off, two fine rubies in the eye sockets of the head. She carried it all on a silver platter, and walked through town in her white silk dress, pearls around her neck, and her wrists jangling with gold bracelets." My grandmother shook her wrists so I could hear those bracelets clatter.

"She knocked on the door, once, twice, three times, and waited patiently.

"When Fate came to the door, with her bright hennaed hair, rubbing her eyes so that the mascara smeared her cheek, she didn't even look at the woman. 'Don't bother me,' she whispered in an irritated voice, 'I'm sleeping, be gone!'" My grandmother threw her head back as she said this.

"The next week, a woman who was poor as those ladies on Eighth Avenue with paper bags knew that it was her day to call on Fate. She lived in a hut in the country, without a dime to her name. All she had was a black dog that she had found dead in a field, and so she dragged it home and cooked it. Even the apple she placed in its mouth was wormy. The next day she went to the house of Fate in a black dress, which smelled like oil and rotten milk. She trembled as she knocked on Fate's door." My grandmother made a knocking motion with her hand. "Fate appeared in a white dress, with diamond brooches in her hair, and she looked beautiful as a queen. The poor woman felt even more unworthy and had to restrain herself from running away. But to her surprise, Fate opened her arms and said in a voice sweet as honey, 'Come in, I've been waiting for you for a long time.'"

My grandmother nodded at me as if to confirm my comprehension, then there was silence. After the timer went off, and we took the *choereg* out of the oven and put it on wire racks to cool, still there was silence. I was beginning to get angry, but my grandmother treated me with such tenderness that I couldn't be angry at her, so I was angry at the story, which excited but baffled me. I wanted to say "Gran, these stories of yours–they're weird, and I don't get them." But I couldn't talk to my grandmother the way I could to my mother, so as I stared at the warm, shiny *choeregs* cooling on the wire racks, I just blurted out: "What's Fate, Gran?"

My grandmother looked around the kitchen and then looked me square in the eyes, as if she were about to attack a melon with her hands to see if it was ripe. "*Pakht,*" she said, "it's *Pakht,*" making the deep, guttural gargle with her throat, as you do with some Armenian words. "*Pakht.* You know, luck, fate. Fate." She paused again, taking a spatula and slipping it under a couple of *choeregs* to make sure they weren't sticking to the rack. "Fate, it's your destiny, it's what's in store for you."

"Uhuh," I gargled back through a swig of 7-Up as I began sliding the *choeregs* off the rack and onto a big dish. My grandmother went on, "It's a force, something bigger than you are."

"You mean like God?" My grandmother looked at me with serious eyes and then down at the *choeregs* cooling.

"No, not God," she went on slowly, "no, *yavrey.*" And just as she was letting me know with her eyes that she didn't want to answer any more questions, my tongue had already slipped out of my mouth again. "What about the dog?"

Animated and clipping a choker of pearls around her neck, she backed out of the kitchen as she looked at her watch, and began warning me that we had to get to the grocery store. "The dog ... the dog, the dog is fate's answer to us–to the human world."

"That dead animal?" I asked, feeling dumb. "A dead black dog?" I heard myself say it again. "Gran, what are you talking about?"

"The dog tells us to have hope. The dog tells us there is mystery."

"Mystery, hope?" I echoed.

Then she pounded her palm on the red Formica counter. "The dog tells us that appearances are deceiving–the world is not what you think, *yavrey.*" Then she grew impatient and began ordering me, "A & P by three-thirty or we won't have dinner ready for the girls."

I wanted to ask why the rich woman was turned away and what happened to the lamb with rubies in its eyes, but my grandmother had drawn the line. She had said all she wanted to say, and even my annoying prodding wouldn't get me anywhere. So the image of a white lamb with two red precious stones in its eye sockets floated in my head as we left for the A & P. We walked and trotted and jogged through her shortcuts, empty lots, alleys, and backyards. My grandmother walked fast and this amazed me, for I–who thought I was the Maurie Wills of my Little League team–had to work hard to keep up with her. With her mended hip and slight limp and manner of pushing off with her cane, the stride of her thin, sturdy legs was relentless. I was manic with joy as I ran alongside her. We always finished our walk at the overpass where the Garden State Parkway was being built. It was 1958 and this Eisenhower highway was being built from north to south along the whole snaking eastern side of New Jersey. As we hung over the railing watching those giant machines gouge out the earth, she peeled the wrapping of an Almond Joy and gave me half.

On these walks my grandmother liked silence, but when she talked, she talked about the stock market or the Yankees, who she had followed since the Babe Ruth and Lou Gehrig days. Her love of Joe DiMaggio made her reluctant to accept Mickey Mantle with open arms. Mantle had a lot to live up to, she said; he was a "playboy," a "prima donna," she complained. "But Casey loves him," she went on. Her feeling for Casey Stengel was inveterate and she loved his head-down-skip-over-the-white-line on the way to the mound; the way he pulled his ear, and signaled to the bullpen. "Manages on instinct," she reminded me.

When she spoke fast with her Armenian accent she had a tendency to leave out the articles, as Armenian immigrants often do, and sounded like Red Barber with his hard, clipped Brooklyn style. When she said things like "Baseball means something; you keep averages, turn off the radio when you want; box scores the next day; it's free," I realized the game was something more than a game to her. I realized she felt the game more deeply than anyone I knew.

My grandmother and I followed the Yankees together, and by the time I was ten it had become an ongoing conversation between us.

Box scores, averages, pitching rotations, prognosis for the World Series–because there was almost never a series without the Yankees. In August of '59, my grandmother walked around our back yard in Teaneck muttering, "the damn Chicago," because by the end of the month it was clear the White Sox and not the Yankees were headed for the series, which would mark the second time in my short life that the Yankees would not be playing in October. In April of '60, she said about the Yankees' acquisition of Roger Maris from the Kansas City A's: "We say in Armenian, one man's luck is another's stupidity."

The Yankees of the 1950s and early '60s were more than a team, they were a mood, an image, a feeling. They were thin blue stripes and elegant numbers on a white uniform. They were a Y spliced into an N on a blue cap. Power and muscle and confidence, and they did what great teams do, they won in ways that seemed inevitable yet magical. Even now when I see the Yankees logo–a red, white, and blue Uncle Sam hat topping a bat inside the white circle of a baseball with the Yankees script across the center, I feel not just nostalgia but a thrill, and I think, too, of my grandmother's quiet, intense passion for her team.

After we had moved to our new house in Tenafly, my grandmother began to appear at the door after dinner when the Yankees were on channel 11–now that she and my aunts lived a five-minute bus ride away in Englewood. In our new, paneled TV room, the two of us sat on a black leather couch beneath big framed posters of the Côte d'Azur and Monaco, while upstairs my mother put my brother and sisters to bed. As the light coming through the sliding glass doors turned purple and then black, the blue-gray of the TV lit the room.

By the early sixties, my grandmother had come around on Mickey Mantle. Perhaps because of his bad knees, his constant struggle to stay healthy enough to play, and maybe because there was something pathetic about this man who undermined his brilliant talent by his own foolish behavior off the field. He was, she said, a *tutoum kulukh*, in Armenian, a pumpkin head, a dumbbell. But by the end of the 1961 Mantle–Maris duel for the Babe's season home-run record, my grandmother came to see Mantle as a tragic figure who endured his own frailties with grace and courage and who was forced to watch from the sidelines in the second half of September as Roger Maris hit sixty-one to break the record.

So as the camera caught Mantle's boyish blond face and zoomed in on his wondrous 17½-inch neck while he took his warm-up swings in the on-deck circle, my grandmother and I grew silent. "His swing is like a great wind," she said, "sheeewwww." And when he sent one out of the park, my grandmother would say "Outta here," and dish into the crystal bowl of pistachio nuts on the coffee table. Splitting the shells with her thumbnails, she would pass me the salty green nuts so that we could celebrate with our teeth.

I remember my grandmother during the '62 Series between the Yankees and the Giants, because that October she decided to watch all the Series games in our new TV room. "It's a bigger screen," she said to my mother about our new RCA, "and I can see better," and although she didn't say so, I think she wanted to watch the games with me. But that fall I disappointed her by listening to every game on the radio with my friends behind the chain-link backstop of our sandlot diamond. We scurried between the field and transistor radio and sometimes stopped our play as we did for the final half-inning of Game 7. I remember how Yankee fans stood on one side of the backstop and Giants fans on the other as Ralph Terry faced Willie McCovey while Willie Mays and Felipe Alou stood on second and third waiting to break the Yankees' 1–0 lead, and how the loud crack of the bat came over the radio as McCovey smacked a line drive that seemed destined for right field and a 2–1 Giant victory to win it all when Bobby Richardson leapt to his left and snatched the ball to give the Yankees another World Series. When I returned home, my grandmother was waiting in the driveway for me, dressed in a beige linen suit and a choker of pearls, with a small, quiet smile on her face. "Good ole Richardson" was all she said.

About two weeks after the Series had ended, the Cuban Missile Crisis took over our lives, and my grandmother began showing up after dinner to watch the news with us. Walter Cronkite's face, slightly worried and avuncular on the big black-and-white screen, followed by aerial footage of aircraft carriers and the shoreline of Cuba. My father mocking Kennedy's Boston accent, saying, "Cuber's just a stone's throw from Florida." My mother passing a tray of dried fruits and nuts that my aunt Alice had just sent from Fresno. In my fifth-grade class everyone was talking about the bomb and the end of the world. Meredith Gutman, sensing my inclination toward morbidity and terror, stared at me one morning and said, "The whole world will go up in smoke," as she wiggled her fingers and raised her arms like a conductor.

That week I had found on my parents' night table a small pamphlet called "A Citizen's Handbook on Nuclear Attack and Natural Disasters," published by the United States Department of Defense. It was written for barely literate people and illustrated with cartoons. Aimed at assuring Americans that no harm would come from nuclear war, it read:

> *If an enemy should threaten to attack the United States you would not be alone.*
>
> *If a person receives a large dose of radiation, he will die. But if he receives only a small or medium dose, his body will repair itself and he will get well. Most of the nation's food supplies would be usable after an attack.... Also, to avoid injuring your eyes, never look at the flash of an explosion of the nuclear fireball.*

Even to a fifth grader this seemed ridiculous; it was clear from the media that nuclear war meant death and destruction. The pamphlet, which went on to instruct families on how to make a bomb shelter, must have been geared for suburbia, for who else but suburbanites would have basements large and fine enough to be converted into bomb shelters? And we were to stock our new shelters: **6 months of evaporated milk, 18 months of canned poultry, 12 months of ready-to-eat cereals in metal containers, 18 months of hard candy and gum, 24 months of flavored beverage powders, jugs labeled "water," pills labeled "medicine."**

3022272l

I was sure my mother would prefer the end of the world to this menu. Disgusted and secretly terrified by the whole Cuba business, I went home each day in late October after playing football, ate dinner, and opened the door for my grandmother and followed her into the TV room to watch the images of aircraft carriers and Cuba on the screen.

I lay in bed one night sweating, filled with images of bomb shelters and cereal in metal containers, and decided to go downstairs for a bowl of Frosted Flakes. As I passed the partly opened door of the TV room, I noticed that my grandmother was watching the late night news. Just as I was about to fling the door open, she took a long ivory pipe out of her purse, filled it with tobacco, and lit up. I was so startled that I stood frozen in the dark hallway, watching her through the two-inch crack between the door and the doorjamb.

I could hear *Kennedy, Khrushchev, Castro, Cuba* from the newscaster's voice. My grandmother drew long puffs on the pipe and put it down on the coffee table, then made the sign of the cross and said some Armenian words: *Der Voghormya, Der Voghormya, Der Voghormya* (Lord Have Mercy, Lord Have Mercy, Lord Have Mercy). Then she crossed herself again, took a puff on her pipe, and said *Sourp Asdvadz, Sourp Asdvadz, Sourp Asdvadz* (Holy God, Holy God, Holy God). She stood up, crossed herself, sat down, and pulled from her purse a dazzling blue and ivory and apricot striped cloth. She placed it on her lap like a napkin and then opened up a big fat biography of Mary Todd Lincoln, in which a '57 baseball card of Hank Aaron was tucked as a bookmark.

For days afterward, I thought of my grandmother's strange ritual in the TV room. Because I felt guilty for spying on her while everyone else slept peacefully upstairs, I couldn't mention it to anyone in my family. Weeks later, after the Cuban Missile Crisis was settled and enough time had passed so that what I had seen seemed like fiction, I told my mother that one night in the summer I had seen Gran take a smoke on a pipe. Seeing on my face that this amazed and somewhat frightened me, she said, "Oh, in the old country, at a certain age, women smoke pipes once in a while. It's a sign of wisdom."

Wheeler Basin Regional Library
Headquarters, Decatur, Ala.

If I was relieved that my mother had given me an answer, I was unsettled that the answer had unfurled more questions. *The old country.* That phrase that came up now and then. A phrase that seemed to have a lock on it. I knew it meant Armenia, but it made me uneasy. If I asked about the old country, the adults would change the subject. Once my mother said, "It's an ancient place, it's not really around anymore." Where had it gone? I asked myself.

If I lived in a house where the old country still had a presence, why wasn't there a map, or photograph, or beautiful drawing of it somewhere, like the one the Zandonellas had of Milan in their TV room? Since there was no picture of the old country in our house and since I didn't have one etched in my mind, the old country came to mean my grandmother. Whatever it was, she was. Whatever she was, it was.

THE WOMAN IN BLUE

WHEN I WAS WITH MY GRANDMOTHER I HAD ACCESS TO SOME OTHER world, some evocative place of dark and light, some kind of energy that ran like an invisible force from this old country called Armenia to my world in New Jersey. It was something ancient, something connected to earth and words and blood and sky.

Now I realize that my grandmother's stories hibernated in me until I was ready to understand them fully. Or maybe *marinated* is a better word, since we are a people so steeped in food; yes, marinated. Or is it cured? Like grape leaves in brine; or lamb cooked in apricots, walnuts, and pomegranate juice and left to soften in hardened fat in an earthenware jug; or long slabs of filet mignons packed in garlic and cumin and left to hang in the dark air of a basement.

My grandmother liked to tell all of us her dreams, but it was to me, when we were alone, that she told her stories; perhaps she had told the same ones to her daughters when they were young, although no one ever mentioned them. I came to realize that my grandmother's stories were part of time and not part of time, part of place and not part of place, part of the stuff that is stored in the mind's honeycomb.

As a dreamteller my grandmother was accorded respect, albeit begrudgingly by my father, the rationalist physician. I remember one morning overhearing my grandmother in the kitchen telling my mother about a dream she'd had the night before about an old friend from the old country, who lived in Fresno, California.

"She was on a hill," my grandmother said. "It was a blue sky and then a huge bird comes flying down at her, making a screaming sound. Next thing I know she is in our old house in Maplewood, sitting in our living room, drinking rosewater. It's spring, because I can see forsythia through the picture window. Then, she asks me to get her shoes; I look down and I see she is *paubig* (barefoot). I say, Nevart, I don't know where your shoes are. She begins to cry. Curls up on the rug. I look up and snow is coming in through the window. I go to shut it and a huge bird slams into the glass, bounces off the glass and disappears."

"It's just a dream," I heard my mother say. That afternoon Nevart, whom she hadn't seen in years, died suddenly.

My grandmother relied on her dreams. She liked to tell them to us as soon after waking as possible. "I had a dream about AT&T; it's going up; we should buy more," she said to my father. "The stock market has nothing to do with dreams," my father said. "Why not?" she clipped back.

"*Yavresie*, things aren't looking good for Mickey."

"What d'ya mean, Gran?"

"Knee or hamstring, I had a dream last night."

She dreamt Man o' War won each of the Triple Crown races before each race. But that was easy. She dreamt something bad was going to happen to my mother in the next five days. Five days later my mother broke two vertebrae slipping down the stairway. "I don't want to know, Mama," I would hear my mother say on the phone. I think we all believed and didn't believe in my grandmother's dreams. She liked to say things like, "I can smell evil in a basement" or "The hawk from the village tells truth in the city" or "Don't trust a snake unless it has two heads."

"It's just coincidence," my father assured my mother in his medical tone of voice, "we know dreams can't predict the future."

My grandmother's stories even had dreamlike qualities about them, and one of them I remember best began with the elk. In Armenia, the elk is magic. With its horns like wild candelabra, the elk was Adam's first partner in the Garden of Eden. But Armenian legend has it that the elk wasn't compatible with Adam, and God banished it in favor of Eve. So the elk grew to hate women. Especially pregnant women, who had to go to bed at night with knives under their pillows in case the elk came to pull out their livers.

"How?" I asked my grandmother. "Through the mouth," she answered. "Elk would have to suck it up?" I asked. "That's right," my grandmother said, "suck it up," and she made a sound with her lips as if she were inhaling on a drinking straw.

Jesus, she told me, caught the elk red-handed with the liver of a pregnant woman in its mouth. Now Elk knew he was done for, so he promised Jesus he wouldn't harm women who cried for help in Christ's name. My grandmother's voice dropped. "I'm not sure Jesus would make that kind of deal."

I remember the story so well not only because it was about liver and the elk but because my grandmother and I had gotten lost on the subway coming home from shopping on Fifth Avenue at Saks and Lord & Taylor, on one of those Saturday afternoon Aroosian shopping sprees during which I was forced in and out of the best stores in New York in order to find clothes that were suitable for me and that would pass the inspection of my grandmother, aunts, and mother. I was ten, and I remember walking up the stairs of the subway station, thin as a pencil, kicking each step with my white bucks. When we emerged above ground we soon found ourselves in a part of the city even my grandmother had never been in. Smaller buildings, grocery stores, barber shops, diners. We kept walking because my grandmother was sure there was a bus we could get that would take us across town. Finally she said, "We're in Harlem, *yavrey.*" She explained that "many colored people" lived here.

Tired and confused, we dragged our shopping bags along the sidewalk past the dark, low tenement buildings and street signs with unfamiliar names. My grandmother stopped next to a man selling ice cream from a silver cart and bought us each a Creamsicle. We sat on a bench, and I felt white for the first time in my life. I don't know if my grandmother sensed my uneasiness, but she started in: "*Djamangeen gar oo chagar*"–a long time ago, there was and there wasn't.

"A young bride gave birth to a boy. The baby was a long time coming out, and she was tired." She paused to make sure I understood her English translation. "A beautiful boy. When the husband returned from his business trip to find his new son, he was like a dancing bear. 'Wife,' he says, 'go get us our best wine for a toast.' The wife said she was too weak to walk to the wine cellar, but the husband demanded, and she went.

"In her green robe, she went down into the cool stone basement where the wine was stored. When she opened the door she saw a woman dressed in blue, sewing a large cloth. She passed the woman in blue as if she wasn't there, picked up a big clay jug, and poured wine into a pitcher. As it spilled over the spout, screams came from the jug, as if they were pouring out with the wine itself. The terrified woman ran back through the cellar to the doorway where the woman in blue was sitting sewing, and she fainted.

"Upstairs the husband was pacing impatiently."

No buses were coming. It was getting cooler and I felt a pang of hunger. "Where's the bus, Gran?"

"It'll be here," she said, annoyed that I had interrupted her.

" 'That lazy wife,' " she marshaled it out, tapping her cane on the pavement. "The husband goes downstairs to the wine cellar, and he finds his wife lying on the floor. He shakes her, picks her up. 'What's wrong, what's wrong!' " My grandmother brandished her cane.

"The wife comes to and tells the husband how voices came from the jug and how they seemed to chase her to the woman in blue. 'Woman in blue? I see no one,' says the husband. 'But she was right here,' the wife protests."

My grandmother and I must have looked odd on that green, blistered bench, with black-and-white shopping bags from Lord & Taylor and Saks piled around us, I in my chinos, Oxford button-down and she in her black lamb's-wool coat, high heels, Ray Charles–style sunglasses, and wand of an aluminum cane. When she realized that no bus was coming, she asked me to hail a cab. Although I'd never done this, I wanted to act grown up, so I stood up tentatively and began waving my arms like a referee signaling a first down.

Women in bright-colored kerchiefs walked past us with shopping carts and bags of groceries. Black kids were playing a game with a ball off a concrete wall. The ice cream man returned to see if we wanted another Creamsicle, the soles of his shoes flapping as he walked.

"That's no way to get a cab," my grandmother said, and got up with characteristic vehemence and began waving her cane like a conductor, and in a minute a yellow checker cab was at our disposal. "G. W. Bridge Terminal," my grandmother said and we got in.

"For the next week, the wife slept and woke." My grandmother interrupted her story with this incantation–"The wind blew in and the wind blew out"–and she continued: "When she woke she told her husband about the woman in blue and about *al* (Elk) who came to pull out her liver." The cab sped through Harlem up Lexington Avenue, past basketball courts, rows of tenements with fire escapes, burned-out buildings, and the thick, colorful tubing of neon signs as my grandmother went on. "Now, the elk is unusual," she said in a deliberate way, so I could hear the cadence of her accent. "It's an invisible animal, only the bells on the antlers can be seen and only at a distance. It has the power of copper claws and iron teeth.

"The wife told her husband how the elk had come every night to take her liver, and she refused to open her mouth. She kept her jaw clenched like an alligator. One day after a fainting spell, the wife saw the woman in blue again, who said, 'Come to my church and I will banish the elk forever.' 'Which is your church?' asked the wife. '*Mairig Asdvadzadzeen.* Notre Dame, Our Lady,'" my grandmother said to make sure I understood. "The woman in blue disappeared. The wind blew in, the wind blew out."

In the cavernous bus terminal, we hiked the long stairs to the Red & Tan Bus Line platforms and sat on a bench behind the Plexiglas shield of the waiting area for no. 14K. "When the woman came to, she told her husband she must go to *Mairig Asdvadzadzeen.*"

Mairig Asdvadzadzeen. It was a phrase that stuck with me. *Mairig* is "mother" in Armenian, and *Asdvadzadzeen* means "of God." The words made strange music, like a good phrase that slides into your ear and hangs around for a while. As my grandmother told the story I kept repeating it to myself. *Mairig Asdvadzadzeen. Mairig Asdvadzadzeen.*

"After some arguing, the husband, who was suspicious of his wife's dreams, now grew worried about her, and he took her over the mountains and down to the church on the plateau. It was winter, and the couple lived on the cold stone of the church floor. Her husband brought offerings of slaughtered lamb and gold coins to the altar. The wife had nights of fever and cold sweat, and her husband rubbed her arms with beeswax, put the milk of the hodad plant on her forehead. One day in spring, she woke to see light flooding the great window behind the altar, and there, on a cross that seemed to float in the air, was the woman in blue."

I dragged two shopping bags up the bus steps. My grandmother paid the driver. We sat near the rear of the bus, our shopping bags packed around us and at our feet, my grandmother's cane wedged in so it looked like a silver shepherd's crook jutting up. I took a window seat, from which I could see the girders of the George Washington Bridge and its great gray towers. I was just settling into the stale odor of bus-seat fabric, which smelled like cigarette smoke and hair spray and carbon monoxide, and was getting ready to hear the end of the story when something hard hit me on the side of the face, so close to my eye that for a second I saw stars. Stunned, I looked up and saw that my grandmother's hat had been knocked off too.

In the seat behind us a fight had started. A man in a three-piece suit and dark glasses was striking with his cane a slightly pudgy man in a motorcycle jacket, black pants, and pointy black boots, who reminded me of Roy Orbison. I ducked, then curled up into the lap of the seat to protect myself from the man's flailing cane, my hands over my head. When I peered out from my crossed arms, my grandmother stood up ready to defend the Roy Orbison lookalike against the man in the three-piece suit. "Stop, stop," she shouted. "Fool," she said.

The man began swinging his cane vehemently in my grand-mother's direction. Now she held her cane up diagonally to block his swing. For a long moment the two locked canes—the man's painted cane and my grandmother's silver cane like crossed swords, he cursing at her and she retorting in Armenian, "*eshou kulukh*" (donkey head).

The Roy Orbison lookalike had backed off, and like me was watching in amazement as the two dueled. Just before the bus driver came back onto the bus (he had gone to fetch another bus driver), my grandmother's cane jarred the dark glasses off the man and for a moment he stood there, craning like a startled turtle, and then I looked at his eyes—they were like pitted fruits sewn up—and I could-n't stop staring into his shut cavities that revealed just a rim of mem-brane. My grandmother stood there, her sunglasses still on; her Sunday hat had been knocked off, her hair pins had been pushed out of place and her bun was coming loose. She picked the blind man's glasses off the floor and placed them in his hand. Then the bus dri-vers took the blind man and the Roy Orbison lookalike off the bus.

My grandmother sat back down. "You OK, ma'am?" the dri-ver asked her after climbing back on the bus. My grandmother nod-ded, and then opened her purse, took out her compact, which had a small oval mirror in it, straightened her hair, and put some tan pow-der on her cheeks. I could see her hands trembling slightly. I could hear her mutter in Armenian under her breath.

As I stared out the window at the cars and trucks and buses flowing by, I felt overwhelmed by my grandmother's courage. What had possessed her? I had never witnessed anyone come to the aid of a person in trouble; but an elderly woman with a limp from the pin in her hip, risking her safety to help a total stranger? As the bus left the Hudson River behind and we turned onto the Palisades Parkway, some images from her story began drifting in my head, and before long I was asking her about the woman in blue. Who was she? How, I wanted to know, could a woman be on a cross? Wasn't that a place for Jesus only? A floating cross? Did things work out OK for the couple? But she just nodded at me as if she were lost in a daze. When we arrived at my house and walked into our front hallway, my grand-mother stared at me so that I understood I was to say nothing of what happened on the bus. Then we began to unwrap the boxes of clothes we had bought and my mother and aunts came in to offer their opinions, and the day dissolved into the noise of home. But the phrase *Mairig Asdvadzadzeen* did not go away, nor did the images of the elk, the jug, the woman in blue, the liver. In time I would come to understand them as a part of my grandmother's story, but only after I came to understand what had happened to her in 1915.

My grandmother died on a Sunday night in the middle of November of 1964. From the bathroom where I was brushing my teeth, after watching "Bonanza," I heard the phone ring and then my mother's scream. I went downstairs to find my father hugging my mother and trying to calm her. My mother through her sobbing was telling me how much I meant to my grandmother. I gazed at them both for a second in their embrace of grief and then turned around and walked back upstairs, slammed the door of my bedroom and turned on the radio.

Every other song now was British. The Beatles, Dave Clark Five, The Kinks, Zombies, Jerry and the Pacemakers, The Searchers. All night a new song by Herman's Hermits: *Woke up this morning feeling fine/ There's something special on my mind/ Last night I met a new girl in the neighborhood.* A refrain, voices from Liverpool or somewhere over there. England. Carnaby Street. Mod. How to have long hair and play ball. Coach Henderson telling us haircuts every three weeks. "None of this Beatles stuff on our team."

The previous night I had asked my mother to take me to my grandmother's. When we walked into her living room she and my aunts had just finished watching Neil Sedaka on one of the variety shows. "He's good," my grandmother said in an animated way. "Good. Good."

"I'm sick of him, Gran," I said, just to bait her.

As if she hadn't heard me, she went on, "I think he's a Turkish Jew. Looks like someone I knew, long time ago."

To which I said nothing, for it meant nothing to me.

"Can we have *lokma?*" I asked.

"Yes, yes," she said and limped into the kitchen to heat up some oil, mix a batter, and put some cinnamon and sugar in a large bowl. I loved to watch her make this Armenian fried dough because it cooked up like magic. As the oil bubbled she let the batter slide off the tablespoon, and it sputtered, then hit the bubbling oil and expanded into wild shapes like outer-space creatures. When they got to be a golden color she fished them out with a small strainer and let them dry on a paper towel before she rolled them in the cinnamon and sugar. I ate a dozen *lokmas* while my grandmother and aunts and mother drank thick coffee out of small porcelain cups and ate cherry preserves.

As I lay in bed I kept picturing my grandmother's hands holding the large tablespoon over the boiling oil. Her skin oddly blotched, long white streaks from her knuckles to her almost colorless wrists. Wrists like the bellies of fish in the kitchen light. With the spoon clenched in her hand, her knuckles looked like bone, and I realized I'd never really seen them before. I lay in bed staring into the dark, feeling frozen, and listened to the wind outside blowing the bare trees against the clapboards, scratching and clawing the window nearest my bed. Through the wall I heard my mother's sobs and my father talking in Armenian, and then it was quiet.

Neil Sedaka, "a Turkish Jew" who looked like someone she knew? What did it mean? What could it mean? I wanted Gran to come back just once more so I could ask her that simple question. Neil Sedaka, the guy who sang "Calendar Girl" and "Breaking Up Is Hard To Do"? A Turkish Jew? The idea that I couldn't ask my grandmother questions anymore flashed through me like a cold current of terror. That she was no more. That there was a big empty space where she once pushed through the world with her quick step. I didn't believe it. Tomorrow, I told myself, she'd be back with her aluminum cane and her thick dark hair pinned up in a bun and her big eyes staring at me through her glasses, telling me her crazy stories.

All night I stared into the black air with its big molecules floating, and the boyish voices of Herman's Hermits and the phrase *Turkish Jew* kept spinning round and round my head like a black 45. My grandmother's hands floated like wings of bone in the dark, then they were birds, then small discs of light and then bones again, and then it was dawn.

FREEDOM, NEW JERSEY

In the years after my grandmother's death, I came to discover there were two kinds of memory. One was a personal web of sensations. That was suburbia: good times, romance, sex, friendship, and the body in motion. That kind of memory–that sense of limitless potential–was inseparable from the rock 'n roll that poured out from the large turquoise-and-gray Zenith transistor radio my grandmother gave me when I was eight or the smaller RCAs and SONYs I later carried in my hand.

To be thirteen and dreaming. Sleepless between the cold water of the morning faucet and the light between curtains. Between dream and homeroom. Believing in "Somewhere beyond the sea." A bra strap graceful beneath the transparency of a white blouse. And when the blue sky over the shoreline and the coconut smell of Coppertone faded and the pubic curls from bathing suits and breasts half visible were gone, the sweet voice of "   " and the saxophones blared.

Eros dueling with death. Paul Anka's agony. Elvis's shaking. Little Richard's St. Vitus's dance at the piano. Aretha opening the campaniles of the jukebox. Martha Reeves's great belts. Roy Orbison's lamentations. Jackie Wilson's tremolos. Billy Stewart's black-scats. Garnet Mims's gospel highs. Bob Dylan's nasal cantering.

When the music was on, the Balakians and their high culture, the Aroosians and their culinary and aesthetic obsessions, folktales, and dreams disappeared. Then life was fun and fast, not slow and deliberate like Armenian time.

To be seventeen in Linda Bloom's basement, smell of warm malt from cans of Colt 45 and smoke hanging from Salems, Luckies, Marlboros, the couches pushed back against paneled walls baby I need your lovin', got to have all your lovin' *Arlene's black pumps kicked off. Heaven Scent. Old Spice. Dampness.* So take a good look at my face, you'll see my smile, it's way out of place, if you look closer it's easy to trace *Someone says Jerry and the Pacemakers for President.*

You love the way the cigarette juts out from between her long fingers and how her red painted nails set off the white cigarette paper. You're breaking training and her parents are in Puerto Rico for the week baby you're so smart you know you could've been a school-book, the way you stole my heart you know you could've been a cool crook *no matter what car you can get, some MG midget or a Spitfire or a bug or a GTO, the top will be down and the warm midnight air of the Garden State Parkway will pour in. The smell of the deep fry wafting over the boardwalk, the surf surging over your throat, and the transistors blaring tinny and static–*

The way she leans now against the yellow counters in the dark kitchen and starts to sing cry baby cry baby welcome back home

But I learned that there was another kind of memory, too. A kind of memory that was connected to something larger than my life. After my grandmother died, Armenia seemed more and more remote, and I lost my direct and visceral sense of the ancient Near Eastern world that she embodied. Yet, no matter how deeply I sank into suburban life and the happy society of teenage Tenafly, my memory of my grandmother was a strange shadow appearing now and then to remind me that there was something else I needed to know. She imploded my present at the strangest moments, without conscious provocation. She had become my *pakht*–the force of fate that called on me, whether I was ready or not, and who, like Lady Fate, was indifferent to my present moment, my station in life, or my need for security and comfort. She was history knocking on the door of the heart, and when she came knocking, her message often was opaque, symbolic, evocative. I was left to make of it what I could, but I could not escape the intrusion.

I'm remembering a clear, cold evening, a few inches of hard-crusted snow on the roadside. It's February 1968, and my girlfriend Rose Germain and I are sitting, arms around each other, in the third-row seats of a Ford Country Squire station wagon on a triple date. We're returning north up the Garden State Parkway from the Milburn Theater, where we have just seen *The Graduate.* I walk out of the theater thrilled in part because the hero was played by Dustin Hoffman. Not a John Wayne or a Steve McQueen or a Paul Newman, but this short, dark guy with a nose that would have been at home on any Greek bas-relief.

Earnest, alienated, and rebellious, Benjamin Braddock was more real to me than Holden Caulfield or James Dean, and until Camus' Mersault replaced him, he was my antihero. His destined love, Elaine, was played by Katherine Ross. A touch of adolescence about her cheeks, blue eyes, long auburn hair, and tentative smile. She was chic as she walked the Berkeley campus in suede boots and blue jeans and an array of Abercrombie & Fitch jackets. I loved the way she popped a few french fries into her sensual mouth from a white paper bag she and Benjamin had taken out from the drive-in, and then smiled as she said goodnight and disappeared into her white house. Against the swarthy Hoffman she was the ultimate *shiksa.*

Everything was white in southern California. The white walls of Mrs. Robinson's hallway against which she shrinks when her affair with Benjamin is revealed to her daughter. The white paneling of the Braddock kitchen; the white empire dresses at Benjamin's college graduation party; white walls of the Taft Hotel's famous room no. 528 (the place of assignation). And finally, the white 1960s First Presbyterian Church of Santa Barbara, where Benjamin rescues Elaine from the white interior of her almost-marriage to the blond medical student. It was more than sixties minimalism; it was the white nothingness of the American Dream.

And Benjamin, depressed and alone, staring into the fish tanks in his bedroom. Benjamin driving forlornly around the posh streets in his new Alfa Romeo after Elaine has banished him from her life. Benjamin in shades drifting on a raft in his backyard swimming pool, a beer sweating in his hand, orange trees above him. The lyrical and melancholy songs of Simon and Garfunkel: *Hello darkness my old friend, I've come to talk with you again/ because a vision softly creeping/ left my dreams while I was sleeping.*

I sat with my arm around Rose in the third seat of the car, elated by the film and feeling the good feeling of being with her on a Saturday night. Then, like sudden cold water, a memory overwhelmed me. I found myself back in the summer of 1962, reliving a scene that no doubt I had repressed from the time it happened. Perhaps my flashback was triggered by Dustin Hoffman, whose Jewish looks were somehow a bridge for me back to my Armenianness, which lived submerged in me. My arm went limp around Rose's shoulder and I stared through the back window of the station wagon into the sky where the red lights of the radio towers were blinking.

I am lying in my bed running a fever that in a few days will lead to the measles. My nose is bleeding periodically onto my tee shirt and I'm rereading a book called *Roger Maris at Bat*, in which I can relive all sixty-one of the home runs Maris hit the previous summer to break the Babe's record. As the fever rises, I'm trying to hold on to the image of Maris's elegant left-handed swing and the white bullet rising into the right-field bleachers of Yankee Stadium.

My grandmother comes into the room, hot late July, the air conditioning on the blink, the windows open and the sounds of cicadas shrill in the trees. "The soul," my grandmother says, "leaves the body. *Sounch* (breath). *Ott* (air). *Hokee* (soul). The soul leaves through the mouth when you die and finds a place to live. Souls are either good or evil. Good souls are connected with angels and saints. Evil souls with suicides or criminals or Turks."

My grandmother is talking in a loud voice and the sun pouring through the window is so bright that she is almost lost in the glare. She keeps speaking. "The unclean souls pursue the living and appear in the bodies of animals. The souls of evil people roam the world; the souls of the good find homes. Souls can hide in anything, a jerboa or a grape leaf; they can fold into coils on a mulberry leaf. Souls are like flowers, so pay attention to them and don't be fooled by nature, don't be fooled by beauty."

She steps out of the light, in front of the big mirror on my wall, and I can see that she has let her hair down. "Everywhere there are omens. When an omen appears near you and you miss it, you have missed your fate. A red rose turns white in April; broom on the hillside goes black in August; sheep change color over night; mulberries on lower branches are soft and inviting. When bread is dear, death is near. Sleep with one eye open; be a half-inch off the sheet. Know the evil eye."

I nod when she says evil eye. Then the door opens and it's my father.

"I'm not going to die," I say to my father. I watch him by the window as he punctures the pink rubber circle of a bottle of serum with the long needle. The glass syringe has a long purple line going up the side. I watch the serum fill the void of the tube made by the slow release of the glass push-stop. From the nozzle the silver needle seems to float in the light.

"You're up to 104," my father says. "It'll come down."

The pain is like a knife in my ear. The needle is long and when I smell the alcohol on the cotton swab, my muscles tighten, then it's cool on the back of my arm, and I clench my jaw and the blue sky in the window disappears as if someone pulled the shade.

When I wake my grandmother is standing over me. My skin is burning, and I am too groggy to talk. I just watch her pull a glass jar off my chest, and I smell the kerosene. My eyes follow a thin swirl of smoke as it evaporates toward the ceiling. There is gauze in the jar and my grandmother stares into it, and I stare at her and then at the college pennants on my wall like flags in the wind making me dizzy. I see the red ring on my chest where my grandmother has just pulled the jar.

"Syringe can only do so much," she says, "now fever will lift soon. *Hokeet seerem, ano-tee-es?* (Beloved soul, are you hungry?)" I nod yes and feel the sweat cooling on my body and my tee shirt damp and cool. Her hand brushes my hair. Her wrist is cool on my forehead.

I think it is morning, because the light seems red against the wall, but the room is dark, and my grandmother is standing by the old black Windsor rocker. When she smiles, she is all gums just like a baby because she has taken her teeth out. Her thick, dark brown hair flares out over her shoulders and spreads like a cape down her back, and as she grins the space of her mouth seems to float in the air, making her look like a hag. In a white slip, her breasts are half visible.

"My father used to say if a sheep goes this far it isn't worth looking for, Nafina."

"There were maggots on the slits of their backs. We lay on the ground. Four of us. Something ran through the brush. The night sky was perfect. I saw a star shoot south to Nineveh, and lightning came and the brush was silver and then it was black again.

"When the sun broke through the gray light, I saw birds like the tail of a huge kite. There were men in black robes on the mountain. They waved far away. Then the birds and the dogs came."

I feel like I am dreaming, but the headboard is hard against my neck and I sit propped up in bed watching my grandmother. Was she dreaming, in front of me?

"Everything smelled rotten. Hagop was on the ground. I kicked him.

"There was something ahead. Hagop was cold. Then there was blood dripping down the side of my leg and I could feel the coins.

"I felt Alice in the sling on my back asleep. The gendarmes began slapping me. One of them used the whip. The blood and milk oozed. Alice was crying.

"The Turk had an ax and a short knife with a mother-of-pearl handle. The blood was warm, then cold. I recognized him from the souk in Diarbekir. He was like a dead animal on me. I watched the dead feathers fly up into a blue sky where my box kite flew at Easter. I fell like a lap of blue beads on the marble floor in the Turkish bath.

"I saw the woman in blue. Beloved mother of God. I saw the woman in blue. Der Voghormya. Der Voghormya. Der Voghormya." My grandmother makes the sign of the cross as she says it.

When the light comes through the window there is a bowl of soup on a mother-of-pearl tray, strands of egg flying through the broth. *Arkayutiun* soup (soup of heaven), my grandmother calls it. Some bones float and the allspice in the rice-stuffed meatballs is sweet in the lemony chicken broth. My grandmother's hands smell of fresh lemon rind as she feels my forehead again.

Sweaty and uncomfortable, I sat like a paralytic and looked blankly into the night as the cars blurred by. I was thinking to myself, "Gran, what the hell are you doing here? I'm on a date, and I know you'll understand if I say I was hoping to have a good time at Rose's after the movie." But I was emotionally wiped out by this reverie. Although Rose and I prided ourselves on being able to talk about ideas and feelings, I would have felt absurd trying to tell her of the memory I had just relived. How could I explain my Armenian grandmother to her, when I didn't understand Armenia myself? So when I stood on Rose's front porch back in Tenafly and she asked me to come in, which meant that we would go down three steps to the TV room of her split-level house and roll around on the couch doing everything we could with her parents sleeping upstairs, I said I didn't feel well and went home.

At home I sat and stared at the dark TV screen beneath the bookshelves. The house was silent, everyone sleeping upstairs, and the air of the room floated with dim molecules of light from the lamp, and I kept hearing my grandmother's voice. S*ouk, Diarbekir, Turkish bath, Der Vorghormya.* Words of Armenia, names of places whooshing around in my head. Had I been a witness to a memory of hers so terrible that it could only be said to me, an eleven-year-old, half delirious with fever, lying in bed between darkness and light? My grandmother had spoken so emphatically that day, in clipped, deliberate speech, as if to say, *this is a moment to listen.*

MOTHER

AN ARMENIAN JEW IN SUBURBIA

We always lingered over dinner after church on Sunday afternoon. In summer we dined on the brick patio in the backyard under the shade of the maple. A plastic tablecloth over the picnic table. The smell of charred lamb. A silver serving dish with some leftover shish kebab and seared vegetables for those whose appetite might reemerge after a while of talking. The pink-and-white azaleas and the little lavender bouquets of rhododendron petals lushly hemming us in. Sunday was family day. On Sunday we seemed more Armenian. Some assortment of relatives—my grandmother, aunts, cousins, uncles—always would be there.

On Sundays I felt like I watched my family as if I were watching a play. My mother passes a tray of *bereks*, triangles of filo filled with sharp cheese and parsley, and Auntie Gladys passes a large bowl of ice in which float black olives and radishes cut into rose shapes. Everyone sits on lawn chairs and chaise lounges. A moment later, my mother opens the sliding glass door carrying a tray of highball glasses filled with *tahn*, a drink of yogurt and water poured over ice and mint leaves. In a white silk blouse and a dark skirt with an apron tied around her waist, my mother is formal and informal, at once decorous and casually suburban, with dark wavy hair cut short against her fair, freckled skin. She is never sitting down but poking and prodding at the food, passing around plates and silverware, and delegating small responsibilities to everyone to make sure we are all within earshot of her voice. At the grill built into the side of the brick chimney my father is fanning the coals, and in the kitchen my mother is seeing the lamb through its last stages.

Since Saturday night the shish kebab has been marinating in a large terra-cotta bowl with slices of onion, coriander, paprika, some crude olive oil, some red wine. As the oil soaks into the paprika, making a rosy hue on the lamb and the pearly crescents of onions and flecks of black pepper and allspice, the whole bowl glistens. Cubed and trimmed of fat, spring lamb is soft and a deep brick color as you glide it up the skewer with chunks of green pepper, Spanish onions, and Jersey Beefsteak tomatoes before it goes over the white coals.

When the vegetables are charred and the lamb slides off the skewers, my father fills the large silver bowl. In a blue-and-white painted dish is a pyramid of pilaf decorated with dried fruits and nuts; there is a basket of bakery rolls and small glass dishes piled with pickled vegetables called *tourshi.* I sit with my hands on my cheeks, scowling and hungry. The only thing that pleases me is the food–its wonderful colors and many fragrances. From around the block I can hear cap guns and my friends playing ball and tag. All I want is to eat in a simple five minutes and get the hell out of this extended ring of adults, but the very idea is impossible because this is an immovable feast, an unquestioned reality of our Balakian Sunday ritual. And I might as well have tar on my butt because I'm stuck here for the day. After the *tahn* and *bereks* and shish kebab, there will be *paklava* or *kadayif,* some melon and grapes and a soft hunk of fresh white cheese, and finally, some cardamom sweet coffee in small porcelain cups; and for the venturesome members of the family, a sip of French cognac.

If Auntie Anna was with us (as she often was), she would proclaim, not too long after *tahn* was served, that suburbia would be the ruin of America, and she was not subtle about letting us know that it would be the ruin of us, too. My aunt Anna Balakian was my father's oldest sister, and although she was married, she used her maiden name professionally, which was unusual for a woman in the 1950s. She was a professor at NYU and her books on French poetry bore the name Balakian on the book jacket.

Auntie Anna spoke with such opinionated emotion that she could cast fallout on the conviviality of the moment. "The whole idea of su-buur-bi-aa is wrong"—she liked to linger on a vowel so that the depth of her opinion was inseparable from each word. "This is how the bourgeoisie will triumph," she said, as my mother grew indignant. "There's more community and goodwill here than any-where in America, Anna, or anywhere in the world, for that matter," she glowered back. "You're lost here," Auntie Anna said, and made it clear that we had sold our souls to a barbarous society that didn't know the difference between Monet and Donald Duck, Mallarmé and Michener. We would become just like everybody else—a thin slice of yellow plastic cheese in the long, soft loaf of Velveeta that was America. Before my mother could erupt, my father interrupted with some comment about how well the kebabs had come out, and members of each side of the family tried to disentangle the two women by urging them to get the dishes and platters and bowls of food around the table. "Peter needs some more 7-Up," my grand-mother said loudly to my mother, "come on, hurry up, hurry up."

I remember a lot of conversation in the family about the sub-urbs in those days, especially in 1960, after we had moved to Tenafly. A book called *The Split-Level Trap* had come out that year written by Dick Gordon, a psychiatrist, and his wife, Kitty, who lived a few blocks away and were friends of my parents. *The Split-Level Trap,* which bore the dedication "To the people of Bergen County, New Jersey," was an insider's guide to the moral decay of suburban life—divorce, alcoholism, adultery, juvenile delinquency—and it prophe-sied doom. Because my parents knew that the Gordons' field work had been done in Tenafly and other neighboring towns I began to wonder, as I listened to my aunt and mother fight it out, why my parents settled here. My aunt's rants against the suburbs were unsettling. I would watch my mother bristle with anger at Auntie Anna, and my aunt staring with fierce disapproval at my father, seeming to me to say, Why did you marry her and come to these suburbs?

Almost every part of Bergen County was an easy commute to Manhattan, but not every part was new suburbia. Our first house was a two-story brick and clapboard built in the thirties. It straddled the sloped corner of West Englewood Avenue and Dickerson Road in Teaneck. Our part of Teaneck was mostly brick and clapboard or stucco and plank, Tudor revival, dating from the decades between the wars when Teaneck had become a fashionable suburb. In 1953 my father set an iron lamppost into the front lawn and hung a sign announcing his medical practice.

The lawns of Teaneck were well manicured, thick and green and edged with privet, forsythia, or hydrangea. My father and our neighbors compulsively yanked and dug and pulled and poisoned weeds out of the cracks between the large concrete blocks that made up the sidewalks. In the driveways of Dickerson Road were Fords and Chevys, some Buicks and Oldsmobiles. I remember Mr. Goldfischer's Caddy, a white '56 with chrome that shined like the bullet noses of the rockets I gazed at in *LIFE* magazine. Every morning I stared out my bedroom window at the driveways separated by a strip of grass and at the Goldfischer Cadillac, which dwarfed the gray '54 Olds my father and mother shared, the seats of which gave off the sour residue of regurgitated milk and infant formula and "a faint uriniferous odor," as my father called it.

Dickerson Road was Jewish, and our neighbors were Blumenthal, Cohen, Berg, Berkowitz, Goldfischer, Oshinski, and Liebowitz–Jews who had moved up from Union City or Brooklyn after World War II. I spent half of my early childhood wanting to be Jewish, in Mark Blumenthal's finished basement with its paneled walls, fluorescent ceiling lights, and Ping-Pong table. On that dank floor with its loose linoleum tiles we flipped baseball cards and sat in front of a small RCA television to watch the Yankees. We played with toys made by Remco and Ideal. A miniature Cape Canaveral, with rockets and missiles, launching pads, and beautifully drawn control panels, was our favorite.

Around four o'clock Mrs. Blumenthal would call us to the kitchen for a rugulach or a cheese Danish and cream soda. Sitting at the red linoleum counter with its chrome edging, I smelled the kitchen filling up with the richness of corned beef boiling in a big aluminum pot on the stove, where it seemed to float in a strange gray scum of fat and bay leaves. I stared at the piled-high white bags from the bakery and the small brown ones from the A & P, oil-stained paper bags of bagels, salt sticks, Danish. I thought the jars of herring and sour cream were jars of marshmallow candy, until I asked for some one day and found myself forcing the slimy fish hunks down my throat. I gazed at the mason jars of yellowish jelly full of gefilte fish and the almost patriotic stack of red, white, and blue boxes of matzoh on which Hebrew letters seemed to climb like spiders. Once a week a Beverages By Hammer truck pulled up to Mark's house and a man in a white uniform disappeared into the Blumenthals' basement with a crate of twelve turquoise spritzer bottles and came out with a crate of empties.

On Saturday mornings I watched from our window with envy as my friends walked with their parents in procession, family by family, down Dickerson Road on their way to schul. I wanted to join the men and boys in their black and white yarmulkes and their silk talliths. A brocade of silver and gold thread on Mr. Blumenthal's yarmulke glittered in the sun. The talliths were decorated with tassels called *tzitzits,* and Mark used to brag that Jews wore talliths so they could feel closer to God. "Wrapped in a robe of light: Psalm 104," he quoted. Talliths were like shawls and were adorned with gold and blue thread and tiny pearls sewn into the shapes of stars and boxes. "Tzitzits are reminders of obedience to the Almighty." Mark sounded like a Talmudic scholar when he said things like this.

I longed to be walking solemnly and confidently with my friends as they moved toward the Beth Israel Temple. I imagined the mystery of being in temple was more wonderful than anything our new, makeshift Armenian church could offer, set up on Sundays at the Teaneck Women's Club. It was strange to be Armenian on Dickerson Road, because we seemed like we should be Jews. We shared a similar feeling about family, a habit of being in the kitchen, a slower, more deliberate sense of time that was part of something I didn't understand at age seven. Dark and scrawny, with my shaggy crew cut and slightly almond-shaped eyes, I even looked Jewish.

One Saturday as I was lounging in front of the TV in my red pajamas with gray plastic feet, after *The Little Rascals* and *Sky King* and *Roy Rogers* were over and the procession of families had disappeared down West Englewood Avenue, I turned down the sound of the television and asked my mother why we weren't Jewish. The fact that it was December and the candles of the brass menorahs in all the living room windows of Dickerson Road were lit had goaded me on. They were more alive to me than Christmas trees.

"Because we're Christians," she answered.

"Why are we Christians?"

"Our people decided to follow the teachings of Jesus." She paused. "There's a legend that Noah's Ark landed on Mt. Ararat in Armenia. That makes Jews and Armenians cousins."

"What's Mt. Ararat?"

My mother exhaled as if she wished I would go away. "Mt. Ararat is one of the highest mountains in the world; it's snow-capped; it's our national symbol."

"The symbol of America?"

"No. Of Armenia."

"Where's Armenia?"

As long as I had known language the word *Armenia* had existed; it was synonymous with the rooms of my house. An assumption. *Ar. Meen. Ya. Armenia.* Like *ma-ma, da-da.* Like *hurt* and *horse. Arm. You. Me. Eat.* The word rolled to the back of my mouth and just as I almost swallowed it, I caught it back near the epiglottis and unrolled it, pushing it forward as my jaw dropped open to the *Ya* and the word spilled into the air. *Armenia.* It was such an unconscious part of my life that I had never even thought to ask: Where is it? What is it?

My mother exhaled again. "It's in another country."

"Armenia's in another country?"

"No, Mt. Ararat . . . well, both. Armenia and Mt. Ararat are in other countries. But, we're American. That's the main thing. We're not like other Armenians. They're too ethnic."

I was more confused now. How could our national symbol be in another country, and if Armenia was where my grandparents had come from, why wasn't it its own country, and why wasn't Mt. Ararat there? My mother went on explain that Mt. Ararat was in Turkey and Armenia was in the Soviet Union. Then she looked at her watch and told me to change and brush my teeth and meet her in the car in two minutes for our trip to the A & P.

I stared at myself in the bathroom mirror. If only we were Jewish, I thought, things would be better. I would walk to schul in the morning with my parents, wear a yarmulke like Mark's. There would be eight candles in December and Hebrew letters on boxes of matzoh. I would light a candle each night, get a present each night. My eyes looked back at me from the mirror, dark, deep brown, like my grandmother's eyes. They were more Jewish than Mark's. And I thought, Jesus, God, did it matter, really? Like my mother said, we were American. We didn't go to church bazaars or Armenian gatherings. We didn't talk about Armenia. I couldn't even speak the language.

Playing ball one day in the middle of March, when the ice had melted from the poured concrete of Dickerson Road, I came to feel my outsiderhood in a new way. We charted our field from the manhole cover that was home plate, a large gridded iron circle that read 1927 Hackensack Waterworks. The rest of the bases we drew in with chalk. We played with anything, a pinkie, a white sponge ball, a putty-colored, hard rubber ball with imitation seams. Sometimes we used the real thing, a cowhide baseball with red stitches, but they were easily ruined from street play, and a foul ball that smashed the Liebowitz's picture window had forced a ban on them.

On Saturdays we played double headers, beginning after schul and going till dinnertime. On this damp, chilly Saturday in March 1959, I had flipped the ball from shortstop to Mark as Ronnie Schwartz came barreling into second base trying to break up a double play. To slide on pavement usually meant a cut knee, so Ronnie threw himself into Mark as a running guard might into a lineman, and a fight broke out. As I ran toward second base to help break it up, I was more puzzled than anything because my friends were arguing about something that was downright preposterous. Their cheeks crimson and the ski-jumps of their crew cuts flattened over their foreheads, they began spitting at each other as they argued about Abraham's wife. I was furious with them for their stupidity and for delaying our game, and I screamed, "Mary Todd Lincoln is Abraham's wife, you assholes!" When I was ignored, I repeated it until Ronnie snapped at me, without turning around, "Not that Abraham, you asshole."

"Who do you think Abraham's wife is?" I asked sarcastically.

"Just get outta here," Ronnie said.

All I could say was "Fuck you," and then he pulled me over to third base and said in a low voice, "Listen, Peter, anyone who thinks Mary Todd Lincoln had anything to do with making a covenant with God and leading the Jews to the Promised Land is a total asshole."

I stood there looking down at the yellow chalk box that was third base, too confused to answer, and walked back to shortstop pounding my glove so as to get on with the game as if this argument had never happened. But the argument already had broken up the game, and as I stood at shortstop I watched Mark and Ronnie, Gary and Arnold and Ira and the other guys walk away in the twilight up Dickerson Road talking intensely in some private language about things I didn't know.

That night I found myself sitting at dinner poking at my *fassoulyah* (lamb and green bean stew) until I worked myself up to telling my father about the discussion at second base over this person named Abraham. My father grew animated and first made it clear to me that this story was connected to Noah's Ark, which had landed on Armenia's great mountain, Mt. Ararat. Then he went on and filled me in on Abraham, Sarah, Hagar, Ishmael, and something called a covenant between the Jews and God. "An agreement," he said.

I stared at my *fassoulyah* and nodded. Sure I knew about the Old Testament from Armenian Sunday School and about Mt. Ararat and Noah's Ark, and even the story of Moses, who was sent down a river in a basket. I liked the idea that Noah was a Jew and he landed in Armenia and the world got a second chance. Jews and Armenians were connected. But the argument at second base over Abraham's wife had intruded on my game and my afternoon and made me realize, as I did when I spoke with my mother on that December morning, that we were born into things; we had "backgrounds," as my friends' parents would say. My Jewish friends had their own language and rituals they carried out each week that were bound up in thousands of years of history and stories and ideas. There was something secret and alluring about it all.

One morning, as I was hunched behind a large blue box of Frosted Flakes and the flaming stripes of Tony the Tiger, my father said casually that we were moving to a new house in the neighboring town of Tenafly. I kept crunching on the flakes as if they were gum. I said nothing. All day I carried around the news, feeling the dread of absence like a sensation of death. No longer to walk those ten blocks up West Englewood Avenue to Whittier School with Ronnie and Mark. No longer to flip baseball cards and eat salt sticks and watch the Yankees in the Blumenthal basement. No longer to run the bases on the white concrete of Dickerson Road.

For the rest of that day I threw a white sponge ball against the brick side of our house, where I drew a chalk box so I could practice my pitching. In a tee shirt, checked bermudas, and high blue Keds, I licked my index finger and went into a windup. I was facing Al Kaline, Rocky Colavito, Ted Kluzuski, Mickey Mantle. I pitched through lunch and into early evening before my father appeared and walked me into the house. At dinner that night, I refused to talk about leaving Dickerson Road. I refused to look at my parents and secretly I was sure something would happen to save me.

A month earlier I had been to Lenny Cohen's bar mitzvah, where I stood all evening at the Imperial Manor on Route 4 watching the adults dance to "Havanagela" and "Mack the Knife" and eating huge pastrami sandwiches with cole slaw washed down with tall glasses of cream soda. As I stood eating and watching, Lenny's aunt Carol began to interrogate me about *my* bar mitzvah. "How old are you? Have you started lessons? Are you Reformed or Conservative?" I just nodded and kept stuffing my mouth, until I managed to make a motion with my lips that suggested the word "reformed," before I fled to the bathroom to avoid having to admit I wasn't Jewish.

The more I thought about leaving Dickerson Road, the more deeply Jewish I felt. If I hadn't been born into the tribe of Abraham, I had become Jewish by the sheer reality of living on Dickerson Road my whole life. I recalled Mrs. Blumenthal once saying to her sister about me, "He's Armenian, but they're really one of the lost tribes." I didn't see why I couldn't become a Jew. After all, I looked like a Jew, even more so than Ronnie Schwartz, who had red hair and freckles. Matzohs, yarmulkes, menorahs were objects of intimacy for me. I would walk with my friends on Dickerson Road to schul on Saturday, and when I was thirteen I would have a bar mitzvah. In the spring of 1960, I told my mother, "I'm Jewish, I belong here. And I know about Abraham and the Covenant."

"You'll forget you were here after a year in Tenafly," she said.

"I'm a Jew," I said. My mother was silent for a moment and then replied, as she did when I had irritated her in a particularly exasperating way, "*Ghe khent tatz ness,*" you make me crazy.

"I'm running away. You stink," I was shouting now.

My mother then said something that struck me as strange. "Don't get too attached to places in life, Peter."

But in the spring of 1960, my need to be a Jew had more to do with leaving Dickerson Road than a deeper understanding of the real kinship Armenians and Jews shared.

TAHN ON CRABTREE LANE

WHEN WE MOVED IN THE EARLY SUMMER OF 1960 FIVE MILES TO Tenafly, I felt strangely more American and more Armenian. We had custom built a house in a new development of about twenty-five houses on an apple orchard that had belonged to a nineteenth-century estate. The builder called our street Crabtree Lane because he mistook the lovely orchard of apple trees for crabapple trees. On either side of our new development were grand nineteenth-century houses and manors set back behind high hedges, stone walls, wrought-iron gates, and huge expanses of lawn off Knickerbocker Road, where, as my mother told us, the robber barons used to live. We had moved from Jewish Teaneck to an older, elite American town with a historical Dutch name to boot. Seventeenth- and eighteenth-century stone Dutch houses still spotted the town and some quite fabulous nineteenth-century estates surrounded our new street. The imposing white pillars of Congressman Osmers's small mansion on Knickerbocker Road, almost opposite the entrance to Crabtree Lane, made me feel that even the lines of government came to our new place on the map.

My mother now seemed to be obsessed with the details of the house, and her intensity about it made me think of 57 Crabtree Lane as something more than just some boards and a roof. The house had to have style or my mother wouldn't move into it; she made that clear. All that year, as the house was being built I watched my mother, with the aid of my aunts Lucille and Gladys and my grandmother, oversee the plans. They fought with the contractor and with his carpenters over the kind of moldings they wanted, over the thickness of doors, the style of sinks and bathroom fixtures, the mullions on the windows. "That is not an ogee molding, get it out!" my mother screamed at the senior carpenter. The marble for the sink wasn't right, the position of the electrical outlets was wrong. "Just move the little box three feet more," she said as she stormed out. "The windows are going to look like someone sat on them if you don't redraw them." Mazzola, Archer, Boyd, Kostelanski; my mother talked about the men working on our house constantly. Some days she brought them Danish and coffee; other days she brought them her aesthetic daggers. Only later did I realize that in saving the house from being without style, like many of the houses going up all over Tenafly, she was expressing the Aroosian passion for the decorative world.

57 Crabtree Lane, a white-shingle and brick colonial, was equipped with an array of new appliances that made leaving Dickerson Road less painful. A built-in dishwasher, whose copper-tinted door you unlatched to light-blue rolling shelves. A sleek white Maytag washer and dryer, with a set of dials that looked like a rocket control panel. Cool air pouring from small vents on hot days. A TV room, with large glass sliding doors that opened to a backyard half the size of a football field. Everything was white and blond and varnished and smelled new. The maple kitchen cabinets with shiny gold handles, the fresh oak floors, the white and pale-yellow walls: everything light, fresh, airy, the way Thoreau described his pad at Walden.

What finally sold me on Crabtree Lane was a small silver rectangle set into the yellow countertop of the peninsula that curved in the middle of the kitchen. An automatic blender with the name

NUTONE in bold black letters. I could whip up a milk shake at the speed of three and watch the ice cream become sludge, or I could blast it to ten for a smooth shake with fine bubbles. It was a small dream. A malt shop in your own kitchen, where we sat that summer around that yellow counter in our wrought-iron ice cream parlor chairs and my father dug into a large tub of T & W chocolate ice cream, added a tablespoon of Carnation malt, and let me and Pam and Jim take turns driving the dial.

On Crabtree Lane, families were larger. Fathers were surgeons, advertising executives, lawyers, Wall Street investors. No one was in wholesale. Fathers came home late on buses or in car pools from Manhattan. Dinner was something kids got through quickly. Our neighbors, the Walls, were masters of the five-minute dinner, which often consisted of minute steaks, four-inch squares of beef thin as linoleum. Mrs. Wall served minute steaks with potato puffs, which tumbled out of a big plastic bag like frozen golf balls before they puffed up on a cookie sheet in the oven. A hefty serving of ketchup and a large glass of Coke or 7-Up, and that was dinner.

In the midst of a neighborhood cuisine of minute steaks, hot dogs, Swanson TV dinners, or tuna whipped up in a blender, my parents became noticeably more formal and regimented about our dining. By the end of the summer I was convinced that moving to Crabtree Lane had triggered some deep Armenian feeling in them. In this cul-de-sac of American families whose parents seemed invisible and whose children owned the new macadam till after dark, my parents reverted. On Dickerson Road we were practically WASPs with our Christmas tree and Easter eggs, and now, amidst the O'Tooles and Wheelers and Walls and Dillsteins, we were something else.

Food for us was a complex cultural emblem, an encoded script that embodied the long history and collective memory of our Near Eastern culture. I didn't know that eating also was a drama whose meaning was entwined in Armenia's bitter history. In 1960 I hadn't even heard the phrase "starving Armenians," nor did I know that my ancestors were among the more than two million Armenians who, if they weren't killed outright, were marched into the deserts of Turkey in 1915 and left to starve as they picked the seeds out of feces or sucked the blood on their own clothes. In 1960 I was unaware of the morality play of the dinner table, but I was aware of how irritatingly intense my parents were becoming about the propriety and ritual of dining.

We were American enough to begin our first course with salad: lettuce, tomatoes, cucumbers, or diced celery marinated in tomato and lemon juice, or grated cucumbers in yogurt with mint leaves. Two glasses walled off each dinner setting, one for water and one for milk or *tahn*, of which the faintest odor made me queasy. Only on rare occasions did my father have a glass of *Miller High Life*, as he called it.

What minute steaks were to the Walls, lamb was to us. Leg of lamb tied up and stuffed with garlic and herbs; shoulders of lamb cooked slowly in the oven so they were falling apart and could be cut with a fork; lamb chops, thick with white fat rimming the knob of tender meat that flowered off the bone; the coveted necks of lamb–which were hard to get–cooked slowly in the oven with garlic and onions, eggplant, and sweet red pepper until the meat was tawny and soft.

And there were always surprises, like the time I found on my plate something that looked like scrambled eggs the color of parking lot gravel. Its musky flavor and chewy texture was so strange I cautiously inquired about its identity.

"Brains," my mother said.

"From what?"

"Lamb," she answered. A "delicacy full of protein," she called it.

There was regular fare: tongue, roast beef, chicken, soft-shelled crabs, scallops, sole, bluefish, and always the weekly dolma. For dolma my mother bought whatever vegetables were fresh that week, cored them, then kneaded ground beef and lamb, onion, parsley, tomato pulp, lemon juice, rice, allspice, and pepper, and stuffed full each tomato, pepper, squash, or eggplant. If there were no worthy seasonal vegetables, she used cabbage or grape leaves. Dolma simmered on the stove, and to keep the juices in, a dish is placed upside-down and pressed firmly on top of the dolmas as a second cover. On dolma days the whole house blossomed with fragrance.

My mother's only concession to fast food was *lahmajoon,* a tortilla-thin crust topped with finely chopped lamb, parsley, red and green pepper, onion, and garlic. They came frozen in packages of twelve from the Armenian grocery store in River Edge, and they heated up in ten minutes. We usually rolled into them thin slices of fried eggplant or diced cucumbers in yogurt. Good as this was, it wasn't frozen pizza or Mrs. Paul's fish sticks.

Perhaps the most interesting things my mother did in the kitchen were hybrids of southeastern Armenia and North America. Hamburgers with fresh mint and scallions, eggplants stuffed with collard greens and black-eyed peas, red lentils cooked into baked macaroni and cheese, homemade pizza topped with sautéed okra and eggplant, steaks grilled with fresh artichokes, turkey stuffed with spinach, pine nuts, currants, and hunks of French bread soaked in wine and ground *sumak* (dried barberry).

At dinner my mother was like a timed toast popping up from her end of the table to refill serving platters and pitchers or check something on the stove, and if there was nothing to get up for she popped up anyway, disappearing into the kitchen with what I think of now as her Armenian need to control the table. She was deaf to my father imploring her to sit. Her passion for food was both cultural and temperamental, part of the way she defined herself in the wake of the Armenian past and the suburban present. A story my brother tells about my mother in a restaurant in France suggests something about her way of negotiating at the dinner table, her way, too, of carrying on what she believed to be the superior sensibility of her lineage from a lost Armenian world.

It happened in what was reputedly one of the finest restaurants in the south of France, in Nîmes, a couple hours north of Aix-en-Provence, where my parents were visiting my brother, who was taking his junior year abroad. When my mother discovered this four-star restaurant, she insisted that they make the pilgrimage north to this lovely *auberge* with broad glass windows and trellissed gardens. They were seated at a round table in the center of the restaurant and my mother ordered fish wrapped in pastry. When it arrived presented delightfully on a stark white plate with fresh herbs and julienned lemons, my mother took one bite and called the waiter. "*Ce n'est pas fraîche.*" The waiter disappeared and returned with the maître d'. "*Ce n'est pas fraîche,*" my mother said, louder now. The maître d' replied, "*C'est impossible,*" and disappeared. A minute later the chef appeared.

My brother described the chef as about 250 pounds and short, dressed in white, with a large white hat. His face was red and sweating and he held a butcher knife. My mother repeated in her clean, college French, "*Ce n'est pas fraîche,*" so that now people in the restaurant were watching, and before she could speak another word, the chef was screaming, in English, "Out! Out! Out! Get out!" To this my mother rifled back, belligerently, "We're not paying for this." Minutes later, when the local police appeared in their blue uniforms, my father, who had been silent, his sense of decorum shattered by my mother's behavior, stood up tentatively as if he were being courteous to a woman entering the room and assured the chef he'd pay.

My brother does not recall how he wound up in a pile of bodies that included the chef, two policemen, and my 165-pound father. As my mother watched expressionless the police pulled the chef off my father. There was some conferring, and when my father said that he would pay and my mother insisted that he wouldn't, the police took my family to the station to settle the matter. At the station, my mother insisted that my father call an attorney her cousin knew in Paris, at which point my father began referring to my mother as someone "completely out of her mind." When the police chief dangled some handcuffs in my mother's face and pointed to the jail cell where "no dinner would be served," a certain fee was agreed on and my father signed some traveler's checks.

The Balakians filed into their rented Citroen and drove in silence back to Aix, not stopping at a restaurant along the way, and I suspect that this was the first time since our ancestors were sent out into the desert to starve in 1915 that any members of our family had gone to bed without dinner. My brother shrugged his shoulders, claiming that "it was just a cultural misunderstanding." This is my brother's way of dismissing it, but his phrase is not without meaning. The culture that was misunderstood was my mother's: her feminine, Armenian, post-Genocide disposition. At certain moments her unacknowledged cultural past became an irrepressible force, a statement of beauty and sometimes rage that asserted itself in the name of things culinary, in the name of the kitchen, the inviolable sanctuary of a culture that had barely escaped extinction. In the kitchen, my mother really was saying: We are alive and well, things have order, the world has grace and style.

If my mother was unreasonable about perfection in the kitchen, it was because she made good things happen there. Even vegetables were a ritual: *Bamiya,* okra cooked with tomatoes and onions; *imam bayeldi* (Turkish words Armenians translate as "the priest fainted"), eggplants stuffed with onions, tomato, and garlic; *fassoulyah,* green beans stewed with tomato and onions, with some cinnamon and garlic; *enguinar,* fresh artichoke hearts, onions, carrots, and potatoes cooked in olive oil and lemon juice.

While the rest of Crabtree Lane seemed to live on potatoes— french fried, puffed, chips, instant mashed—we tended to give potatoes a back seat to rice, which we call *pilaf,* cooked with chicken broth and sometimes made aromatic by adding chopped dried apricots, currants, and pine nuts. If my mother didn't make pilaf it was *bulghur* (cracked wheat) or *bulghud*—I had to go deep into my throat to say it—earthy brown and cooked with angel hair noodles and onions in chicken broth. Her rice-cooking technique was exquisitely specific. The flame had to be just so low, it had to be turned off after so many minutes, then the rice needed to stand with a paper or cloth towel under the pot lid to absorb the extra steam. The pilaf had to be light and fluffy, not sticky like Chinese rice, and had to have texture and flavor.

So much of Armenian cooking is tied in with onions that a whiff of onions in the air today reminds me of the chopping board of my mother's kitchen. The stinging whiteness of raw onions, the slivered rings falling out of each other as they were sliced, and their tubery translucence as they were diced and minced before disappearing into the olive oil of the cast-iron skillet. In the evening their unmistakable pungency would leave a lingering scent in the air.

Whether we finished with melon and some goat cheese or piles of string cheese with black seeds, figs, strawberry shortcakes, crème caramel, Jell-O, or Whip and Chill (my mother's concession to the palate of Crabtree Lane), or with the sweeter delights, such as *paklava* (a pastry made of layers of paper-thin dough stuffed with walnuts, cinnamon, and sugar, and served with a sugar syrup), *kadayif* (a torte made of shredded wheat with a stuffing of cheese or walnuts, cinnamon, and sugar), *titoomov* (chunks of pumpkin hardened in lye—bought in vials at the drugstore—cooked in syrup and covered with walnuts and cinnamon), *sujuk* (a roll made of walnuts covered with hardened grape juice and powdered sugar that arrived every now and then from Aunt Alice and Uncle Ed in Fresno), dinner took a long time to get through.

So when I asked my mother one day that first summer after we moved why we couldn't just have casseroles for dinner—things like tuna noodle or Johnny Mazetti—my mother said "Casseroles?" and then snapped back, "If the Americans want to eat that way, let them." The Americans. The phrase slapped me in the face. Like "the old country," it was a phrase that popped up now and again. "The Americans," or "typical American," my mother would say, referring to neighbors who would wander down the block for a cocktail with new neighbors, leaving their children alone after dark. "American," she would say, holding up a piece of Wonder Bread as if it were some object from another planet. The old question had been dropped in my lap again. Weren't we Americans? Congressman Osmers lived two hundred yards from us, and the stone Dutch houses spotted Knickerbocker Road. If we weren't American on Crabtree Lane in our colonial house, from which my father drove in his Chevy dressed in his dark Brooks Brothers suits each morning, what were we?

Among children, the hierarchy of a new suburban development evolves quickly. There are no histories and no alliances. The kids who are oldest, strongest, and most cunning come to power instantly. New in town, in the summer of 1960 the neighborhood became all-consuming for me. Andy Wall, the oldest kid on a block that included twenty children in the four houses surrounding us, quickly became the tyrannical leader.

The Walls were a family of seven children, and the two oldest, Andy and his brother Dan, were a year or two older than me. They ran the block by bullying and by manipulating their knowledge of the new. They were up on everything: the latest 45s–Del Shannon, Dion and the Belmonts, the Shirelles, Chubby Checker, and the Crystals. They wore the latest Keds. On hot days they appeared in surfer trunks–the kind the Beach Boys wore on their album covers. They collected weapons from the great wars of the century: hand grenades from Iwo Jima, a Nazi helmet, a piece of a Panzer from the Somme, a Japanese saber. They subscribed to *Famous Monsters of Filmland*, a slick journal of Hollywood gothicism that made them connoisseurs of horror and authorities on Lon Chaney and Boris Karloff; they had seen *Psycho* so many times that their imitations of Tony Perkins in an old woman's dress wielding a knife were closer to Steve Allen than to Hitchcock. They stayed up past midnight to watch *Invasion of the Body Snatchers* and *The Blob*. They walked around chugging cans of Mountain Dew.

One evening, after arriving late to the night baseball game because dinner had dragged on in its deliberate Armenian way, I was rebuked by Andy, who liked to mock me by asking, "You guys dining with the President?" I tried to survive that summer by ignoring Andy and playing hard, and that evening I hit three balls into the oaks–which meant they were homers–and we beat Andy's team and I walked home enjoying summer dusk on Crabtree Lane, feeling a bit superior, smelling the sweetness of cut grass and the rhododendrons and lindens and azaleas still dripping from the water of the sprinklers. As I slipped into the row of hemlocks that separated our yard from the Walls', I was collared and dragged to the ground, and when I could see again I was looking at Andy and Dan Wall sitting on top of me as they ripped open my tee shirt. I struggled, expecting to be punched in the stomach, only to find that they offered up their hands like small fins and began patting my stomach. "You're getting a pink belly," Andy said.

"It's Chinese torture," Dan chimed in. "They used it in Korea." They played on my stomach as if it were a bongo until their wrists were tired.

"Next time we'll use toothpaste or mustard," Andy threatened.

"Fuck you," I said, and threw a lame punch at Andy, who ducked it, laughing, and then I fell back to the ground exhausted and lay there for a minute looking up at the sky as it turned dark purple.

When I reached home I was covered with dirt and grass, my tee shirt was a strip hanging off my shoulder, and my mother was waiting for me in the hallway under the large hanging lantern. Angry as she looked, when she saw me her anger dissolved. "Get off my back," I snapped before she could open her mouth and disappeared upstairs, where I sat on my bed listening to my parents referring to the Wall children as juvenile delinquents and suburban brats. My father insisted that the neighborhood needed time to gel, and my mother began carrying on about casseroles. "What do you expect if they eat casseroles and minute steaks? What kind of people are these?" And they began speaking in Armenian.

The next morning, as we were finishing breakfast at the kitchen table near the windows that looked out on the backyard, we saw a cluster of towheaded kids behind our new fence. The seven Wall children, led by Andy and held up in the rear by the youngest, a three-year-old in diapers, began pelting rotten apples, from the apple tree in their yard, at my mother's beefsteak tomato plants. My mother, at the sink washing dishes in her yellow rubber gloves, threw down her Brillo pad and charged into the yard, the yellow rubber on her hands flaring in the sunlight as she pointed and admonished them. The Wall children ran, except for Andy, who stood there with an apple and a churlish look. "Just try it," my mother warned, and he dropped it and walked away.

"The problem is," my mother said to my father that night, "there's no parental guidance." My father now hurled back phrases like "excessive permissiveness," "laissez-faire morality," and "split-level traps." He was sounding like Auntie Anna. And my mother, whose anger quickly turned to word repetitions, kept saying, "Casseroles, he wants casseroles."

In this newly excavated orchard amidst the white-shingled and brick-faced neocolonial houses with their thin hairs of new grass, children seemed to rule, or at least be uncontested in public. Parents were noticeably absent, especially when compared with Dickerson Road, where Mrs. Cohen and Mrs. Bernstein and my mother were always somewhere visible. On Crabtree Lane, fathers left early. Mr. Dillstein went to work in a chauffeur-driven limo at 6:00 A.M. Mr. Wall left for Madison Avenue in a carpool of New York executives at 7:00. Dr. O'Toole left for morning surgery at Mt. Sinai at dawn. None of them returned till dusk. Only my father, who left at 9:00 A.M., was home at 6:00 for dinner. While other physicians were seeing patients until 7:00 P.M., my father poured *tahn* while my mother hopped between the kitchen and the dining room.

The mothers of Crabtree Lane were full-time mothers. I thought of them as cool, modern mothers, at home in the morning when the maid came to clean, in their bathrobes and curlers, chain-smoking and sipping coffee as they did some half-baked exercises along with Jack Lalanne on TV. But most of the day they were on the road—that is, driving children to school, music lessons, art classes, Little League. The duties of consumerism kept many of them, including my mother, perpetually at the malls of Route 4 or at the A & P, Grand Union, and Shop-Rite. Some mothers had active social schedules. They were at the club, the hairdresser, the golf course, or having luncheons and teas at the Clinton Inn. Some of them retreated into alcoholism. Some of them had affairs while their husbands were at work and having affairs. But I had no knowledge of those matters then; I only knew that my mother seemed less in the swing of Crabtree Lane life than her neighbors.

My mother had the charm of Jane Wyatt on "Father Knows Best" or the buoyancy of Donna Reed as she darted in and out of her pink-and-white '57 Chevy wagon to drop us off and pick us up from our events of the week. But she was more entrenched in the house than the other mothers, and she gave her children very little space.

When I woke up in the morning she was in the kitchen, breakfast on the table, lunches packed, prodding us to move. When I came home from school she was in the kitchen, a box of Lorna Doons on the table, glasses out for milk, dinner preparations under way. When I went to bed she was anxiously hanging around the bathroom, nagging us about washing faces, brushing teeth. Because my parents rarely went out on weekends and never on week nights, and never vacationed without us, my mother was an immovable presence 365 days of the year at 57 Crabtree Lane.

The kind of autonomy and freedom that existed for the Wall and Dillstein kids was exotic to me. It was exhilarating to sit at Bobby Dillstein's kitchen table eating Mallowmars and drinking Coke while watching Godzilla on *Million Dollar Movie* on a portable color TV perched on the kitchen counter. Or to be at the Walls' with my feet on a hassock on a Saturday night, watching the whole of *Love Is a Many Splendored Thing* or *Town Without Pity,* a box of Oreos and a six pack of Mountain Dew at hand and not a parent in earshot. Such indulgences were impossible at our house, where an Armenian-American Puritanism was beginning to rigidify as our first year on Crabtree Lane came to a close. Inside our new rooms with their marvelous appliances, my parents were ordering our lives – or perhaps were being ordered by the old habits of Armenian culture, in which the lines of authority between parents and children are clear and rituals of dining primary expressions of cultural continuity.

Still, I had hope that one day I would come home from school and find my mother sitting on the patio in white slacks, a turquoise blouse, white flats, her hair in a bubble-cut. She'd be smoking a Salem and sipping a cocktail. "Hon," she'd say casually, "I'm meeting your father at the club for dinner. There are some Swansons in the freezer, just pop one in the oven. They take twenty minutes."

If life appeared to me more complex and contradictory at 57 Crabtree Lane, one ritual we performed right in the center of suburbia embodied the strange dovetailing of new suburban life with our ancient Near Eastern culture. In the way that a scene comes back like a tableau, this comes back to me from July of 1960. On an ordinary summer evening in the middle of the week, the *Der Hayr* (the priest) and his wife (*Yeretsgeen*) from the newly built St. Thomas's Armenian Church appear at our front door. They are in summer clothes: *Der Hayr* in his clerical collar and black short-sleeved tunic, and *Yeretsgeen* in a tight low-cut lavender suit. With his silvering goatee, he is slightly debonair in an Old World way, and *Yeretsgeen*, with her jet-black page-boy, is chic. They stand in the doorway checking out the large black-and-white diamond-shaped tiles of our new foyer, and the cool air of the house mingles for a minute with the dank July evening and the smell of just-spread fertilizer.

In front of the new walnut sideboard in our freshly painted yellow dining room, standing on a new Kirman rug, the *Der Hayr* chants in Armenian. We stand around the new dining room table, attentive, and when he crosses himself, we cross ourselves. I am self-conscious, bringing my properly pointed three fingers from forehead to solar plexus, and fearing I'll go to my right shoulder before my left, I cross myself quickly twice to make certain I've covered all the stations of the body. He has a Bible in one hand and takes out of his pocket a cross and what looks like a silver flask, studded with jewels. He makes motions with the cross in the air and sprinkles holy water from the flask onto the rug. I watch my mother grimace at this small assault on her new Kirman but she holds her tongue. *Der Voghormya, Der Voghormya, Der Voghormya:* Lord Have Mercy, Lord Have Mercy, Lord Have Mercy. He chants it several times, recites a prayer, and we cross ourselves again. Then he looks at the five of us as we make an arc around the dining room table–the new gold chandelier slightly obscuring his face from where I stand–and he proclaims our house blessed.

The table is set, and while my father lights the candles my mother comes out of the kitchen with platters of *plaki* (white bean salad), *yalanchee* (cold, meatless dolmas), shrimp and cocktail sauce, chicken salad, *paklava*, marinated quinces, a bottle of French brandy, and crystal snifters. I eat in silence. I feel like I'm watching a play being put on in my own house. If the Walls and the O'Tooles

THREADS OF SILK

ARAX AROOSIAN. MY MOTHER'S NAME. UNPLACEABLE SOUNDS TO THE American ear. A name that must have baffled teachers in Paterson in the 1930s when they stared at it on the top of the class list. Arax: a name of eastern Anatolia and the southern Caucuses, where the Araxes River flows from the Ararat plateau eastward and makes a border uniting Armenia, Turkey, and Iran. A name that means turbulence, synonymous with the river.

Aroosian, a name part Arabic and part Armenian, meaning "son of the bride," or more idiomatically, "son of beautiful ones." A name of southeastern Anatolia, north of Nineveh, where the Tigris hooks around the ancient stone-walled city of Diarbekir, a city the Hurrians, Urartians, Assyrians, Armenians, Persians, Greeks, Romans, Arabs, and Turks all controlled at one time or another. Diarbekir: a linguistic estuary where Armenian, Kurdish, Turkish, Arabic, and French mingled, forming a creole language that Armenians spoke. *Dikranagerdsi* Armenian, they called it, because they called their city by its Armenian name, *Dikranagerd*, the city of King Dikran, who was the most powerful king of the Armenian

Empire at its height, circa 50 B.C. Diarbekir: a killing city where the Turkish government slaughtered more than a hundred thousand Armenians in 1915. Today, it is an impoverished city of modern Turkey where the PKK–the Kurdish Worker's Party–is based and where the Kurdish movement for civil rights is centered. A place where thousands of Kurds have been killed by the Turkish government in recent years.

The Aroosians: my mother, grandmother, and aunts. They were the queens of the aesthetic domain. No dinner or family gathering was without their constant conversation about presentation, style, quality, and taste. "He has good taste." "She has no taste." "How tasteless." Such phrases made loops and whorls around me. "That Kashan has a bad blue in it." "The cranberry in that Sarouk is gorgeous." "That shirt looks sleazy." "That button is poorly sewed on." Auntie Gladys would say to my mother every Sunday dinner, as if she were saying it for the first time, "Ary, I just love this Limoges."

The strangest things were worthy of obsession: the pattern on some old china my mother set for dessert, the presentation of pilaf, the filigree in the lace curtains, the colors of flowers in the yard, and our clothes. "Those lapels are cut poorly." "That's good cotton." "Silk will last forever if you treat it well." They always talked about silk and they always wore silk: raw silk, refined silk, silk and linen mixed. And they talked about cloth: seersucker, linen, cotton, wool, madras, rayon, nylon, dacron, and other new synthetics.

The fact was that I couldn't have any piece of clothing until I passed through the Aroosian gauntlet. Twice a year my mother took me clothes shopping to Best and Co., Bloomingdale's, Saks, and Lord & Taylor. We always bought twice as much as I would keep, and when we came home with large shopping bags of shirts, pants, sport jackets, and sweaters, my aunts Lucille and Gladys and my grandmother would be sitting on the living room couch, waiting impatiently for the fashion show to begin.

I would go to my bedroom and put on a shirt, a pair of pants, a Harris tweed jacket, and dutifully walk down the stairs into the living room and stand in front of them while they voted yes or no on each item. Although I felt like a jerk as I stood there like some boy

fashion model, I also secretly loved their doting attention, their endless passion that went into preparing me to go into the world. "Loud
color," "poor seams," "wrong kind of buttons," "sort of cheap-look-
ing." Up and down the stairs on a Saturday afternoon, changing into
new clothes just off the racks and still slick with their tags and labels
and store-bought smell.

Sometimes I was horrified at the vehemence with which my
aunts and grandmother pronounced verdicts, as if to humiliate my
mother. "Don't even *think* about it," Auntie Lu would declare about a
certain shirt. "Get that back to the store," my grandmother would
command about a jacket. They glowered at my mother. Such passion. Such conviction. I wondered if they were acting out some rite
of sibling hierarchy, since my mother was the youngest, and my
aunts and grandmother perhaps wanted to make clear the absolute-
ness of their aesthetic authority. Yet my mother enjoyed making
those returns to those stores, because they confirmed the superiority
of the Aroosian eye, making it clear that even the finest retail clothing stores in the United States were dealing in cloth that was coarse
and far from their Armenian expectations.

What I didn't know then was that my mother's father's family, the Aroosians, and my mother's mother's family, the Shekerlemedjians, were silk growers, silk refiners, and silk merchants back
in Armenia, in Diarbekir. The Shekerlemedjians owned acres of
mulberry trees near the Euphrates River basin and produced those
great horned worms that differed from the others, to borrow a
phrase from Aristotle. In the Byzantine era, Justinian attempted to
monopolize the silk industry by sabotaging the traditional Persian
trade route into eastern Europe and rerouting it through Constantinople. Although he failed to do it, he succeeded, in about A.D. 550,
in persuading two Persian monks who had lived in China to smug-
gle silkworms out of the country in the hollows of their canes and
bring them to him in Constantinople.

Thus sericulture came to the Near East, and sometime
thereafter the Shekerlemedjians began raising silkworms. My grandmother once told my aunt that the Shekerlemedjians had been
involved in the silk trade for centuries. Silk: fat mulberry leaves, the

larval worms, flossy filaments, spinning enzymes, the magical cocoons, trays of eggs, soaking skeins, the emulsions, the washing, the thrown yarns. When my grandmother was growing up in the late nineteenth century, her father, Karnig Shekerlemedjian, traded on the silk routes between Ispahan and Athens. I think of the silk routes winding down from the Himalayas across Persia and into Armenia, then snaking across the central plateau of Anatolia to Constantinople. The well-worn paths of merchants who brought the coveted thread from east to west, and my grandmother's father and his father, and his father before him, and on and on back into the fissures of those fought-over routes.

In the last decades of the nineteenth century, the Aroosians were in the silk-processing business, mostly in reeling, which involves the culling of threads from cocoons in order to produce the uniform strands that constitute commercial raw silk. When my grandfather, Bedros Aroosian, arrived in the United States in 1903, he went to work in the silk mills of Paterson, New Jersey. An Armenian Genocide survivor, my grandmother in 1916 supported herself and her two daughters in Aleppo by working as a tailoress. In 1920, when she married my grandfather, they opened a French Cleaning and Tailoring business in Paterson, where they cleaned and tailored, among everything else, a good deal of silk.

And so the ritual of critically evaluating everything material and aesthetic was part of some long-inherited past. Dinners, for one, were always a subject. No matter how gorgeous, flavorful, fine, and textured the food, it was discussed in detail. More salt, less salt, too much allspice, olive oil too coarse, pine nuts too chewy. Lamb strong, lamb underdone, lamb done two minutes too long; chicken too gamy, chicken too stringy, and on and on. My mother would say, "That Grand Union is going to hear from me first thing in the morning." Auntie Lu would say, "They have some nerve." That was a favorite phrase of all the Aroosians: establishments that sold us anything less than the finest meat, fish, or produce *had some nerve*. It was taken as a personal affront. Auntie Gladys would say, her voice squeaking with irritation, "You just tell them that we won't pay for lamb like this."

All matters concerning decoration consumed hours, weeks, months, and even years of intense round-robins of consultation and opinion. Wallpaper, upholstery, lighting fixtures, furniture, and rugs. Swatches of cloth for drapes and upholstery, clippings of wallpaper, trial carpets and chandeliers and sink fixtures went back and forth, back and forth from stores, dealers, and warehouses, as if our house was a small Middle Eastern *souk* here in the wealthy suburbs of New Jersey. Whole weekends were devoted to discussing these objects, in tones of moral highness.

Until I was about twelve and no longer so easily bent to their will, I was their companion on Sunday drives devoted to looking at houses. These drives always were predicated on the hope that my grandmother and aunts would find the right house to buy. The way it comes back to me now, I can smell the musty seat fabric of the cream-colored '54 Olds. It is 1958 and I am sitting in the backseat between Auntie Gladys and my mother, skinny as a reed, twitching my legs. We are driving the streets of East Orange, West Orange, South Orange. The windows are rolled down and everyone is speaking intensely, so that the owners of these houses, who are trimming hedges and sweeping porches, can hear us. I feel embarrassed but certain no one can see me as I slump down in the middle of the backseat. The Aroosians are holding forth on roof lines, doorways, moldings, shingle color, landscaping, the shape of front porches. We pass Queen Anne, colonial revival, Victorian houses, and the four Aroosian women say things like, "Those Queen Annes get too busy in the front," "most colonial revivals look tacky," or "those Victorians with the flat roofs, they've had their heads chopped off."

Most houses failed inspection, although there was a grading system delivered as we slowly passed by, sometimes so slowly that we seemed to come to a standstill before each house, as if casing the joint for a robbery. *Ugly, OK, Good, I'll buy it* approximated a grading system of F, C, B, A. The blackest mark you could give a house was something called "hum hum," a designation I had invented when I was five and first joined them on these Sunday drives. *Hum hum:* Auntie Lu loved that sound, and she roared with laughter as she delivered a *hum hum* on a house. There were many *Ugly*s and

*OK*s, and an occasional *I'll buy it,* but it was clear that such a house, were it for sale, was out of price range.

As the years wore on and I found myself sitting in the backseat of a '60 Chevy Bel Air and then a '63 Buick as we wound through the streets of Tenafly grading split-levels, ranches, and colonial revivals, my aunts and grandmother still had not found a house good enough to buy. There was something vicarious, voyeuristic, and sublimated about their harsh opinions of what were to them clear failings of the houses of northern New Jersey. Or was it that nothing in the material world was good enough for the heiresses of the family silk fortune lost to the Turks when the Armenians were driven from their homeland?

PART III

FATHER

SATURDAY AUTUMN I

IN MY FATHER'S LIFE, MT. ARARAT AND BAKER FIELD ARE STRANGE bookends. On Saturday afternoons in the autumn, the only place my father wanted to be was Baker Field, in section 16, row BB, which meant on the forty-yard line on the Columbia side. And from the age of five until I began playing football in high school, I was with him.

My father grew up on the corner of 116th Street and Broadway, and from his bedroom he could see the iron gates of Columbia University and through them the walkway to Butler Library, where students gathered and dispersed. I'm convinced that my father, who came to America at the age of five in 1926, fell in love with his new country because of the Columbia Lions, and especially because the "boys in baby blue" won the Rose Bowl in 1934. And they won it in Horatio Alger fashion. A small, twenty-nine-man squad, outweighed seventeen pounds per man by the number-one-ranked Stanford Indians, they were eight-to-one underdogs, but on New Year's Day they managed to hold Stanford scoreless and come up with one touchdown.

My father loved to talk about that one touchdown–a naked reverse–known in the Columbia playbook as KF–79. A simple play in which quarterback Cliff Montgomery faked a hand-off to the full-back, Ed Brominski, diving off right tackle, and as he followed Brominski he seamlessly slipped the ball to Al Barabas, the halfback sweeping across the backfield in reverse direction. By the time anyone realized what had happened, Barabas was in the end zone for a seventeen-yard score. I grew up hearing a nostalgic litany of Columbia football names: Cliff Montgomery, Al Barabas, Sid Luckman, Paul Governalli, Paul Zwiacki, Mitch Price, and of course, Coach Luigi Picolo, called Lou Little.

My father never entered the stadium without a program and saved every one, starting with a Columbia–Navy game in '29. At Baker Field my father performed his rituals, always sitting in the same seat, always buying a program at the same entrance gate, always buying a Coke and two hot dogs wrapped in aluminum foil for each of us from the vendor at the entrance to section 16, who carried a large aluminum box on a strap around his shoulder.

Though my father had no interest in the social part of Ivy League football, I loved walking through the tailgate field behind the scoreboard area of the parking lot. I was dazzled by the dress and ceremony of food, by the alums in Scotch-plaid pants and blue blazers and the women in gray skirts and bright cashmere sweaters. I loved how the gates of the station wagons hung down under the weight of thick blue blankets and portable bars on which glass cocktail shakers of Bloody Marys and whiskey sours and cans of beer were stacked. Some had sterno stoves on them with chicken and sausage grilling, others had plaid tin coolers stuffed with sandwiches, dishes of olives and pickles and radishes and celery. I wished my father was among these happy, well-dressed people reminiscing about the Yale game of '42, shaking hands, laughing, pouring drinks, and talking with their mouths full.

He seemed oblivious to all of that, and privately I resented it. We always walked briskly to our seats in time to study the program before we would rise to sing the National Anthem and the Columbia alma mater, which my father sang in his usual high-pitched off-key voice, just as he sang "Who Owns New York" after each Lion touchdown and "Roar Lion Roar" at strategic intervals of the game.

Perhaps it is not surprising that my first recognition of my father as a public person happened at Baker Field on a balmy Saturday in October of 1958. Because he was late leaving the hospital that morning after his rounds, we arrived at the stadium behind schedule and soon found ourselves jogging alongside the Columbia team as they came out of the locker room, the players' steel-capped cleats throwing up dirt against our trousers. As they moved past us, a small bald man, dressed in a suit, collapsed like a marionette. When he hit the ground, his hand fell in the path of the last player's spikes. I watched the bald man lying on the spike-pocked ground and saw thick crimson blood pouring down his wrist onto his dark suit and into the earth.

My father dropped the program and ran to the collapsed body. On his hands and knees, he undid the man's tie and shirt and began pressing his hands on his chest. Then he put his mouth on the man's mouth and began blowing into it. Within seconds a crowd formed around the two of them, and I stood there staring at the game program in my hand: "Columbia–Harvard" and "homecoming," a word my father had repeated that morning, and a drawing of a man in a raccoon coat, a pipe in his mouth, arm in arm with his flapper girlfriend–college nostalgia that was lost on me at seven. When I looked up, the police and an ambulance had appeared. As the back doors opened my father disappeared with the stretcher and the bald man, who was wrapped in a blanket. Then the crowd broke up and my father returned to talk with the police, who were writing down his every word.

Then my father walked briskly toward me as if he had just remembered I was there. He was sweating and smiling, and I noticed that his sweater was gone. "Kick-off time," he said, and we jogged into the stadium and snaked through the crowd to section 16 just in time to see a wobbly, short, end-over-end kick land in the hands of the only black player on the field, a halfback named Harvey Brookins, who returned it a few yards into a pile of white and crimson jerseys.

As I sat in the clear October light looking down on the green field and the colorful uniforms, I felt sick in my stomach. I wrapped my hot dog back into its aluminum foil and stuffed it in the pocket of my windbreaker. I looked at my father, who was immersed in the game, and I kept thinking of the bald man on the ground with the blood pouring from his wrist. I flipped through the program, then looked back at the field where the uniforms were running and piling up on one another. When Columbia could not move the ball ten yards and had to punt, I turned to my father and said, "Is he dead, Dad?"

My father just stared at the high spiraling punt that landed deep in Harvard territory.

And so I waited for the next series of downs, and when the Harvard punter got the snap and began his punt, I turned to my father again.

"Dad, did the man die?"

My father looked down at me and I up at him as he squinted in the bright autumn sun. "Arm tackles, arm tackles, arm tackles. Ever since Lou Little left."

So this time I asked again immediately, after the Lions had returned the punt a few yards but before they began their first play from scrimmage, "Dad, did the man die?"

My father clicked his tongue, and when he did this he made a sound, by brushing his tongue briskly against the roof of his mouth, that sounded like something between a cluck and a kiss. It was a subtle, almost delicate gesture, often made with a slight look of disgust, but it was an iron command and meant simply that you were asking an inappropriate question; it meant No Trespassing. It was my father's way of keeping order, and so when my father clicked his tongue, I had learned by seven, I was not to get an answer. But then he surprised me and said, "He'll be all right. Now watch the game."

All day I sat in the stands and watched the shadows grow on the field as the gold and scarlet leaves on the hillside in the distance seemed to blur and glow. Cigar smoke, coffee, hot dogs, damp turf, the good smells of Saturday afternoon like a distant world as I sat in the stands thinking about the small bald man and my father, and the ambulance with its eerie bed on wheels. I kept seeing his hand and the blood leaking onto the ground. By the end of the fourth quarter, when my father realized that we had not analyzed plays or forecast Coach Donelli's calls and that, in fact, I had said almost nothing all afternoon, he turned to me and said, "The man will be OK, he won't die, he had a small heart attack," then he brushed his hand over my crew cut and said, "you gotta be tough as nails, son."

On the way home we listened to the scores of other games on the radio: LSU, Alabama, UCLA, Ohio State, Notre Dame, the names of power and success in the great stadiums in other parts of America. As we drove across the George Washington Bridge and the purple twilight settled on the tall buildings of Manhattan, my father was relaxed and content, humming one of his favorite football songs. I wanted to ask him: "How can you be singing the Georgia Tech fight song when a man almost died on the soft ground of Baker Field? You, Dad, who put your lips to his mouth. Did you taste death? What was it like?" The image of the man on the ground with my father bending over him kept appearing in my head as I slumped in the seat and the next thing I knew he was carrying me from the car up to my room, the smell of dolma on the stove wafting over me as we moved through the kitchen. Then I fell into a deeper sleep as he undid my shoes and pulled the quilt over me.

ISTANBUL WAS CONSTANTINOPLE

B<small>Y SEVENTH GRADE MY FATHER AND</small> I <small>BEGAN OUR ERA OF STRAINED</small> relations, and it was the telephone that came to symbolize the wedge between us. In the years before formal dating, my romances with girls began and often ended on the phone. While there were school dances and parties at the houses of my more socially precocious classmates, whose parents would turn over the chic dens of their split-level houses to us on Saturday nights, mostly we talked on the phone.

I loved the magic of dialing the baby-blue phone in my parents' bedroom as I lay on the soft Kirman rug. My heart pounded as I dialed and asked, as quickly as I could when a parent answered, for Sally, or Adrian, or Kathy, or Julie. When I try to picture them now in their middle age, with their teenage children or their careers or husbands, I only hear their twelve-year-old voices, playful and flirtatious, coming through the perforated holes of the receiver.

After several days of observing my new evening phone calls, which I made behind closed doors in a quiet voice, my father used a phrase he liked to use at such moments: "Peter, I'm putting my foot down." As a physician he lived by the phone, he told me. "If the phone is tied up," my father said, "people who may be dying cannot reach me." He told me I could talk on the phone for five minutes each evening, and then I must finish my sentence and hang up. Even though I took dying seriously, I shouted back, "Goddamit, take your five minutes!" and stormed up to my room.

"He's so out of it," I complained to my mother, "he's a god-damn square."

As I proved incapable of limiting myself to the five-minute plan, the evenings turned into cat-and-mouse games between me and my father over the phone. The struggle for the phone was my first move away from the autonomy of the family and the first challenge to my father's control. Since the phone was the nexus of Tenafly teen culture—a precocious, affluent world embodied in the songs of Tenafly's Lesley Gore, whose hits like "It's My Party" and "You Don't Own Me" expressed the troubled hearts of indulged adolescents—such lack of restraint was most unwelcome in our house. To my father, who had different notions about growing up, there was something indecent about his twelve-year-old son talking to girls on the phone for twenty, forty, or sixty minutes at a clip. As the year progressed, my father and I grew further and further apart, and I spent time every evening planning my phone life around his evening schedule. My phone problem, as my mother came to call it, hit my father on some primal level. His reaction was more than an expression of normal parental authority to my new seventh-grade identity. Although some of my friends' parents expressed vicarious delight in their children's first nudge toward sexuality and some did not, none seemed as hostile to this passage to adolescence as my father.

The more aloof, distant, and disapproving my father became, the more I thought of him as Armenian. The truth is I never thought of my father as an immigrant, nor did he consider himself one. His English was perfect Manhattan American. In his dark Brooks Brothers suits and starched white shirts he looked Ivy League as he moved through public life with the serene confidence of a suburban doctor. He was formal, but always at ease at his office, PTA meetings, or a Little League game. He was so thorough about not identifying with ways that might be thought of as "ethnic"–that generic word Americans like to use to refer to "the other"–that he refused to speak Armenian at his office, even with those Armenian patients whose English was rough and who longed to bond with their physician in their native tongue. "There's only one language at the office," he told my mother whenever she would beg him to give the elderly Armenians some extra attention. He sometimes told people he was born in New York City. "It makes it easier," he said. "When I die, just put 'born in New York City,'" he told me once when I was in college. Around his Armenian friends he never said such things; they all knew he was born in Constantinople.

I often played with the sound of the word: *Con stan tin ople.* I liked rolling it around in my head. Secretly it came to obsess me. I found it difficult to believe: my father, whose passion for football was Vince Lombardiesque, had not been born in the United States. I had a picture of my father's birthplace in my head, from tidbits of overheard adult conversation, a painting by Sarkis Katchadourian hanging in my grandmother's dining room, things I read in the *World Book.* Constantinople. The name wasn't even on the map anymore. There is a song by the Ames Brothers called "Istanbul," one of those forties-sounding razzmatazz songs that joked about the names of changing places or the names of places changing: *Istanbul was Constantinople/ Been a long time gone, Constantinople/ Now it's Turkish delight on a moonlit night . . . / Why did Constantinople get the works?/ That's nobody's business but the Turks'.*

I hummed the tune to myself, flipped the words in my head– Constantinople, Istanbul. Asked myself: Why did Constantinople get the works? *Turks. Works. Nobody's business.* It was a city in Europe and Asia, a continental estuary. An imperial center of trade for merchants from Scandinavia to China. An uncovered *souk* where for millennia things came and went: silks and brocades; sacks of cardamom and myrrh, saffron, wheat and barley; the slaughtered cattle, the brass wares and carpets piled and hung as the pleasure boats and schooners and caiques floated in and out.

There was an Armenian restaurant in Greenwich Village, The Dardanelles, named after the famous strait that links the Sea of

Marmara and the Aegean. We drove there in rush-hour traffic for *midya,* cold mussels in their shells stuffed with currants, pine nuts, and rice. And there was The Golden Horn on 56th Street, named for an inlet of the Bosphorus. Why were Armenian restaurants in New York named after parts of Constantinople?

The painting by Katchadourian showed the gold dome of Hagia Sophia. "The greatest monument in Christendom," my grandmother said. The minarets in loose brush strokes gold and green. My grandmother said they were Islamic. Sun-flecked caiques in the harbor or boats on fire? My grandmother said it was a night of fireworks in old *Bolese,* what Armenians called Constantinople. Red and gold Roman candles in a deep blue sky. A summer night of fun in Constantinople. Sarkis and Vava Katchadourian, both painters, were friends of my Balakian grandparents, and though Sarkis died young in Paris after complications from an appendectomy, we talked about him often. His bright post-impressionist still lifes hung in our living room. He was the man as pure artist, for I had no image of him except as impasto oils on canvas. Yellow wildflowers. The rouge of apples. The pistachio light of morning.

My father was born in September of 1920, while his parents were vacationing on Prince Island in the Sea of Marmara. In September the mussel shells wash ashore, and the light makes silver cups of the tepid tide. Powder-blue sky. The bronze spray of light on the eucalyptus, olive, and apricot trees, and on the minarets, the domes of Hagia Sophia, and the Blue Mosque. Constantinople was colonized by the Greeks as Byzantium, and in A.D. 330 the Roman emperor Constantine the Great turned the city into the imperial residence and the eastern capital of the Roman Empire, before it became the seat of the Byzantine Empire. In the sixth century, Justinian built Constantinople anew on seven hills. His magnificent monument was Hagia Sophia, with its porphyry and Thessalonian marble, braided gold chains hanging with lamps and crosses, which made light and shadows on the mosaicked walls and dome.

The Middle Ages brought Persians, Arabs, Russians, Bulgarians, and the first Turks, the Seljuks of central Asia, who deforested Anatolia in order to graze their horses and sheep. Between 1095 and

1195, three Crusades passed through Byzantium on their way to defend the Holy Land from the Muslims and plundered its riches. Such was the European envy of the great city that during the Fourth Crusade, Crusaders attacked the city, gorging themselves on Christian artifacts. Shortly thereafter, Baldwin of Flanders set up a feudal state within the city walls and Constantinople was made so unstable that encroaching Turkish tribes, called Ottomans, coming from as far east as the Gobi Desert, were able to conquer the city by 1453. Then Hagia Sophia became a mosque, the mosaic stories of Christ were whitewashed, and by the mid-sixteenth century, the Turkish sultan Suleiman the Magnificent had consummated the city's new Muslim era.

When my father was two years old, my grandparents left Constantinople with their three children. My grandfather, Diran Balakian, a physician for the Berlin to Baghdad Railway, arranged for his family's passage to Europe. My father told me that his family left in 1922 and mentioned countries they passed through–Bulgaria, Serbia, Hungary. In Vienna, my grandfather joined the staff of a hospital. Later they moved to a small town in the French Alps.

The Armenian writer Gostan Zarian records in his diary at the end of the summer of 1922, the month my father left the city:

> The shores of the Bosphorus are agitated. There is a scent of opium and mastic in the wind. The air around my lips bubbles like water in a hookah.... Like enormous decapitated crocodiles, streetcars glide up and down the street.... Though he continues to be present, the Armenian has ceased to exist here.
>
> In the shadow of the Sublime Porte, Armenian printers collect muddy beams of light from puddles in the street. From their holes in the walls of winding Byzantine alleys, Armenian booksellers peddle reproductions of Mother Armenia and Casanova's *Memoirs....* A couple of streets down, sheltered by the Genoese and Venetian missions, stands the

Armenian church. Stands there like a heap of stones, a graveyard of memories. There is horrible misery on the shores of the Bosphorus. In the streets, fragments of humanity with terror in their eyes. Sinister glances from Turks. Whispered talk. Every day I am assailed by new memories. Our loss is so enormous that it is impossible to write about it.... It is not easy being an Armenian. Perhaps it is our function to illuminate some dark corner of the universe. Darkness itself is on the move. At daybreak the sun looks at ashen faces. Everyone is still alive for the time being.

My father recalled nothing of his birthplace, and little about his passage out, but images of Europe slipped into conversation now and then. In Collonges, a small town in the French Alps, they ate bread and chocolate for breakfast. Cowbells rang from the fields of yellow and red flowers around their house. On a clear day he could see the snowy top of Chamonix. He grew nostalgic talking about a Viennese amusement park, the Prater, with its carousel of huge hand-carved and painted wooden horses. And about a Wiener schnitzel his mother made, a dish my mother could never make to his satisfaction, until she realized it was a dish too mythic to be re-created.

Three days before my father died, he told me of two dreams he'd had, as we sat in the TV room watching replays of the assassination attempt on Ronald Reagan. My father looked shrunken, his face graying from the eroding heart disease, his feet up on the black leather ottoman, he was sipping orange juice. In the first dream, he is with his cousin Armine and his sister Anna in their house in Collonges, leaning out the window flinging pastries to the ducks, and a church bell begins to ring plangently, echoing wildly, hurting his ears. In the second, he is on a train departing Constantinople. Smells of garlic and wool and body odor. The nostalgia of train whistles. Steam and hissing. His mother says, "When the train starts the lights will go out. Don't be scared, we're right here." I knew it was a dream about death, and I wish he hadn't told it to me.

My father's Aunt Astrig recalled that as the Balakians
boarded the *Berengaria* in France for America, my father was com-
plaining about the wrinkle in his woolen trousers. He was shouting,
"Il faut repasser mon pantalon." He was making a commotion.
Because my grandfather had gone ahead to set himself up in the
practice of medicine, my grandmother was alone with her three
young children and a family passport from a country that no longer
existed. *Republique Armenienne* in flamboyant script. A ten-by-
twelve-inch piece of parchment with a three-by-five-inch photo of
the family. My father with a Beatle haircut wearing a sailor suit. His
eyes dark and playful. It's the spring of 1926. I think of him, not yet
six, annoyed by the crease in his trousers. Trying to create order. The
name of his birthplace has disappeared from the map, and the
meaning of that map, too, has disappeared. I picture him leaning
over the railing of the *Berengaria,* the Atlantic Ocean in the background.

THE OTHER SIDE OF THE BRIDGE

O~N~ S~UNDAYS~ ~WE~ ~WERE~ ~OFTEN~ ~SUMMONED~ ~TO~ 395 R~IVERSIDE~ D~RIVE~, Auntie Anna and Uncle Steve's river-view apartment on the Upper West Side of Manhattan near Columbia University. Life in Tenafly was separated from the Upper West Side by the George Washington Bridge, which loomed with its gray towers and huge steel girders and cables as I sat in the middle of the front seat of our pink-and-white Chevy wagon in a blue blazer and tie and tan Levi cords. I was angry and sullen because I was pried away from a Yankees, Giants, or Knicks game on TV. "Do we have to go there?" I asked several times.

Going to 395 Riverside Drive was going to high culture. Even as I stepped across the threshold from the dark hallway into the narrow entrance hall of the apartment, I was overwhelmed by bookshelves that were crammed not with books but with magazines, "scholarly journals," my father called them, their bindings yellowing white, cracked, and well-used. Most of them were in French, shelf on shelf to the ceiling. In the foyer to which the hallway opened there were more bookshelves filled with the colorful bindings of books, and on the open areas of the walls hung drawings by Surrealist artists Marcel Jean and Yves Tanguy. If the coat closet was full, we had to take our coats into my aunt and uncle's bedroom, where my sister Pam and I found ourselves bewildered, for most of the surfaces—including the bed—were piled with manuscripts, books, and journals. "Is this a bedroom?" my sister asked.

My aunt Anna, called by her Armenian name, Anahid, in the family, was my father's oldest sibling. Her husband Steve was an electrical engineer and businessman who was born in the ancient Greek city of Smyrna and narrowly escaped with his family in 1922, when the Turks burned the city in order to wipe out all the resident Christians—the Greeks and Armenians—before changing the city's name to Izmir. Years later I listened to him recall how he stood on the prow of a French steamship in the harbor and watched the buildings peel apart in the fire as he and his family escaped across the Mediterranean to Tunis, where he grew up speaking French as well as Armenian and Arabic. At 395 Riverside Drive, French, Armenian, and English were the chosen languages.

Auntie Anna was a professor of French in the Romance Language Department at NYU, and her sister, Nona, was a longtime editor at the *New York Times Book Review*. They both wrote books. Auntie Anna wrote about French literature, especially French poetry, and Auntie Nona wrote on American literature and sometimes on Armenian-American writers. In my childhood memory Anna and Nona are inseparable. It was always Auntie Anna and Auntie Nona; we were going to Auntie Anna and Auntie Nona's. When they walk up the flagstone walk to our house they are always together, Auntie Anna six inches taller than Auntie Nona, walking side by side.

Auntie Anna loved big parties, especially birthday parties, which she made occasions for family gatherings. Her passion for the extended family was limitless; the more family present at any gathering, the happier she was. Usually 395 Riverside Drive filled up with: Mrs. Nalbantian, Uncle Steve's mother; my great aunts, the remaining sisters of my late grandmother, Vergine Tante and Astrig Tante, as they were called by my father and his sisters; and their husbands, Miran Uncle and Ostanig Uncle; and then Uncle Steve's brothers, Jack and Henry, and their wives, Rose and Zabel, and their children, Eddie and Ara and Nancy and Carol; and my father's cousins, Laura and Ronnie Sarraf, and their spouses, Jack and Ruth, and their children, Paul, Christopher, Malina, Caroline, and Edward; Auntie Satenik, who lived upstairs and who would live to 104, was always there, as was Auntie Lucy, the widow of Krikor (George) Balakian, my grandfather's brother; my aunts Lucille and Gladys and my grandmother; and my cousins, Suzanne and Haig, Auntie Anna and Uncle Steve's children. If you were Auntie Anna's friend and you were in town, you were invited. Auntie Nona's good friend, Ross Parmenter, the music critic at the *Times;* Auntie Anna's writer friends, Anaïs Nin, Daisy Aldan, and Marvin Cohen; and what I thought of as oddball professor-types who spoke French, Italian, Spanish, and wore dark suits, horn-rimmed glasses, and mustaches and beards. So this throng of people all speaking strange languages, stuffed into this overheated apartment, created for me such bewildering cultural density that I found myself drifting off to the side of the room to watch.

A long buffet table was set with a white tablecloth and platters of ham and turkey and beef and silver trays of *bereks, yalanchis, midya,* and *pasterma* (thin slices of cumin and garlic-cured beef), *plaki* and pilaf, glass plates of *paklava, shekarjee* (almond-stuffed sugar cookies), and *kadayif.* Everyone had a highball glass, which Uncle Steve made sure was always full of scotch or gin, and we children had highball glasses of ginger ale and Coke. When my aunt determined the moment was right, she would ring an empty wine glass with a spoon to call us to order for the concert to be given by my cousins Suzie, who was a year older than me, and Haigie, who was three years younger. Suzie in a dark dress and black patent-leather shoes and Haigie in a suit and tie. They were serious about their music and played with pride.

When Auntie Anna clinked the wine glass, Haigie stood erect with his violin under his chin, his bow poised, staring at the music on his stand, and Suzie sat at the piano, her hands arched and ready. Then Aunt Anna gave the signal and they would play Beethoven's Spring Sonata, or Mozart's fifth violin concerto in D major. Sometimes Auntie Anna and Uncle Steve would spontaneously go to their bedroom and return with their violins and join their children. They were all good. Very good. Not quite good enough to be professional musicians, but almost that good.

I watched them with a mixture of respect and resentment, not because I couldn't play like them (I had no interest in playing an instrument) but because I could see Auntie Anna smiling at my mother, seeming to me to say, *Your children can't compare with my prodigies,* and I felt the thrust of this competition directed at me, the oldest of my father's children, who was not in the least interested in high culture. I was twelve and had taken cello lessons for several years, and when the concert was over my mother beat Auntie Anna to the punch by blurting out, "Peter is making wonderful progress on the cello." I wanted to break in, but just shook my head at my mother in disgust at this untruth. The only progress I was making on the cello was wearing a hole in the puck of resin I used on my bow. Auntie Anna then launched into a small lecture on Pablo Casals and said, "Arax, you and Peter must come to New York and join us when Casals is in town next." These moments of cultural rivalry made me wish I had my cello right there so I could kick a big hole in it and make it very clear where I stood on the matter.

As these exchanges between the Aroosians and the Balakians heated up, I found myself listening to two sides of the George Washington Bridge. Auntie Anna and Auntie Nona spoke in literary language: *Proustian, coterie, Hemingwayesque, la nausée, ennui, nihilist, Dadaism,* and so on. And when the Balakian sisters assailed the suburbs for being banal and philistine, which I took to mean that we were not part of a world that was as cultivated and civilized as theirs, the Aroosian sisters turned up their lexicon and claimed their own moral high ground.

The Aroosians prided themselves on their aesthetic refinement and sense of style, and preferred Taylor Caldwell and William Saroyan to Virginia Woolf and André Breton. They were champions of Protestant Christianity, around which their sentimentality, too, was wound. I often would hear Auntie Lu and Gladys invoking God in pious whispers under their breaths, "Dear God," "God bless," "God save." Like many Armenians, my grandparents' families had been converted to Protestantism from their own Armenian Orthodox Christianity by the American missionaries who went to Turkey in the nineteenth century with hopes of converting the Turks from Islam. By the time the Aroosians and the Shekerlemedjians had come to the United States, they were already on the road to being American by virtue of their Protestantism – a Protestantism that had, as well, nearly two thousand years of Armenian Christianity behind it.

Auntie Lu and Auntie Gladys were single businesswomen who worked on Wall Street and who found in Dr. Norman Vincent Peale the perfect marriage of their faith in capitalism and their Christian piety. The work ethic, free enterprise, self-help psychology, and American Protestantism were all rolled into one with Dr. Peale. Every Sunday they attended services at the Marble Collegiate Church on Fifth Avenue, where he bellowed his triumphal sermons over the well-groomed heads of his affluent congregation that sometimes included President Nixon. So when Auntie Anna lorded over them the alchemical transfigurations of poetry to suggest that the light of French symbolism was not shining in suburbia, or when Auntie Nona made an appeal to the tragic vision of her friend, the novelist Carson McCullers, my mother and aunts rifled back with their own visionary rhetoric. It could go something like this:

"You see," Auntie Anna says, emphasizing her favorite vowels, "the Romantic poets fled *ennui* through intellectualized sensualism. Back then they understood the problem of the petite bourgeoisie," to which Auntie Lu replies in a taut voice, "Dr. Peale believes in the *actual* power of words. Words in the mind of prayer give us access to the power of something larger than ourselves – 'all things through Christ which strengtheneth me,' Phillipians 4:13."

As Auntie Anna heats up she enunciates, "You see, my dear, the poet has taught us that the abyss is the gateway to man's imagination, and it's imagination which gives us power over ourselves."

Then my mother, in her tone of controlled, in-your-face belligerence, says, "Stonewall Jackson was a man afraid of nothing, because he never took council of his fears" – something she must have picked up from a Peale sermon on the radio, because she never attended his church.

Auntie Gladys adds, "He [meaning Stonewall Jackson, or Dr. Peale, or perhaps Jesus Christ] believed in the *power* of prayer."

My mother continues, "Life in Tenafly is just what America is *about*, Anna. And, I don't know of a better country than America," insinuating that all is well where the Aroosians come from back in New Jersey, but at the same time asking, What in God's name is this country at 395 Riverside Drive?

Then Auntie Nona chimes in, in her high, gentle voice, "We must remember that whether it is God or the imagination, and perhaps they are the same, that we're all resisting crass materialism for a higher ideal. I was talking with Eudora yesterday—" (Eudora Welty, her old friend in Mississippi), but before Auntie Anna can break in, my mother says "Nona, I think you better bring in the paklava, and I'll get the coffee."

On and on it would go on those Sundays. Literary Romanticism versus middle-class Protestantism. Democratic suburbia versus high culture. The Aroosian women and the Balakian women fired their opinions back and forth across the symbolic bridge of the dinner table. Each camp defending its side of the George Washington Bridge with vengeance and pride, and at some level of their cultural beings they seemed to be guarding their territories like Old World Armenians defending their particular province or city. The Aroosians, wealthy merchants from the Armenian hinterlands of Diarbekir, would not be upstaged by the intellectual Balakians of Constantinople. Country fierceness and cosmopolitan arrogance. So back and forth it went, Mallarmé, Peale, Baudelaire, Thomas Edison, Eudora Welty, Stonewall Jackson.

At these showdowns my father sat at the table and grew remote. He looked as if he were watching a tennis match, turning his head to one end of the table and nodding, then back to the other and nodding, smiling uncomfortably. Finally, he would get up and drift into another room and let the women fight it out, caught between the high culture of the Balakians and his new life in suburbia with the Aroosians, whom he liked quite well.

By evening I would be slumped in the corner of a stiff couch sipping ginger ale out of a highball glass, a wet coaster in my lap, feeling beleaguered by the contentious women on both sides of my family. I was thirteen and growing my thick dark hair longer now. In my blue blazer and Levi cords, which looked like clam diggers because I was growing by the month, I felt like a misfit. The sun was gone and the Persian carpets too dark, the sound of steam kept knocking the radiators, some Chopin was on the stereo, and the general conversation persisted with talk of the better colleges, music camps in Provence, expectations for our futures; and I was sunk in depression, not only because the great promises of the weekend had dissipated but because it had come to this—this place of strangeness and confinement—and my soul wanted to rise into my mouth and proclaim to all of them that I hoped my future would include just one thing: the beach at Seaside Heights, where Bunny Russo and I would disappear under the boardwalk and watch the sun set while we drank Colt 45 and ate clams. When the moon rose and lit the smashing waves, our beach fire would smolder and we would make love while Roy Orbison's voice on the radio poured over us in the velvet air.

When we leave 395 Riverside Drive in our Chevy wagon, the winter wind is raw on my face, and my father turns the key in the ignition so that the car radio, which had never been turned off, blares into the cold black air lit by the lights of the dashboard. In a fog of breath my father says, "If you can't turn it off, turn it *way* down." I turn it down, but the voice of Cousin Brucie, WABC's evening DJ, skitters into the black air of the front seat, and I'm free again.

· · · · ·

To make sense of my father, I had to piece him together. More than the mystery of personality, it was a collision of cultures. Wasn't my father American? Wasn't he also European—not a European national—but European? Wasn't he an Armenian from Constantinople, the youngest of a family that fled to Europe in 1922 as refugees of the Armenian Genocide? And weren't the Balakians part of an

intellectual tradition that was both Armenian *and* European? In
Constantinople, Armenians had absorbed European culture into
their own for centuries, since the time of the Enlightenment in particular, from which ideas about political and social freedom sus-
tained Armenians seeking reform from an oppressive Ottoman
society. My father grew up in a family that idealized artists and intellectuals, that believed universities were salvation. My father's father
left his native city of Tokat, in the interior of Turkey, to attend Ner-
sessian College in Tiflis, then to medical school in Leipzig. My
father's mother, Koharig Panosyan, graduated from the American
Women's College in Constantinople before doing graduate work in
Chartres. The Balakians and the Panosyans believed in the intelli-
gentsia and culture with religious fervor. In the Ottoman Empire, the
Balakians and the Panosyans had been clergymen, teachers, physicians; and now, the Balakian sisters, Anna and Nona, were in the
business of high culture in the United States.

At thirteen I thought of my father as a square. His dicho-
tomies bewildered me. Formal, aloof, interior, he was like an Edwar-
dian gentleman. He was also the doctor who moved to Bergen
County because he wanted to be part of suburbia. He would joke,
"God made the country, man made the city, that's why I moved
here." Once he told me that he left the Upper West Side to flee high
culture, just as he fled it on those Saturday afternoons of his childhood when he jumped the fence at Baker Field to watch the Lions
play. He made it clear that he fled Manhattan as well, because he
had no interest in the kind of medical business practiced by Park
Avenue physicians; he liked the looser, more human tone of medical
practice in Teaneck and Englewood. He was an admired physician
whose efforts on the boards of education and health and with the
local sports teams gave him pleasure and a sense of community.
Although he had few close friends, he enjoyed people and people
were fond of him and often asked me about him. They found him
unpretentious and kind, and, perhaps, a little different, and that
interested them.

At home my father was meticulous, formal, deliberate. Not
until mod styles infiltrated Brooks Brothers did I ever see him in

anything but a gray or blue suit, white shirt, and a red or blue tie. He wore black shoes and topped his neatly parted, fine black hair with a cocoa Stetson hat. For dinner he took his tie off, but when he came downstairs around nine in the evening to put the cars in the garage, he would stop by the coat closet take a tie from a hanger and put it on before proceeding out to the driveway.

In the world of my friends' dads, my father stood apart. No backslapping or hearty handshakes, or greetings of "old buddy" or "man." No polo shirts or khaki pants or slip-on canvas sneakers, or buddies for golf on Wednesdays, when doctors were supposed to be riding the fairways in orange carts and lime-green pants and white visors. No weekend cocktails with the McKays or the Wheelers. Nor did my father joke with me about macho ideals, the kind that Hemingway and John Wayne embodied. He made no jokes of the kind my friends' fathers would tell, in sly moments when mothers were out of the room and fathers and sons bonded. Because he was 4-F in World War II owing to high blood pressure, something he never mentioned, he had no war stories either.

Sometimes it seemed that the whole physical world made my father squeamish, and for a physician this seemed to me strange. Anything suspected of being unclean, any surface of the world that might harbor fungus, virus, bacteria, a mote of something dangerous, was combatted with alcohol, Lysol, Clorox, hydrogen peroxide, Mr. Clean, Janitor in a Drum, SOS soap pads, Comet, Babo. My parents were both fanatical about germ-theory conspiracy. Our house was a place where germs were to be wiped out with ruthless passion.

In my father's world, things were always incubating. "Don't eat chicken salad at the delicatessen, it's been incubating." "Don't order desserts with cream or custard"; "Don't take mints from a bowl in a restaurant"; "Don't shake hands with anyone if you can help it"; "Check for stray hairs in everything when you eat out." A sneeze would drive my father out of a room. Once I saw him use a paper towel to pick up ice cubes for his own glass. In his office, he wiped the doorknobs with alcohol after patients left. He rarely passed a sink without washing his hands. We were forbidden to drink from each other's cups or glasses at home. No sips from friends' Coke cans or bites from a communal Twinkie–there was always spinal meningitis or hepatitis going around.

In all of this germ madness there seemed to be some deeper, more pervasive anxiety being expressed. Some pathological fear that I sensed in my grandmother when she hovered over me, incessantly brushing her hand over my hair and asking me, How are you, what can I do for you, are you OK? *Eench, eench, eench.* For my grandparents' and parents' generation, perhaps the world was a place conspiring to kill you. After the Genocide, the fear of death was different from the fear of mortality. In this atmosphere of deep anxiety, our family was far from the optimistic mood of suburbia. As my grandmother said to me as I lay on my bed recovering from the measles, "Sleep with one eye open; know the evil eye."

At thirteen, I often watched my father as if he were a stranger. These are scenes that come back like little frames of eight-millimeter film. Scenes that made me realize my father had several selves. On a Greyhound bus in Oregon after midnight, a young woman is telling my father that she wants to leave her husband, a forest ranger, because he beats her. I wake from time to time as the bus jerks along small country roads. She's about twenty-five and looks like Kim Novak, although her hair is black and her eyes are the shade of her light-blue Idaho State sweatshirt. She's in blue jeans and white sneakers and is chewing gum, and I thought she was beautiful the minute she walked on the bus. I hear her tender, anxious voice, and I hear my father calmly talk with her all night. In the morning I pretend I've slept soundly.

On Christmas Eve of 1965, a phone call comes in the middle of dinner, a common event in our house, and my father disappears till morning. He spends the night fishing a hypodermic needle from the trachea of one of the town's notorious greasers. When I ask my father to tell me what a hypodermic was doing in Pascarelli's throat, he makes a clicking sound with his tongue. But the fact remains that my father has spent hours with Pascarelli on Christmas Eve–the famous Pascarelli who has been suspended from school and for whom beautiful blondes fall. When I see Pascarelli in the hall in tight sharkskin pants and his greasy pompadour, I want to ask him:

"What did you and my father say to each other on Christmas Eve?" At thirteen I was in awe of my father's access to the secret world of disease and death, to the human places of hurt and pain and suffering. I always wanted him to talk about his work when he came home at the end of the day. But he never said a word about any of it.

Men were scarce in our family, and it made my father's remoteness from me more complex. My mother's and my father's families each were dominated by women, all of whom in some way or other presided over our clan. I had come to think of family as woman's invention. Both of my grandfathers died before I was born, and in lieu of patriarchs we had aunts. To add to this, three of my aunts never married, instead becoming mothers to my siblings and me. So when my father was remote, he left me to the women, and the women had tireless passion for me.

A CREATURE OF ROCK 'N ROLL

As phone calls to girlfriends and Tenafly teen culture enveloped me, my father became increasingly concerned with my future, which was inseparable from his vision of college. Regularly, now, he reminded me that "if you are going anywhere in this life, you have to go to a good college." As reports came home from teachers indicating that I was distracted in class, passing notes to girls, and not working to my potential, my father became obsessed with private schools.

With increasing frequency he mentioned Andover, Exeter, Horace Mann, Lawrenceville–places where serious people went. Franklin D. Roosevelt went to Groton, and John F. Kennedy to Choate, my father reminded me as he asked me to pass the *tahn*. Soon the brochures for private schools in the metropolitan New York area began arriving on our mail table; I walked past them each day on my way upstairs. At night, my father liked to drop by my room to see how my homework was coming, and drop as well some tidbit about a Lawrenceville quarterback getting a scholarship to Princeton, or an Andover shortstop turning down the big leagues for

Amherst. In private school, he believed I would be free from the fast crowd of Tenafly public school and my new friends who lived on the affluent east hill, where driveways had Cadillacs and Jaguars and the houses came with swimming pools and maids.

My father was particularly concerned about my friendship with a new boy, Frank Haskell. Haskell was a good-looking, blondish, muscular, talented athlete who at the age of twelve was nearly six feet tall. The Haskell house on Carmel Court–only several hundred yards from the new St. Thomas's Armenian Church, of which my father was a founding member–was a sleek ranch with a T-bird and a black Caddy in the driveway, decorated in a combination of French antiques and '60s suburban fashion. I loved Haskell's bedroom, which was done up in wall coverings, pillows, and bedspread all of synthetic orange-and-black leopard fur. I was even more fascinated by a large walk-in closet with mirrored walls, steel-and-gold cabinets, and shelves of liquor with spouts– the kind of bar where at any moment you expected Dean Martin or Sammy Davis, Jr., to walk in. Although the Haskells were Jews, Carmel Court made my childhood Dickerson Road seem like the shtetl.

Mr. Haskell, who owned a country club in a neighboring town, had a butler and maid, a black couple named Al and Daisy, whose black Fleetwood was always in the driveway. And after Mrs. Haskell's early death from cancer, Al and Daisy ran the house. Simply by ringing a bell from their bedroom, each of the three Haskell boys could summon Al or Daisy. If we were hungry, Haskell just shook the bell and Daisy appeared in her white uniform. "Na, what ya hungry boys want?" her words whistled through her nearly toothless mouth in her soft Southern vernacular. She was sweet and warm and always at our service.

In seventh grade Haskell usually requested shrimp scampi, "Enough for me and Peter, Daisy." Half an hour later, Daisy rang her bell and we went to the marble-floored dining room, where we sat at a long table under a gold chandelier. There before us were plates of jumbo shrimp in garlic sauce, some vegetables and rice and glasses of milk, and a chocolate cake waiting on the buffet. "There's plenty more, boys, when you done," she said. At the Haskell house, we talked on the phone with our girlfriends for hours and disappeared for more hours into his basement to lift weights with his Joe Wider deluxe barbell set. By high school, we were pouring seven and sevens, whiskey sours, and screwdrivers in the walk-in bar. And the leopard-skin bedroom and its adjacent rooms were swank spaces where we brought our girlfriends as if we were checking into a hotel. During the winter of our senior year, Mr. Haskell returned home one night around midnight to find that every room in his house—his own bedroom too—was occupied by a high school couple. And for the only time I ever saw him express any emotion, he stood in the hall and shouted through the house, "What the hell is this, Haskell's Haven?"

Indeed, my father had reason to be concerned, for Haskell's Haven was an absurd fantasy come to life; it embodied the misguided path my father believed my life had taken. As I basked on that island of material pleasure at Haskell's Haven, my father began to drop phrases like "excessive permissiveness," "laissez-faire society," "decadence." This stodgy language goaded my retorts: "It's what any good house is like in this town"; "It's the way we live these days." My father now sounded like Auntie Anna on Sunday afternoons. He started in on my English, too, which he said was for the gutter because I had become "a creature of rock 'n roll."

His obsession with private schools was further fueled by his discovery of a pamphlet called "The College Rater," a publication that ranked the top 200 colleges in the United States. Tabulating endowment, library holdings, faculty research, admissions standards, and alumni satisfaction, the College Rater provided my father with a grid of statistics that would help him measure his idea of my future. On Friday night, as I lounged in the big stuffed chair watching "77 Sunset Strip," my father would drift in to announce that "Kalamazoo should be higher than ninety-fifth," "Dartmouth's overrated," and "Harvey Mudd is better than its name." I thought he had gone mad.

At dinner he began to direct conversation to the world and its events. The Aswan Dam, Nehru, Martin Luther King, Jr., the Jews and Arabs and the Middle East, and sometimes there were history lessons, like Eisenhower and the Nazis, the fall of the Roman Empire, Napoleon at Waterloo, Custer's Last Stand. Nightly he would ask: "How are things going in class?" So, when in the winter of eighth grade I told him that for our social studies project I was to write about a Near Eastern culture, he brightened up and said, "Here's a chance for you to learn something about Armenia."

"Armenia?"

"It's a perfect opportunity," he said. "To learn."

"OK."

The next day I went to the *World Book* and found the entry on Armenia. About 200 words and a picture of an Armenian girl in a checked dress sitting at a schoolroom desk with an open textbook. I remembered my father's disappointment when he purchased the encyclopedia in 1960. "Not much on Armenia," he said to my mother, and continued to place each red-and-blue vinyl-bound volume in alphabetical order on our bookshelf in the TV room. No, there was not much on Armenia. Knowing that Armenia was once in what was now Turkey, I decided to see what there was on Turkey: a sizable entry with colored pictures, maps, a list of export products. I checked the sources in the bibliography at the end of the entry and went to find them in the stacks of the Tenafly Public Library. I kept reading and reading and reading. The wealth of the sultans, the military might of the Ottoman Turks, who had come from around Mongolia and had conquered the Christians of old Byzantium. The rise of the Ottoman Empire, the waning of that empire during World War I. A great deal about Ataturk and the rise of modern Turkey. The reforms of medieval Islam and the modernizing of the alphabet.

Two weeks went by and I found that I had read several books on Turkey without ever once coming across a reference to Armenia. I thought it strange, because Armenians had lived in the land now called Turkey long before the Turks had come. For a minute, the American Indians flashed through my mind. I knew they had been in America before the Europeans came, so I went to the *World Book* and checked under U.S. history to find that the American Indians were mentioned often and with cross-references, and I thought it odd that there were no references to Armenia in all these books on Turkey.

But there was no time to think about this. My paper was due in four days and I hadn't written anything. I had no choice now but to write about Turkey. In slanted, angular script I wrote twenty pages on blue-lined, white loose-leaf paper, skipping every other line. I recounted the history of Ottoman Turkey from the time of the conquest of Constantinople through the rise of Ataturk and the solidification of the Turkish Republic. My teacher thought I wrote well, and gave the events a narrative that showed a cause-and-effect relationship during periods of change. I got an A.

I brought the paper home that night and announced at the dinner table that I had received an A for my social studies project. My father, his voice rising with a modicum of excitement, asked, "So what have you found out about Armenia?"

"I wrote about Turkey," I said.

My father stared at me, and silence hung over the table.

"What?" His voice cracked as he lingered on the t. "You were supposed to write about—"

"I know," I cut in, "but I couldn't find anything."

He was shouting now. "Don't you know what the Turks did to us?"

"Of course," I said, but I was too hurt and confused to admit I didn't know what the Turks did to us. Although I recalled the word *massacres* coming up in conversation every once in a while, when children were not supposed to be around, no one ever attached the word to a meaning.

"Would your Jewish friends write about the Germans like this?"

"Maybe," I answered, trying to save face. Then I went numb with humiliation and left the table. When I returned, the family had finished eating. I stood by the dirty dishes as my father picked up my term paper and began skimming through it. No mention of the Armenians, and no serious evaluation of Turkish history. After a few minutes he put the paper down. And for a while he sat quietly. As I watched him out of the corner of my eye, I saw an inaudible gesture of anger frozen in his face and it made me feel as if he were holding something back, something more than just disappointment with my paper. His silence seemed to open inward and I knew I couldn't speak to him then. For a moment I felt afraid, and then my fear became anger. Then my anger became indignant thirteen-year-old rage. If my father wanted me to know about Armenia, why hadn't he said, "Here, Peter, read this," or "Son, did I ever tell you about what happened to Armenia?" I held back tears and walked out of the kitchen, and as I scuffed up the red oriental runner to my bedroom, I heard my parents speaking in Armenian.

We never spoke about the Turkish term paper again. By the weekend it was as if it had never happened. I had earned an A, and I was happy for that. I told myself it was just history that had happened long ago. Outside spring was beginning and the Yankees were winding up training camp in Fort Lauderdale, and I was throwing the ball around each day to get in shape for Babe Ruth League. I had grown almost five inches since last season, and outside the mud was thawing and becoming sweet with the new grass, and nothing smelled sweeter than the dirt of the infield. But the Turkish term paper marked a turning point; in its wake, my father became even more alien to me.

Now my father's conversion to private education compelled him to denounce the failures of public school at the monthly meetings of the Tenafly Board of Education. He told our townsmen and women that peer-group tyranny and the encouragement of excessive social skills were the downfall of public education and part of the problem with the suburbs. On the way to school on the mornings after those meetings, my friend Ed Harrison, who had heard about my father's performance from his father, who also was a board member, would rib me. "Pete, your father's not exactly democratic, is he?" or "Why is your father such an elitist?" The word *elitist* hung in the air like a big sting, and I had to defend my father. "You don't understand; he doesn't mean that," I said. "It's more complicated than that." Ed was half mocking and half self-righteously indignant, and privately I was embarrassed and angry about my father's public declarations. Mr.

Harrison, my old Little League coach, was an Oklahoma liberal, and by contrast, my father seemed to me positively un-American. As much as I wanted to explain my father to Ed, I couldn't. "Ed, he's just trying to point some things out. He's not against democracy!" I said, and knew as I said it that I wished my father were more like Mr. Harrison.

By June of that year, as I was finishing eighth grade and nestled in the cocoon of junior high, my father decided my fate. He informed me that next year I would attend The Englewood School for Boys, the private day school in the next town. Because it was only a ten-minute drive from Tenafly, my father reasoned, I would feel the break with my friends less badly, but in the spring of 1965 I felt myself soaring into the teen life of Tenafly Junior High. I moved with a pack of friends who lived in the three-season rhythm of football, basketball, and baseball. Six days a week, three sports seasons a year.

That my sense of loyalty to my friends was decidedly greater than my sense of loyalty to my family was also at the heart of my father's disgust with my world. My friends and I lived for each other, planned our days around each other's. When my father spoke to me about my future, I felt I had none, apart from swaggering down the halls of Tenafly High School with my friends in our black-and-orange letter jackets and riding through town after games with our girlfriends. So when my father announced that The Englewood School for Boys was to be my destination in September, the arguments between us became bitter. "I'm getting the fuck outta here," I said, "no father could hate his son like this." I was revolted at the thought of attending the Boys School, which I thought of as a runtish place for sissies who were required to wear blue blazers with an insignia on the breast pocket, who walked to chapel with thin-lipped teachers still smelling of last night's sherry. It was a humiliation, and worse than that, an emasculation. I made it clear to my father that I would not go.

That summer my father and I did not talk. Dinners passed in silence between us, and my sisters Pam and Jan and my brother Jim grew increasingly taciturn as well. When my father and I passed each other in the hallway and when we sat in front of the TV, we did not recognize each other. I spent most of my time in my bedroom playing 45s and doing push-ups and sit-ups to get in shape for football. By July, my mother had become so alarmed at the silence between my father and me that she interceded, and in doing so, took my side. At first, she tried diplomatically to entreat my father to listen to me. At night, after we were in bed, I would hear her through the wall talking to him in a low voice, alternating Armenian and English. As her entreaties failed and my father grew more quietly aloof, our house became icy with tension. August came and I grew more desperate and estranged, and my mother became more vociferous in her pursuit of changing my father's mind.

One evening at dinner in mid-August, when the air-conditioning was on the blink and the windows were open and the filigreed glass curtains seemed almost wet, my mother brought it up for the first time in the civic arena of the dinner table. "Gerard, he can't go; it's just not that important. You're ruining him." My father squinted and said nothing, but before my mother could start another sentence my father said, in a voice of condescending anger, "I never want to hear another word about this again from either of you."

Even now I can't picture how it happened, but the next thing I knew I had taken a swing at my father across the table. He blocked it with his forearm, and as my momentum carried me forward I reached with my left hand and grabbed his starched white shirt and ripped it down the middle. I took three strides into the hallway, opened the front door, and ran until I was walking up East Clinton Avenue. By the time I had arrived at the Haskell house, Daisy was waiting for me on the front porch to tell me that my mother had called to say that it was not only fine for me to stay overnight but preferable.

All August I refused to come out of my room when my father was in the house. At dinner I ate quickly and left. My anger was smoldering into the grief of a fourteen-year-old who believed his life had been snatched, just as it was blooming, by his father's inscrutable Armenian elitist views. As I sat in my room and heard the cicadas grow shriller in the maples I realized that if I was going to private school I had to play football; it was the only thing that could make life bearable. At the Boys School, freshmen were eligible to play on the varsity, and in this bleak moment that thought was mildly soothing. Since a letter from the school informed me that pre-season tryouts began the last week of August and every candidate had to arrive with a completed medical form from his physician, I would have to break the wall of silence with my father.

One evening in the final days of August, I walked into the TV room where he was watching Walter Cronkite and looked at the floor and then at the TV and said: "Dad, I need a physical for football." I heard my sentence fall out into the air of the room and sit there like a frozen balloon from a comic strip. I stared at the floor and looked back up to watch Walter Cronkite mouthing words on the tube. And then my father said, as matter-of-factly as if we had just spoken a minute before, "Come down to the office tomorrow. We'll get you ready." In one sentence the summer came to an end.

After a week of August practice on The Englewood School for Boys' Solomon Field, it was clear that I would make Coach Sakala's varsity team and that I might even see enough playing time, as a defensive back and a punt returner, to earn a varsity letter. The idea of having a varsity letter as a freshman, of displaying it on a blue jacket with white leather sleeves, distracted me from my self-pity. But when my anger returned the next week as the first day of school approached, I made one last effort to subvert my father's plan.

With my short-cropped hair still bristling from the locker room shower and my muscles pleasantly aching from four hours of practice, I walked in a gray tee shirt, blue jeans, and a pair of white Cons up a flagstone path to a Victorian clapboard building and knocked on the headmaster's door. "Sir" [I had already learned some private school manners] "my name is Peter Balakian."

"I know who you are," the headmaster said. He was a plain, dry-faced man with tan-rimmed glasses whose look of piety reminded me of a Protestant minister's. Yet in his madras sport jacket, white shirt, and thin red tie, his sandy-colored hair parted neatly, he was a modern version of Mr. Chips.

"Dr. Moore, sir," I continued, "I can't attend this school."

He nodded as if to indicate that he understood my feelings.

"I cannot leave my life in Tenafly."

I stood staring at Dr. Moore, and as he stared at me I looked around the office and realized I was in a strange place. The room had an oddly rustic feel about it. One wall was lined with bookshelves, another with nineteenth-century prints of the Hudson River and the Palisades; a lacrosse stick was propped in a corner, and the smell of cherry pipe tobacco hung in the air. It was not public school and I realized, as I watched Dr. Moore watching me, that I was in a new world. I realized, too, that my father's decision was nonnegotiable. He was convinced he knew what was right for me, and he wouldn't be dissuaded by my mother's sentimentality or by my adolescent will. Although it would be years before I understood that my father was right, I felt impotent as I stood there looking around the headmaster's office.

"Peter, give us a try. You might like it more than you think right now." He gave me an avuncular smile. "Let's keep in touch," he said, as he shook my hand.

SATURDAY AUTUMN II

My FATHER AND I STUMBLED THROUGH MY FIRST YEAR OF PRIVATE school in a cautious peace. We were closest during football season and maintained a respectful distance in the winter and spring as my social life with my Tenafly friends continued. My father was happy that I was making good grades and playing varsity basketball and baseball as well. On the last day of school that year, I was awarded a trophy for being freshman athlete of the year, and my father shook my hand politely at the awards assembly and carried the trophy into the house. That night, we stayed up and watched the now-failing Yankees on TV.

The next evening my friends and I had planned a midnight swimming party on the posh grounds of Mary Jo Albright's house on the east hill, where a gorgeous pool was flanked by a cabana and a two-tiered deck. The previous year, Ed Harrison and I had devised a little ritual of sneaking out of our houses at 3:00 A.M. to explore the strange emptiness of the night world. With our parents duped in their beds asleep, we walked down an empty Tenafly Road feeling the strange freedom of night, and on to the Tenafly Diner, where we ate French toast and watched the night crowd trickle in. This year, fifteen-year-olds, we decided to push our freedom a bit further and drive Ed's parents' car up East Clinton Avenue to the Albright house.

Because Ed had forgotten to put the headlights on, the Harrisons' new Olds Vista Cruiser station wagon appeared as a dark apparition drifting down Crabtree Lane as I waited at the end of the block. We drove to Tenafly Road, where we picked up Ray Lane. There Ed got out of the car, walked to the passenger side and said, "It's your turn, Pete." I slid over to the driver's seat and drove four blocks to Westervelt Avenue. As I began turning right on Westervelt, I found that I was not rounding the corner smoothly. I found myself unable to let the steering wheel slide back through my hands in the easy fashion it was supposed to, and so the car kept turning until it was making a nearly forty-five-degree angle and heading for the fence of the house on the corner. I jabbed my foot toward the brake pedal but hit the accelerator instead, and the car lunged forward, racing through the fence and into an oak tree directly behind it.

Blood was pooling from my face into my hands. Ray had hit his head against the windshield and was curled up moaning beneath the glove compartment. Unscathed, Ed got out of the car and ran home. When he burst into his parents bedroom and broke the news, his father sat up in bed and said, "Don't worry, Ed, you're dreaming."

I stood outside the car, my lip like an inflated balloon still pouring blood and I watched the dust swirling in the headlights, the front wheels spinning in the air, and the tree seeming to jut from the engine. I kept thinking, this is somebody else's life. The car doors were open, Ray was moaning on the ground, the radio was blasting a song by the Rolling Stones. A police car drove up, and a cop got out and put his hand on my shoulder and said, "Son, those trees don't move." Seconds later, Mr. Harrison appeared in his slippers and bathrobe, looking on in disbelief at his car, a recent gift from his parents in Oklahoma.

At the hospital emergency room, the nurses asked me my name, and when I told them, they asked what they already knew: "Are you the doctor's son?" I nodded, and they puckered their lips with disgust and suggested that I call my father and tell him where I was. Horrified at the idea, I made it clear by sign language that my mouth was unusable, and the head nurse agreed to call my father while I was on the operating table being stitched up. When she returned she was almost gloating as she informed me that my father had said, "I'm sorry, you have the wrong boy; ours is fast asleep."

My father arrived in the emergency room dressed as if he were starting a day of work. He walked over to the attending physician and the nurses to get the report. I had broken several bones in my face, and my lip and the inside of my mouth had taken a dozen stitches. Ray had suffered a concussion and was being kept overnight. My father stood at the emergency room door and waited for me to rise from the operating table, and we walked with two policemen in silence to the police car. My father followed us in his Buick. At the police station, we were booked for car theft and driving without licenses, and I was charged with reckless driving. A date in the Hackensack juvenile court would be set for the fall. When I arrived home at about 6:oo A.M. with my father, my mother was standing on the front lawn in the silvery morning mist in her pink bathrobe, her eyes sleepless and red.

When I think of the most humiliating moment of my adolescence, it's what happened the following Monday. Eager to be out of the house as much as possible, I walked down to Tenafly Junior High to meet my friends as they were getting out for the day. My lip was still like a salami with black stitches and hurt like hell when I laughed. As I stood on the corner by the Esso station, about to cross the street to the school, Mr. Harrison came riding up beside me on a girl's blue Schwinn, carrying the dry cleaning over his shoulder on a hanger, the plastic wrapping fluttering in the wind. He slowed down, smiled, and said, "Pete, how are you feeling?" He looked at my lip and said with compassion, "Don't worry, the swelling will go down soon." Before I could think of anything to say, he was pumping the Schwinn up Tenafly Road, and I stood there numb and speechless.

Back at home, my father had not forgiven me, and the ground we had gained over the past year was lost. The car accident drove a new wedge between us. My father's fears about my life of suburban indulgence were coming true. My silence that summer was shame, and my father's silence was Old World disgust for the eldest son who had disgraced himself. When the news of the car accident reached the other side of the bridge, my father reported that Auntie Anna declared reform school, not college, was my most likely future.

. . . . .

At the end of another silent summer, football again helped to heal the rupture between my father and me. It happened because one day in August, while doing wind sprints for preseason training, I hit the dusty ground in mid-stride. I felt like someone had thrown a knife into my calves, and when they didn't loosen after ten minutes, my friends carried me home and dropped me on the kitchen floor. My anxious father hovered over me. "Heat stroke, heat stroke," he kept saying. "You can die from it." Within a week, my father had come up with a solution for heat stroke and muscle cramps, and in the early autumn weeks that followed, he turned our kitchen into a lab. Every day when I arrived home from football practice, the kitchen table was buried under plastic containers, bags of powders, scales, measuring cups, and other odds and ends of my mother's cookware. My mother, who had been a chemistry major in college and had worked in labs, pitched in. Every evening that fall we ate on the patio, and in the morning we ate standing at the kitchen counter and stared at the mess on the kitchen table, until sometime in October the gray Formica of the table was visible again, and my father announced that he had a formula that worked and a name to go with it: "Sportade." He called it an electrolyte drink.

After a year of selling Sportade from the house by mail order to professional and college teams, my father sold Sportade to Becton-Dickinson, a pharmaceutical company that had done wonders with the plastic syringe and the Ace bandage. He thought of his invention as a medical product and not a food item, like his then-unknown rival, a Dr. Cade in Gainesville, Florida, who had sold his new drink, "Gatorade," to a pork and beans company, Stokely–Van Camp.

Overnight, my father had become scientist and inventor and was written up in newspapers and magazines. Every week new professional and college teams were ordering Sportade. Envelopes from Notre Dame, USC, Syracuse, Texas A&M, the New York Giants, the 49ers, the U.S. Open, Olympic teams, even the Kenya Safari Club and NBC News in Saigon arrived daily. Invitations to lecture came from around the world. The Sunday *New York Times* sports section ran a half-page story on Sportade, illustrated with a photo of me and a teammate and my father at practice. All through this, my father and I were patching up our relationship. Later that fall when we were all summoned to juvenile court my father, to my horror, told the judge he hoped my driver's license would be delayed a year. When it wasn't, he wrote the judge to let him know he had erred.

But the culmination of our healing process took place the next August, when the New York Giants asked my father to do some Sportade testing on the team during summer practice. When he asked me if I would like to join him at the Giants preseason camp and see "what goes on in the big time," I began organizing plastic Sportade containers in boxes and going over the height and weight stats of Tucker Fredrickson, Homer Jones, Spider Lockhart, and Fran Tarkenton. On a hot afternoon in August, my father and I stood in the Giants locker room, small, wiry Armenians amidst giant black and white men who were peeling off their girdle and shoulder pads, undoing helmets and cleats, and stepping naked and sweating and exhausted onto the scale to be weighed. My father and I in the hot, wintergreen-smelling locker room, rock 'n roll blaring from the radio, as we held out plastic containers and the players peed into them. We were a pair as we placed each cup of urine in a metal tray.

· · · · ·

Although I knew how football kept me and my father together then, I've come to see it more deeply now that I know how the Balakians survived the Armenian Genocide. I've come to see how when the sun shined on the damp green grass of the football field in October, when I played left halfback for The Englewood School for Boys, all

Armenian silence, anger, and misunderstanding between me and my father dissolved. On those days, my father woke early to do his morning rounds at Englewood Hospital so he could take his place on the bench as team physician.

As we jog onto the field my father is already standing on the sidelines. He is dressed just as he is every day when he leaves for the office, in a dark suit, white shirt, red tie. He carries his small brown medical bag as he walks over to the bench to greet the coach. As we warm up, he paces the sidelines, reads the program, watches us intently in our practice formations. At halftime he is in the locker room, and if there are no serious injuries he maintains a cool distance from the coach's halftime skull session and pep talk. In fact, my father seems slightly embarrassed about the whole halftime thing, as if he were an eavesdropper on some sacred rite, and so he backs up into the entrance hall and discusses the first half with the custodian.

During the game he rarely speaks to me or looks in my direction. He checks on the boys who have injuries. He watches and paces the sidelines.

After the game he disappears, and when I arrive home he is in his big stuffed chair that sits on the Kashan in the living room and he is reading the paper. When I appear with my hair still wet in my blue-and-white leather-sleeved football jacket with the letters CAPT and LHB on one sleeve and the number 20 on the other, my father rises from his chair and shakes my hand, a firm handshake, and says "Good job." He is always smiling and sometimes I think he would like to hug me or just put his arm around my shoulder, but he never does—can't, it seems. Just as when he lay dying in his hospital bed, his heart damaged beyond repair, his face ashen, and I wanted to kiss him and put my arm around him and tell him I loved him, I couldn't.

Whether we win or lose, he greets me in the same way. Whether I am a sophomore 2-back—the wingback who blocks and catches a pass now and then or runs a counter play in an odd moment—or the 4-back—the primary running back—and cocaptain of an undefeated team, who is named to an All-State team, my father reacts the same. He is happy for the occasion, for the game, for the effort, and happy to have been there. And then he sits down and returns to his paper. It is on Monday at dinner that he wants to discuss the game in detail. He has wanted to let it all sink in, I think, to enjoy the moment, to keep his distance so as not to seem like those fathers living out their childhoods through their children. I love this gentle, calm way about him. I love the tact with which he respects my space. And I love to talk with him for hours about particular plays of the game, about the opposing team, about our game strategy. During these moments his Armenian silence and formality dissolved, and we expressed our love for each other.

PART IV

CHAIN OF WORDS

BENZENE RINSINGS FROM THE MOON

I'VE COME TO SEE POETRY AS THE CHAIN OF LANGUAGE LINKING LANDS and events, people and places that make up our family story. Poetry has been a deep well of thought and feeling and language lushness that the Balakians have lived by. As far back as I can remember, whether it was Mother Goose, Grimm's fairy tales, those beguiling Armenian words spoken around the house, the vernacular whizz of a DJ, the lyrics of a rock song, a sportscaster's clipped phrases, language was always the realest reality for me. But it wasn't until high school that the sensory and spirit power of poetry appeared to me. It was as if a bird flew out of the dark into my head. It flew into my head like the force of fate my grandmother called *pakht*, and neither football nor Haskell's Haven could interfere with its flight into my life.

. . . . .

I'm sitting in the back of Mr. Schroeder's English class thinking about our last football game of the season. It's a cool November afternoon and I'm staring out the window at the bare oaks and

maples and the sharp blue November sky. For 1967, my hair is rea-
sonably short, and I'm feeling kind of muscular in my blue school
blazer. I carry myself like a good jock near the season's end, walking
around simianlike to prove to the world that my lats are big and my
arms can't quite fall naturally down the sides of my body.

We're discussing a poem by Hart Crane. A weird, alluring
name, I'm thinking, like the name of someone who might play free
safety for the Cleveland Browns. The sound of Hart Crane going
around my head, because last night I read "Repose of Rivers" more
times than I realized.

> The willows carried a slow sound,
> A sarabande the wind mowed on the mead.
> I could never remember
> That seething, steady leveling of the marshes
> Till age had brought me to the sea.
> Flags, weeds. And remembrance of steep alcoves
> Where cypresses shared the noon's
> Tyranny; they drew me into Hades almost.
> And mammoth turtles climbing sulphur dreams
> Yielded, while sun-silt rippled them
> Asunder.

I'm half slumped in my chair, staring out the window,
when Mr. Schroeder asks me what I think of Chip Allen's view of
this poem. I haven't been paying enough attention to know what
Allen just said about it, but I blurt out, "I don't think he really gets
it." I realize I'm dumping on Allen, one of the nerdy A students in
the class who I know thinks of me as a dumb jock. "Could you
explain what you mean, Balakian?" Mr. Schroeder continues.
Again I blurt out, because I don't know what I mean, "He doesn't
get the deeper meaning." Mr. Schroeder, a preppyish hippie with a
bushy beard in a brown corduroy suit, is peering at me now as he
leans back in his chair and puts his feet up on his desk. I'm staring at his work boots, and he keeps peering at me. "And what is
that, Peter?"

"The idea," I enunciate, "that the swamp is about what's going on in the poet's mind."

"Interesting, Balakian." Then he turns to Allen and says, "What do you think, Chip?" The class is silent. Some of my friends turn around and stare at me. Allen and I go on to talk about the poem for the rest of the period, to the astonishment of the class. As we mill out of the room, Mr. Schroeder stops me and says "Balakian, images really blow your mind." For a second I feel some pride, as if the jock has proved himself a literate being, and then his comment hits me, and I rather like it.

In the locker room, my friend and fellow linebacker, Ray Brown, who has been in class with me, tosses a jockstrap in my face as I'm pulling up my girdle pads.

"Poetry, wow," he says.

"What's your problem, Ray?"

"Heavy stuff, man."

"Maybe you could use some."

I fling the jockstrap back at him and it catches his ear and hangs there. Some of the guys start laughing. Ray comes at me, playfully slap-boxing. In our half-laced girdle pads and shoulder pads we begin to slap each other around, then the slapping gets serious and as we tumble over a bench and into the side of the lockers, our teammates break us up. One of the seniors pulls me into the corner of the locker room, stares at me as if I've gone loco, and says: "Is this whole thing about *poetry*? We got a game to win, Pete."

Sometime after the season had ended, I was out on a Friday night with Ellen Duffy. We were doing our usual Friday night thing. A movie, then a spin in my father's Skylark down along the Hudson River in Englewood Cliffs beneath the Palisades, where we ended up on a thin strip of sand along the river, a beach we called the Boat Basin. An early December night, the air still warm enough for us to take out a woolen blanket and lie looking across the river to the lights of Manhattan and the Bronx. The moon white in a black sky, the lights of the city and the moon flashing on the water. I smelled of Canoe and Ellen of Heaven Scent. The radio on low. Some kissing and maneuvering of bra hooks and belt buckles. And I kept stopping and looking out over the water to the lights and watching the moon-light fan across the Hudson. I turned to Ellen and began to recite some lines from another Hart Crane poem: *Whitely, while benzene/ Rinsings from the moon/ Dissolve all but the windows of the mills.* I knew the night view of the city had helped me pull up those lines I had been reading since that day in Mr. Schroeder's class. I turned to Ellen with the eagerness of a kid needing applause. "Well, what do think?" Ellen shrugged her shoulders. "Come on, do ya like it?"

"I don't really know what it means."

"It's called 'Lachrymae Christi,'" I said, like a manic boy. "It's the real thing."

"Maybe if I saw the whole thing it would make more sense."

"Ya don't need to see the whole thing. It's incredible just by itself."

Ellen grew sullen and annoyed. "You're just putting me down."

"No, I'm not, Ellen. I wouldn't do that. But what about Hart Crane?"

"I think you want to break up."

"No, I don't," I said, sounding very earnest. Then we stopped talking and starting kissing. But the night ended on a depressed note, and our conversation about Hart Crane seemed to be the beginning of the end. On our waning dates, the matter of poetry kept coming up.

"You're an elitist," she said.

"Poetry is about all of us," I said. "It's goddamned life we're talking about."

"Just 'cause I don't get it, you're putting me down," she said.

In the wake of this new feeling about poetry, I came to think more about my aunts Anna and Nona. All those years of listening to their rants about culture and literature, all those strange literary words – and those French words. Those words, words, words. Auntie Anna and Auntie Nona, smoking Parliaments and talking about books in high decibels around our dinner table.

At first, I came to know my aunts as books more than as people. I began reading around in their books in my own chaotic way. I picked Auntie Anna's first book off the shelf and felt the gray paper jacket, its lovely ridged surface, its dark red type. *Literary Origins of Surrealism,* beneath which was a drawing of weird futuristic characters by Yves Tanguy, then, in elegant red typeface, *Anna Balakian.* On the inside flap of the jacket, it said that my aunt had been "born in Constantinople of Armenian parents," held a "Doctor of Philosophy from Columbia (1943)," and was an "Assistant Professor of Romance Languages at Syracuse University." There was something noncommercial and beautiful about the book. The ivory-colored pages, the feel of laid paper, the drawing on the cover. 1947. Price: $2.75. *Surrealism. Literary. Constantinople. Armenian parents. Balakian.*

There were other books of hers on the shelves in our TV room, *The Symbolist Movement* and *Surrealism: The Road to the Absolute.* They had flashy trade-book jackets, and *Surrealism* was decorated with an image of a human head swirling with psychedelic colors, a hallucinogenic skull that would have fit on my new Jefferson Airplane album, *Surrealistic Pillow.* On the back of the jacket was a table of contents in bold lowercase type to suggest the modern: *out of the forest of symbols, lautréamont's battle with god, saint-pol roux and the apocalypse, apollinaire and l'esprit nouveau, pierre reverdy and the materio-mysticism of our age.* I loved the playfulness of the phrases and the mystery of whatever my aunt was getting at.

On those days when my father looked up from the *Times* he was buried in after dinner to mention that Auntie Nona had a review in the paper, I returned to the living room later in the evening to take the paper to my bedroom to read the column *Books of the Times.*

I found the reviews opaque, beguiling, exciting. As I got a taste of my aunt's language, I came to sense her life. Her columns had good titles: *Carson McCullers: Love Perverse and Perfect; Beautiful and Undamned: Stories by Fitzgerald; God Bless You, Mr. Vonnegut; Realists of the Interior; Despiritualized Americans: Soviet Views of American Literature; Bitches and Sad Ladies; Poets, Printers, and Pamphleteers.* I played with the phrases, looked up words I didn't know. I also flipped through *The Creative Present: Notes on Contemporary Fiction,* a collection of essays edited with her colleague at the *Book Review,* Charles Simmons. Its red, orange, and black cover glowed on the bookshelf. Essays on post–World War II novelists: Diana Trilling on Norman Mailer; Granville Hicks on Malamud, Gold, and Updike; John Chamberlain on Mary McCarthy. I took it off the shelf regularly, turned the pages, browsed in it, but its language was abstruse and not nearly as exciting as Auntie Anna's exuberant proclamations.

One day in French class, Mr. Prouty asked us each to name our favorite French writer, and when it came my turn I said, "Lautrea-mont." Although I had only read a few pages of my aunt's chapter on Lautréamont, I loved the obscure sound of his name, the letters, the shape of French. When Mr. Prouty asked me if I would care to recite anything by this interesting French poet of the nineteenth century, I said, "Yes, sir." I didn't know a line by Lautréamont, but I did know a few lines by Apollinaire from my aunt's chapter on him, and they appeared on my tongue:

> *"Oiseau tranquille au vol inverse oiseau*
> *Qui nidifie en l'air*
> *À la mimite ou brille déjà ma mémoire. . . ."*

But before I could confess I had forgotten the rest, Mr. Prouty, looking at me in astonishment, said "Very good, Peter," and I sat down, not sure whether I had stumped him or whether he was letting me off the hook in appreciation of my resourcefulness.

THE SIOUX CHIEF

Walking for miles through mud in a new pair of bell-bottoms and a rain-soaked tee shirt. Santana and Richie Havens echoing and blaring all day in the drizzle and rain and sun. A stranger passing me a clay pipe of hash, from which I took a toke and passed it to one of my friends. I felt odd with pumped-up biceps from a summer of weight lifting for football, and I wasn't sure if I belonged here, but I began to feel that day at Woodstock that college wasn't going to be what I had thought it would be just two months earlier, when my friends and I signed each other's high school yearbooks swearing that we would meet on opposing sides on the college gridiron in the coming years.

After freshman football season at Bucknell, I came home at Thanksgiving with a stack of new paperback books, and my father and I began our era of long, late-night talks about socialism, Marxism, communism, capitalism, civil rights, and the Vietnam War, which he was against. The ease with which my father engaged me in talking about ideas created a new feeling of closeness between us, and my adolescent struggles with him gave way to a feeling of pride in his knowledge. By spring semester I had taken to writing him letters about what was happening on campus and what I was reading. One day, in response to a letter I had written him about a racial flare-up among some of the football players over Eldridge Cleaver's *Soul On Ice*, my father wrote:

> Dear Peter,
> Books are the most powerful things in the world. I am sending you an article concerning our own people–which unfortunately time and circumstance have not allowed me to talk about. In an era in which the misfortunes of other peoples are in the headlines constantly, it is most necessary and worthwhile to know about your own people. We have a tremendous historical ancient background with strife against odds, bravery against treachery, but eventual triumph. 50 short years ago it was felt that the Armenians were finished after World War I.
> It is also a fascinating story about a civilization that is showing tremendous progress with its own energy and without outside dollars. It is most ironic that the Soviet Union, which is supposed to take away freedom from other countries, has given the Armenians their first *freedom* and safety in modern times. They have been able to live in peace, have their own language, customs, laws, freedom of worship in a so-called atheistic system and have the protection from a divided world which undoubtedly would have made a Korea or a Vietnam out of Armenia–had it been an independent republic. All this should give you lots of food for thought and a desire to see this land some day and study it.
> Sportade is sponsoring the ski reports on WHN 1050 at 10:55 pm Wed–Fri. Also, I'm enclosing a check for your fraternity dues, $88.65. Hoping to hear from you soon. Love from us all, Dad.

My father had enclosed an editorial from an Armenian-American newspaper about the fiftieth anniversary of the Soviet Armenian Republic. It was devoted primarily to the Armenian triumph of rebuilding a world in the aftermath of "historic suffering."

I stared at the letter, and skimmed the article. What was I to make of my father's letter? Where had it come from? What did my father mean by "time and circumstance" not allowing him to talk to me about "our own people"? Hadn't we spent every day of my life together? For the first time since eighth grade, I thought of the term paper about Turkey. A feeling of humiliation and anger rushed through me and I wondered, why hadn't we talked about Armenia then? How was I to respond to my father now? Did he expect me to? "Hoping to hear from you," he wrote. Did he expect me to go and read some books on Armenia and write him back?

After a long, silent period, Armenia had been dropped in my lap again. I was forced to remember that I belonged to this thing called Armenia, and that my father–the good doctor, the inventor, the team physician, the man of ideas–was still an enigma to me. I didn't respond to his letter, and when I saw him months later at spring break I said nothing about it. But the letter triggered another long-forgotten memory of 1964, when my father decided that my "bar mitzvah," as he called it, would be a cross-country trip by Greyhound Bus. Just the two of us spending time together.

We boarded a Greyhound bus at the Port Authority Terminal on 42nd Street in New York with our $98 tickets for all-you-can-see-of-America. Pittsburgh, Detroit, South Bend–to walk the hallowed ground of Knute Rockne and kneel in the Notre Dame football team's prayer grotto–and Chicago; Wassau, Wisconsin, to visit med school friends; then to Minneapolis, then through miles of wheat fields into the Badlands of South Dakota, and on to the West Coast.

At Teddy Roosevelt's lodge in the Black Hills, now a museum and restaurant, we ate buffalo burgers under mounted bear heads, and on our way out we stopped at a souvenir stand where an American Indian dressed as a Sioux chief with a huge feathered headdress was standing. His face was creased with lines and ruddily tanned, and he was large and thick as a pro linebacker. My father went up to him, introduced himself, and said, loud enough for me to hear, "Chief, we have a lot in common." He pulled me next to him. "Chief, this is my son, Peter Balakian, he's quite a football player."

My father then handed me his prized Bell & Howell movie camera and ordered me to hold it very still and press the button as he stood with his arm around the Sioux chief. As the film began to record and the machine made its clicking sound, I watched my five-foot-eight father almost lunge as he embraced the Chief around the neck. Bemused, the Chief returned my father's gesture with a weak embrace. From where I stood I could hear them talking about how old, great nations could be pushed off their own land, "their homeland." The Chief nodded emphatically, yes, yes, "homeland," he said, and my father said it back, "your own homeland."

I stopped the camera and walked over to them. My father gave the Chief his business card. I too shook his large, warm, fleshy hand, and we said good-bye. Back on the bus, I was so paralyzed with astonishment that I didn't ask my father anything but waited for him to offer up some explanation. Instead, we sat silently as the air blew from the side vents and cooled the sun-heated nylon seats. As the bus picked up speed, the blue sky and the Black Hills blurred like a beautiful painting, and my father and I were silent till we reached Yellowstone National Park. Nothing was said about the Sioux chief, about homelands, about what Armenians and Indians had in common. The next thing I knew I was standing in front of Old Faithful as it spouted to the sky while my father got it all on his Bell & Howell.

When it came to Armenia, there was a pattern of ruptured gestures between us: my father would offer a fragment of knowl-edge, then retreat into silence. A half-statement and then strange quiet. Should I have been more aggressive? Was I frightened? Did I not want to know? So in 1970, when my father wrote me at college the most articulate statement he had ever made to me about Arme-nia, it was still a strange half-statement, and still I could not answer him.

"KADDISH"

By the end of that year, things in my life had changed. On a Friday in May 1970, I was a pledge doing kitchen duty at a frat where most of the football team resided. I wore an anti–Vietnam War armband, a piece of white cloth with a red fist and the word *strike*, because Bucknell students, like college students all over the country, were protesting Nixon's bombing of Cambodia. The chef, Sam Clad, was grilling T-bone steaks when I walked in. Clad was a wiry, middle-aged man with a crew cut, who chain-smoked while he cooked. Without looking up from the sizzling meat, he said in a mock-effeminate voice, "Ball players aren't peace faggots."

"Up yours," I said playfully, trying to dismiss his comment.

In a venomous voice, he shot back, "Peace, love, and fairy bullshit," and as I moved along the stainless-steel counter to get the salad bowls he lunged at my arm, grabbed the armband, and dunked it in a big metal bowl of salad dressing. I backed off, picked up the nearest object, a dinner plate, and flung it at him like a Frisbee. He ducked, the dish smashed, and the two of us squared off before a couple of the guys rushed in to break it up.

"Fuck this place," I said to the bulky defensive tackle who was my pledge trainer. As I heard the kitchen door swing on its hinges, I knew I was through with frats and football. Now college seemed open and uncertain and a place to be free. By my junior year, poetry had replaced football in my life and I had become friends with Jack Wheatcroft, a poet and novelist, whose courses were legendary on campus. In the Bison, the campus coffee shop, Jack spent endless time talking over drafts of my poems. By the time I was a senior, I had decided that I didn't want to spend my life helping to merge Frito-Lay with Pepsi or living on Crabtree Lane or any other phony pastoral street of suburbia, and so I pulled the plug on my plan to go to law school and signed up to do an honors thesis on Allen Ginsberg and Jack Kerouac with Jack Wheatcroft and a brilliant young historian, Leo Ribuffo.

Sometime in the fall of my senior year, I began to correspond with Allen Ginsberg. I sent him my poems, and out of the blue he wrote back with comments and suggestions. When I invited him to come and read his poems at Bucknell, he answered promptly through his agent that he would be there on April 5 and that the fee would be $1,500. Bucknell's president, Charles Watts, a literary critic himself, was excited about Ginsberg's visit and agreed to fund it. As the dogwoods bloomed by the fountain on the academic quad, we read *Howl*. Even my friends who were students of Professor Fell, and read only one thick, black book by Martin Heidegger called *Being and Time*, read *Howl*.

With his beard and hair bushing at the sides of his balding head and his horn-rimmed glasses, Ginsberg looked serious and vulnerable as he hobbled onto the porch of 208 South Seventh Street with a broken leg in a walking cast under his blue-jean overalls, accompanied by his friend Peter Orlovsky, whose biceps bulged from a tee shirt with a huge American flag on the front. They arrived at 4:30, and I wasn't surprised when my mother drove up a few minutes later in our Vista Cruiser station wagon. She told me on the phone the night before that she was thinking about making a visit to her alma mater and that this seemed like the perfect excuse, and she said she would bring dinner. I must have been expecting her, because all I had on hand was an aluminum bowl of Lipton's instant soup onion dip, some potato chips, and a couple of gallons of cheap wine. She walked into my college apartment bright and cheery as some friends were passing joints and Ginsberg and Orlovsky were holding forth with teachers and students. My mother: in a blue suit and suede pumps, carrying two trays of lasagna covered with aluminum foil, some French bread in white bags, plastic bags of lettuce, and a jar of her own salad dressing.

Before I could introduce her, she broke into the circle around Ginsberg and Orlovsky: "Allen, I'm Arax Balakian, Peter's mother; your father taught my sister at Paterson High in '33; he was her favorite teacher." My mother and Allen Ginsberg began exchanging Paterson High gossip, town gossip, northern Jersey gossip, and my mother, who had dug up the titles of a few of Louis Ginsberg's poems my aunt liked, began praising them. Ginsberg seemed so delightedly caught off-guard that he now turned his sole attention to my mother, leaving the professors and students to themselves.

Still chatting with Ginsberg, my mother began dishing up lasagna, imploring everyone to eat because the reading was in less than an hour. As she darted around the kitchen, trying to consolidate our motley collection of silverware, plates, and half-cleaned glasses, she turned to Ginsberg and said, as if she were asking him if he wanted some croutons with his salad: "Allen, would you like to see the review Helen Vendler wrote of *The Fall of America*? The *Times Book Review* is giving it the front page next Sunday." Before I could protectively nudge my mother back to the lasagna, convinced that she was making a fool of herself, she pulled out of her purse the galley proofs my aunt Nona had given her with the review of Ginsberg's new book.

I realized my mother had come with this document uncannily timed to establish her relationship to the poet and his work, to words and texts, in a way that quite frankly blew my mind. Did she wish to show me that literature was a territory she too could navigate? Faculty and students stared at her in disbelief, and Allen stared for a second and then said, "Arax, may I see that?" The bond between them was now unbreakable, and I watched as students and teachers closed in around the two of them.

"Allen, it's not a bad review," my mother went on, as if she were a literary critic. "I hope you're not disappointed," she said, sounding motherly. Now in the inner circle with Ginsberg, she was enjoying herself immensely, and I stood there sipping some cheap wine, astonished and wondering, had my mother really read *The Fall of America*?

Old Larison Dining Hall filled up with students in faded blue jeans and tee shirts with slogans on them like "Make love wherever you are," "Stop the war now," "I brake for marijuana." Some wore bandannas, some love beads. Some were barefoot, some wore moccasins. Faculty came in tweed jackets or torn jeans and sandals. Everyone was sitting on the floor, as joints were circulated and bottles of Boone's Farm apple wine and Mateus rosé were chugged and passed. My mother sat cross-legged in a navy skirt and a pink blouse, her hair styled like Mary Tyler Moore's, a blue purse in her lap. She looked serious and was taking things in. When I went to the mike to introduce Ginsberg and Orlovsky, I saw her sitting in a crowd of students who were passing bottles and joints in front of her, behind her, and over her head.

For the next three hours Ginsberg and Orlovksy sang songs and recited poems, opening with "Hum Bomb," a chant that went like this: *Whom bomb?/ We bomb them!/ Whom bomb?/ We bomb them!/ Whom bomb?*

Not long after came "Please Master":

> please master can I wrap my arms around your
>   white ass
> please master can I lick your groin curled with
>   blond soft fur
> please master can I touch my tongue to your rosy
>   asshole
> please master may I pass my face to your balls
> please master tell me to lick your thick shaft
> please master press my mouth to your prick-heart

After this, some people filed out, especially conservative students and local Republicans who held the college in suspicion anyway and had only come out to see if the counterculture was as sick as they thought.

When Orlovsky recited a poem called "Peter Jerking Allen Off," and stood up to make motions as if he were stroking an invisible penis, more people left. He kept stroking and they kept leaving. I looked over at my mother, who sat impassive in the midst of the crowd, occasionally helping a bottle of wine across the aisle, and I felt awkward and embarrassed, as if I were a teenager with a parent in a situation that was, as Henry James might have put it, "out of context." Or was it that she was back in the dining hall where she had waited tables as a Bucknell student in the '40s?

The poets sang on, oblivious to the audience, Ginsberg playing his squeeze box and the two of them swaying back and forth. After three hours, only a handful of people were left and I wished the whole thing were over. I was on the verge of signaling Ginsberg to wind it up, when out of nowhere, he began to recite in a beautiful, resonant voice: "Strange now to think of you, gone without corsets & eyes, while/ I walk on the sunny pavement of Greenwich Village./ downtown Manhattan, clear winter noon, and I've been up/ all night . . . listening to Ray Charles blues shout blind on the phonograph." It was "Kaddish," his epic poem about his mother. A poem that I loved.

Into the tired, nearly emptied littered hall the rush of images began to flood. I sat staring at the old linoleum floor in the slightly blue light coming from the '40s fluorescent fixtures above. I watched my mother sitting cross-legged in the middle of the near-empty room, intent and poised as a young student.

> Nor your memory of your mother, 1915 tears in
> silent movies weeks and weeks–forgetting, aggrieve
> watching Marie Dressler address humanity, Chaplin
> dance in youth, . . .
> Or back at Normal School in Newark, studying up
> on America in a black skirt–winter on the street

without lunch–a penny a pickle–home at night to
take care of Elanor in the bedroom–
    First nervous breakdown was 1919–she stayed
home from school and lay in a dark room for three
weeks–something bad–never said what–every
noise hurt–dreams of the creaks of Wall Street

As Ginsberg's words echoed in the cavernous dining hall, I
buried my head in my hands and began to weep.

When the reading broke up and things continued at my
apartment, my mother appeared, still fresh and perky, and picked up
where she left off, pouring wine and greeting guests. Before long she
further intruded into my domain by giving her verdict on my girlfriend, Charlene Mills. Charlene was from a small town in western
Massachusetts, five foot three and petite, and her straight blond hair
was now frizzed like Janis Joplin's. In her tight blue jeans and work
boots, her blue denim workshirt neatly tucked in, she looked as
much like Patti Page as she did Janis. By the end of the semester she
would make summa cum laude and high honors in French for her
thesis on Proust.

In the kitchen, before the party, Charlene had been eager–
perhaps overeager–to assist my mother: "Let me get the plates for
you, Mrs. Balakian," "The silverware's here," "It's a tricky oven."

"I'm fine," my mother said in a flat voice, which let me know
that she was repelled by the mere presence of Charlene in the
kitchen.

Back in the kitchen cleaning up, just as I was about to have a
cup of wine and reflect on the evening, my mother said in a sharp,
soft voice: "Charlene's a hick, I hope you know that."

This was not the first such statement my mother had made
about Charlene or other girlfriends of mine. Although I could hear
my mother saying, "We're American, you know," "Stuffy Armenians," and "Too ethnic," when it came to the issue of the girls in my
life, whether at thirteen or when we were college seniors, my
mother was defined by the *odar* syndrome. *Odar* means "other" in
Armenian–those who are not Armenian. It's a word that defines the

limits of the tribe; *odar* is also used by Armenian mothers to signify any outsider who has designs on entering the circle of the family. My mother's *odar* anger had been unleashed from the time I brought my first girlfriends home in junior high school. Even then, girlfriends were greeted with a cool disdain, dismissed as "ridiculous," "silly," or "sweet but dumb."

Since I had never dated a woman of Armenian descent, I had never tested the depth of my mother's *odar* convictions, but I wasn't convinced many Armenian women would pass the test either. For my mother, a woman had to qualify by being *jarbig*, which meant she had to have energy, wit, vitality. She had to be *achgapatz*, open-eyed, so that nothing could get past her, for she was keeper of the gate, the protector of things sacred: family and husband. If a woman wasn't *jarbig* and *achgapatz*—clearly my mother thought she possessed these qualities in abundance—she wasn't worthy, she wasn't, in the existential sense, "Armenian."

So her rude, invasive comment came as no surprise to me. But it was the manipulation, the timing, the way of wielding power that sent rage into my face, because I knew that if I answered her my evening would come apart and I would regress to my worst adolescent self, which might not have displeased her too much either. She counted on my sense of decorum, and knowing I was hamstrung, she used the moment to get in the unretorted jab.

When my mother barged into my room quite early the next morning, I don't know what she expected to find. Charlene and me? Or me under the covers, alone in pajamas? She found neither, because I had neglected to tell her that I had given my room to Allen and Peter, and that I was staying at Charlene's. What she witnessed exactly—that is, the precise details—I've never been able to find out, but my apartment mates who lived in abutting rooms said they heard her scream and run down the hallway and the stairs, and from their windows, watched her get in her car and drive away. Ginsberg and Orlovsky were in bed. Ginsberg had a walking cast on. The rest remains between Peter and Allen and my mother, and it seemed clear that Peter and Allen were unruffled by the intrusion.

When my mother called the next day, she was effusive with the afterglow of the occasion. "It's amazing," she said, "how much Jews and Armenians have in common. I felt so at home with Allen. Please tell him and Peter that they must come to dinner the next time they're in Jersey."

"I will, Mom," I said sullenly. "Thanks for everything."

"And one other thing," she said. "That poem 'Kaddish,' I want to get a couple copies of it; can you find it in your bookstore?"

"Yeah," I said, and then there was silence.

"You know," she went on, "that poem, I can relate to it."

"You can?" I said reluctantly.

"In some way it's about Armenia, too."

Still hurting from what had happened over Charlene, I did not feel like talking with my mother at this moment, when she seemed to want to say something serious about herself to me.

"That's good," I said. "See you at graduation."

I hung up the phone feeling ambivalent. I did not want the poem, the evening, Ginsberg, to be a bridge between us, not just then, because I was sunk in my own spite. I did not tell my mother that I had wept listening to "Kaddish" in Larison Dining Hall, did not want her to know how much the poem affected me. But I was also sorry I could not talk to her just then.

A PRINCESS IN BYZANTIUM

Nᴏᴛ ʟᴏɴɢ ᴀꜰᴛᴇʀ Aʟʟᴇɴ Gɪɴsʙᴇʀɢ ʟᴇꜰᴛ ᴍʏ ᴀᴘᴀʀᴛᴍᴇɴᴛ, Aᴜɴᴛɪᴇ Aɴɴᴀ arrived on our campus to give a lecture on surrealism in painting and literature. In a large lecture hall in the Vaughan Literature Building, where I had sat through many classes, I watched my aunt. She stood there with the remote control to the slide machine in her hand, in a blue dress on which a large gold pin was affixed near the collar, a big white screen behind her. Her hair pulled back in a bun, glasses hanging on a chain around her neck. Then the lights dimmed and the images came on the screen:

Chirico's terrified shadows running in the airless landscapes of cities. An elephant that looked like an exploding water tank, that was Max Ernst. The anatomical squiggles of Miró, the sci-fi forms of Tanguy. A head with breasts and pubic hair? That was Magritte. The melting clocks of Dali. The images kept coming, and they were better than the images created by LSD. My aunt was talking at ease, without looking at her notes, about the relationship between the painters and the French Surrealist poets. Her tone was emphatic and her voice exuberant. From time to time she would break in on herself and recite passages of poetry in French from Apollonaire, Rim-baud, Mallarmé, Breton. The audience was caught up in her passion, and she was having fun. In the years to come I would hear again and again from her former students what an extraordinary teacher she was, how she made literature into an existential experience for them. That day at Bucknell, I felt as if I was seeing my aunt for the first time. I felt a great excitement, the kind you feel when you watch–like a stranger–your kin perform in public. Near the end of her talk, she mentioned her friend Anaïs Nin and urged the audience to read her work, for she was the heir to the Surrealist tradition.

Anaïs Nin. I hadn't thought of her name in years, but now in this lecture room with the lights out and my aunt's familiar voice ringing in this familiar classroom, I thought back to when I'd first met her at 395 Riverside Drive. Standing in the midst of my large, noisy family, impassive, alert, slightly marmoreal, with a faint, sensual smile. Her face was out of *Un Chien Andalou,* and if you had asked me her age, I couldn't have told you. All afternoon, she and my aunt spoke in French and English on and off. When *The Anaïs Nin Reader* was published, my aunt's preface served as the red carpet between Anaïs and America. I saw the book every-where in bookstores, "Introduction by Anna Balakian." I was proud to see the word *Balakian* in all those bookstores, my name, my father's name. I was glad my aunt was reaching a more popular audience. One day a few years later, when I was teaching high school English at Dwight-Englewood School, I picked up a copy of *The Anaïs Nin Reader* off the desk of one of my colleagues and began reading.

My aunt called Anaïs Nin "a princess in Byzantium–the mythological concept of Byzantium, a place of beauty and impend-ing downfall." She described Nin's art as "the isle of non-reality ... a distinct evasion of the brutality of exterior reality," a world of "blurred, misty visions," of "freedom from heritage, freedom from binding memories." I was surprised by my aunt's mystifying roman-ticism, because I always suspected her trenchant attacks on the sub-urbs were political. Also, I had come to believe that poetry needed to encompass the harsh realities of the century.

My aunt saw Nin as more European than American. "Litera-ture in America," my aunt wrote, "was no longer a reality in itself but the written documentary of events." In other words, American writing was not real art but sociology. I was astonished she thought so. Saul Bellow, Eudora Welty, Ralph Ellison, Flannery O'Connor, James Baldwin, Carson McCullers, William Styron – just documen-tary writers? I found Nin's writing so un-ironic and self-indulgent; why did my aunt like this stuff?

In time it became an issue between us. As my poems began appearing in literary magazines, she let me know now and then in her blunt way that they weren't surrealistic enough. Too many real-istic images. Too much logical syntax. Too American. As I read through the Surrealists (albeit in translation, and quite liked Apolli-naire and some of Desnos), on the whole I found it contrived, pre-cious, and romantic in the worst sense. By 1976 I decided to make an even more public statement about my taste in poetry, when with my friend and colleague, the poet Bruce Smith, I started a poetry jour-nal, *Graham House Review,* named after a grand Victorian stone house on Lincoln Street in Englewood, New Jersey, where I lived in a third-floor apartment that Dwight-Englewood School rented to young teachers.

So when I picked up my aunt's best-known book, *Surreal-ism: The Road to the Absolute,* I was a poet and editor seeking to understand her. In her preface, she proclaimed that French Surreal-ism was the revolutionary movement of the modern age, and it brought us news that the world could be whole, harmonious, redemptive. It was a revolution in language and consciousness, and through the power of surrealist imagination humans could achieve a new zenith of being, a new mysticism for "the here and now."

While acknowledging that American poetry could be "vivid and powerful in other than metaphysical dimensions," she saw most American poetry as merely descriptive. Most American poets were failures, she suggested, because they were creating "circumstantial works containing direct communication of social protest, relevant to precise abuses and particular conditions." This poisoned art, she believed, and at the close of the preface, alluding to Apollinaire, she advocated that "artists, instead of facing problems of any particular society, must confront the universe itself," and seek the "emblem of the philosopher's stone in *2001: A Space Odyssey.*" Did she mean the universe without the world?

As I closed the book, the names of American poets spilled out of my head. Hart Crane, T. S. Eliot, Wallace Stevens, John Berryman, Theodore Roethke, Sylvia Plath, H. D., Marianne Moore, Louise Bogan, Karl Shapiro, Robert Lowell, Allen Ginsberg, James Dickey, Adrienne Rich—all born in the U.S.A. They had given voice to the age. Weren't Homer, Dante, Milton, Whitman, Keats, Shelley, Yeats, García-Lorca, Auden, Mandelstam, Neruda, all guilty of representing "precise abuses and particular conditions" in their work? Stylistic innovations couldn't obviate politics and history. Hadn't great poetry always had a moral imagination?

Why, I asked, was she grading American poetry with a literary yardstick that had little relevance here in the United States? And why would she grade American poetry against a handful of French poets from the first half of the century? I kept hearing my aunt's voice on those Sundays at our house excoriating the suburbs, American middle-class life. Her voice, absolute, shrill, definitive. "You're lost here," she said to my mother. I pictured Auntie Anna in Nice and Paris every summer. My aunt, who was born in the real Byzantium (the city from which Armenians looked to Europe for their cultural cues, to France especially) in the year the Turkish government began its genocidal slaughter of the Armenians. I thought now that, when it came to poetry, she hadn't really come to America, and that her exiled soul was part of the historical trauma of the Armenian diaspora. But it wasn't until a year later in Paris that I would come to understand something of the bigger picture.

OWLS FLYING IN THE DARK

A FEW DAYS AFTER MY MOTHER HAD RETURNED WITH A HAPPY REPORT to Auntie Nona about the Ginsberg event at Bucknell, I received a letter from Nona inviting me to her apartment in early May because William Saroyan was coming to dinner. "Now," she wrote, "you and Bill will be able to really talk!" I couldn't say no, so in early May in the midst of exams, I hitchhiked Route 80 to the George Washington Bridge and appeared halfway through the evening.

When I open the door to Auntie Nona's apartment, Saroyan is leaning against one of the dozens of bookshelves that cover the walls. He sips alternately from two tall glass tumblers, one of dark tea and the other of vodka. He is thick and broad-chested. His buffed and polished fingernails glisten against the tumblers. His receding hair is long, black, and slicked back, curling up at the back of his neck. The handlebars of his ivory mustache bush down to the bottom of his jutting chin. In his black shirt, navy pants, and black shoes, he looks like an Old World peasant.

When I walk in, in blue jeans and a tweed sport jacket, I see a group of writers dressed more formally crowding around him as he cracks jokes and laughs in his baritone voice. A group of Armenian-American writers: Marjorie Housepian Dobkin, Michael Arlen, Peter Sourian, Leo and Linda Hamalian, Jack Antreassian, Harry Keyishian, Nishan Parlakian, Fred Asadourian, the jazz and blues producer George Avakian, and, of course, Auntie Anna. For all his fame as an American literary star and Broadway playwright, Saroyan means something more to Armenian Americans. He's an embodiment of a particular sensibility that Armenian Americans feel close to the bone.

Saroyan: master of the short story during the Great Depression. "The Daring Young Man on the Flying Trapeze," "Two Days Wasted in Kansas City," "Seventy Thousand Assyrians," "We Want a Touchdown," "The Armenian and the Armenian." Saroyan: who brought together the essay, a confessional autobiographical voice, and lyrical language and invented something new. An Armenian American from Fresno, California, whose parents had emigrated at the turn of the century from the ancient Armenian city of Bitlis in the eastern part of the Ottoman Empire, a city the Turks wiped clean of Armenians in 1915. A flamboyant autodidact, who invented a style and democratic spirit in which Americans saw and heard themselves. Saroyan: Armenian peasant as American iconoclast, who turned down the Pulitzer Prize in 1943 for his play "The Time of Your Life," the same year another Armenian American, Arshile Gorky, was becoming central to the revolution of American abstract expressionism.

He talks compulsively as he sips compulsively from both tumblers. He talks about racehorses. "Do you know how many horses owe me money?" He talks about his grandfather's vineyards in Bitlis, in old Armenia, which he has never seen, about growing tomatoes and figs in his backyard in Fresno, about his "rival," Hemingway, about living on pita bread and yogurt during the Depression. His eyes are wetly luminous, dark, excited, slightly vulnerable. I sit down next to my mother and father, and my father pours me a tall scotch.

It is a steamy night and the windows are open and the curtains hang like stiff dresses, and everyone is sweating and drinking scotch and eating smoked salmon and bereks and dolmas. Not long after I greet Bill, Auntie Nona tells him that I'm writing poems and asks him what kind of typewriter I should have. I'm feeling somewhat embarrassed, and asking myself, Why do I need Saroyan's opinion? His blessing? Can't I just call my local business-machine store and buy something? What does Saroyan know anyway? He still stuck in the '30s.

"What should I get?" I ask reluctantly, now that my aunt has pushed me out on the carpet. Saroyan slams his tumbler of tea on the mahogany console. "Not goddamned electric! You see how strong these hands are?" As he holds them out, I stare at the fine hairs on his fingers, the odd shine of his polished nails, and the fleshiness of his palms. "That's fifty years of typing on a real typewriter. I'd do anything to have my Underwood of 1928 back. Typewriters have souls, they have magic, something comes out of them. Certain keys have luck, and certain cylinders zing. You know what comes then? The real stuff. The voices of people. The hearts of men and women. Life comes like a rhythm of sounds, like a clippety clicking, like a tap-dancing genie." He sounds like a character in one of his stories. Romantic, nostalgic, verbose. And I, not sure whether Saroyan is an old kook or a prophet and still deferential enough to the Armenian patriarchal mode, go out the next day and buy a manual typewriter. The best manual typewriter I could find, which turned out to be a piece of junk, and I cursed Saroyan every time its bolts came undone. I pitched it a few years later in a dumpster off an exit ramp on Route 80.

But Saroyan was a literary patriarch, and Auntie Nona, who always encouraged and praised my writing, wanted me to connect with him. I was grateful for her love and spirit and her embrace of my young poetry, but I was not a Saroyanite. "Bill did a great thing," I said to Nona, "in his day. He invented something. But I don't think we have a lot to say to each other about writing. He likes a different thing."

"Oh, he'll love what you do. Just show him," she insisted.

She was persistent, and one night a couple of years later after a huge Armenian feast at her apartment, Auntie Nona announced, looking at Bill, "Peter's poems have been appearing in some very good magazines lately, and I hope he'll read one for us tonight." I looked in disbelief across the carcass of a leg of lamb at Auntie Nona. I was sipping wine fast and nervously and kept shaking my head no.

"I don't have anything with me," I said.

"Oh, you must have something in your head, Peter dear, all poets do."

"Really, Auntie Nona, I don't."

As the evening went on, she kept prodding me and whispering in my ear, "Just a few lines, Bill will love it." "Please, I can't, Auntie." And sometime around midnight, when my head was spinning from booze, my aunt held up her wine glass and began tapping it with a spoon.

"Peter is going to read us a poem!" She was smiling her cherubic smile, and I looked at her and looked at Saroyan, who was grinning with his big white set of ivories, and I said okay. "It's a poem, Bill, that uses an image from your story 'Seventy Thousand Assyrians.'" If I had a poem that had anything to do with Saroyan, this was it. It was a dumb poem and I was angry with myself for letting Nona dragoon me into this. I stood up in front of the mantle, wobbly and sweating in my tweed jacket, and recited it. When I finished, everybody clapped, and I felt like a seven-year-old who had just performed Song of the Volga Boatmen on the cello for his adoring aunts. Bill got up and shook my hand and said, "That's great, Peter. I'm a poet—you understand that, don't you?"

"Of course," I said.

"That's what I've done with my life. I'm a poet. That's what the image is about."

"Yes, yes," I said, "the image."

Before I could get another word out of my mouth, Bill was talking again about himself in the thirties when he was at work on his first stories, and as I slumped into a wing chair I watched him happily take over the spotlight. He was frenetic and I thought a bit sad, talking so loudly and drunkenly about himself for as long as anyone would listen.

. . . . .

By the time I graduated from college, I came to understand why my aunt Nona knew so many writers, and why so many writers wanted to know her. She did more than assign books for review at the nation's most influential book review, and she did more than write reviews in the daily *Times;* she was an aider and nurturer of writers. Writers from around the country sent her manuscripts as well as books. From the moment she stepped into her apartment after work until some time after midnight, she was on the phone with writers. She gave as much time to unknown writers she believed in as she did to established friends, and lived through the emotional roller coasters of her friends' writer's blocks, post-book depressions, pre-review anxieties, early-, mid-, and late-career despair.

Nona's parties introduced me to the idea of literature as a public occasion, a place where writers came together to eat and drink and talk about what they believed in. I met many of her colleagues and friends there: Eudora Welty, Kurt Vonnegut, Michael and Alice Arlen, Erica Jong, Walter Abish, Marguerite Young, Daisy Aldan, Harriet Zinnes, Bill Henderson, Marvin Cohen, Muriel Reukeyser. Nona was an exuberant hostess, always dressed immaculately in a suit or a floral dress, a Parisian scarf around her neck, and she moved like a hummingbird between groups of people with trays of bereks, dolmas, smoked salmon, anchovies on crackers. She was tiny, several inches under five feet, because of her disfigured spine, the result of a childhood illness.

Almost nothing was ever said about Aunt Nona's bowed back, but I knew that my grandparents sought the best medical care possible in Vienna and Geneva in the early 1920s and decided against spinal surgery because the risk of death was too great. When the Balakians arrived in New York, Nona was not sent to school, and my grandmother continued her education at home. Aunt Anna brought home her own school books, and Aunt Nona read them. My grandmother taught her mathematics and grammar, and her sister's homework assignments provided a structure for a curriculum, which her mother shaped and added to.

An émigré, a refugee from this century's first genocide, born on a Turkish army base, transported in fragile health from Asia Minor to Europe to North America, Nona spent her youth indoors. Sharing a bedroom with her younger brother and older sister in an apartment in which her father had his medical practice, she read her way through childhood. She once told me, "Until I was eighteen, I literally lived through books. Everyone I met was filtered through a literary equivalent–Proust, James, Chekhov. Reading wasn't just pleasure, it was an introduction to life, to myself." By the time she was fifteen, my grandmother had persuaded the administration at Horace Mann School for Girls that her daughter could keep up with anyone. At first, the Horace Mann administrators said, categorically, "no" to my grandmother. A handicapped immigrant girl, who had never been to school, enter the ninth grade at one of the elite prep schools of America? How many immigrant girls were there at Horace Mann in 1933, in the worst years of the Depression? My grandmother refused to take no for an answer, and after several appeals, the administration at Horace Mann School for Girls consented to let Nona Balakian become a freshman, and with a scholarship at that.

It is September 1933, and my aunt Nona is wearing a navy skirt and a white blouse. She walks in patent-leather shoes, spindly legged and petite, her silky black hair curling at her earlobes. Her torso is top-heavy due to her bowed back, and she carries a school bag in one hand, looking carefully both ways as she crosses the side streets on her four-block journey to school. She has never been to school in the New World–or in any world, for that matter. Buses and cabs and cars speed by her. A colorful scarf she wears around her neck blows occasionally into her face. The façades of buildings seem to waver against the blue sky. It is warm and humid and a faint breeze comes off the river. She is careful as she walks over sidewalk cracks and up and down the curb.

Nona did well at Horace Mann, and from there went to Barnard, where she majored in English and wrote plays. In 1942, she went to the graduate school of journalism at Columbia, where one of her teachers was John Chamberlain, then the leading book reviewer for the *Times*. He liked her work and suggested she apply for a position at the *Book Review*, and her public life began.

My aunt never spoke about her physical deformity. Only at the dinner table, when she needed a phone book or a pillow to raise the height of the chair, was it ever acknowledged. Had anyone suggested that she was handicapped or needed any special consideration, Nona would have been insulted. She commuted every day from 116th Street to Times Square, and moved briskly through the crowded streets and packed buses and subways. She was one of the first women at the *Book Review* and she rose in the patriarchal world of journalism.

More than anyone, William Saroyan defined my aunt's notion of the hybridization of literature and her feeling about the meaning of exile. Not long after Saroyan's death, after she had already begun her book on him, we were having dinner at Sardi's, where she often took me when I was in town. It was her favorite place, a *Times* hangout just yards from her office on 44th Street. As we drank our martinis in the air-conditioned restaurant, my aunt told me that she had dreamt about Saroyan last night.

"We were at Gristede's, an old one on Broadway in the 90s. Bill picked up some fresh figs and said–shouted, the way Bill does– 'Nona, a fig is a fig, you can't change it. It grows like a big sac of seeds and only the sun can change it, only the sun can make it sweeter and tougher. Isn't that right, sweeter and tougher. Isn't that what we want to be, sweet and tough.'"

"I said, 'Bill, you've got better ones in your own backyard.'

'You mean back in Fresno?'

'Of course.'

'Well, what good will they do me now, I'm in New York.'

'Bill, you can always go back to Fresno and pick them.'

'Hell I can.' And then he picked a fig from the bin and bit into it, and his mustache was full of the juice and pulp.

'Listen Bill,' I said, 'you see those apples, each one is different. Each bin a different skin, a different texture, a different juice.

Delicious, Macintosh, Cortland, Golden, Northern Spy, Rome, and so on. Isn't that America for you? An apple in each state. A state in each apple.'"

My aunt looked at me and began laughing.

"He looked at me and began to laugh. 'Hey Nona, that's it, I got my figs in the sun and my apples in my pockets. What more do I need? What more does a writer need?' Then the lights went out in the store, and when they came back on again, there was no one in the store, but a bird, flying around the fluorescent lights and then swooping down through the aisles and round the stacks of cans and bins of fruits and vegetables. It was a big owl-like bird with a great white walrus mustache, which is how I knew it was Bill.

"'Bill, Bill,' I began shouting, 'come down now. This is Gristede's. You can't do this here.'

"He just kept flying and flying in great swooping circles. And I just got dizzier and dizzier until I woke up."

My aunt paused and looked down at her drink, from which she had not taken sip, and she brought it to her lips. And as tears began to roll down her cheeks, she picked up the white napkin on the table and wiped her eyes. I realized how deeply she missed Saroyan.

"You see," she went on, composed again and talking like a critic, "I believe that Saroyan, like all Armenians, was a natural utopian. We have a dream instead of a country. Because territory has eluded us, we have a freedom to invent that most people don't. The more our geography shrinks, the more our imaginations expand, the more we're like owls flying in the dark."

WORDS FOR MY GRANDMOTHER

THE JOURNEY INTO HISTORY, INTO THE ARMENIAN GENOCIDE, WAS FOR me inseparable from poetry. Poetry was part of the journey and the excavation. I've never believed in poetry that expresses polemical ideas. I was a young poet devoted to immersing myself in the plasticity and lushness of words and making the best language I could. But I learned that when words collide with memory unexpected things happen, as they did one day shortly after I began my first adult job.

I was teaching English at Dwight-Englewood School, and because my third-floor suite of rooms in Graham House was only a few hundred yards from my classroom, I slept as long as I could and made it to homeroom just before the students arrived. The phone was ringing early that Monday morning. It was my mother on the phone, in her cheery morning voice, informing me that on Sunday at church she and my aunts were having a *hokee hankisd* (memorial service) for the tenth anniversary of my grandmother's death.

"I can't come," I said. "I'm going to Cambridge to spend the weekend with April."

"This is more important than being with some stranger."

"She's not a stranger."

"She's some girl who means nothing to any of us!"

I slammed down the phone and walked down the huge staircase of Graham House, three flights, to the cavernous kitchen. I lit a match to start the old gas stove and boiled some water for a cup of awful instant coffee. I sat at the small Formica table staring at the long glass doors of the cabinets and the faded blue walls, sipping coffee. I was making it clear to myself that I wasn't going to let my mother force me to this *hokee hankisd*, not when April and I had a weekend planned. I kept sipping coffee and saying to myself, I'm not going. And I kept hearing the words *hokee hankisd*. A very Armenian sound. *Hokee*, soul. *Hankisd*, rest. The soul's rest: a memorial.

Armenians have a special sense of the word *hokee*. It's a word that captures the Armenian feeling for the soul, for the spirit life, the invisible, the numinous. My grandmother addressing me: *hokees*, my soul, my beloved. During my night of fever in '62 when she had her flashback, she said: *Sounch* (breath). *Ott* (air). *Hokee* (soul). *Hokeet seerem:* I love your soul. *Hokeet dal:* to have soul-energy. *Hokvov yev marmenov:* body and soul. *Sourp hokee:* holy spirit. *Hokee kaloust:* coming of the spirit.

"Who the hell cares about a fucking *hokee hankisd* ten years later!" I said to my mother when she called again.

Her voice turned icy. "Have you forgotten how much your grandmother loved you?"

"I'll think of her all weekend," I said as I hung up.

On Friday afternoon after coaching J. V. football, I got into my new brown Toyota Corolla and drove to Cambridge to spend the weekend with April in her dorm at the Harvard Business School, where she was finishing an MBA. I was feeling grown up with my new paycheck and sense of independence. We took in a couple of movies and ate at a chic restaurant in Boston. We drove the streets of Cambridge after midnight in my new car, and wound up in some bars off Central Square. We slept late and lounged under the sheets reading to each other while we drank bad instant coffee.

I pulled into the long circular driveway at Graham House late on Sunday night feeling good about life. As I walked up the staircase, I realized I hadn't thought once about my grandmother all weekend. Not about church, or family, or *hokee hankisd.* I opened the French doors to my apartment, chucked my knapsack on my bed, sat on my garage-sale turquoise couch, and opened my notebook. I just needed to write, and I began.

> The trees are bare
> with abandoned nests.
> Small swarms of birds
> break, dive, and rotate
> in a cloudless sky.
> I make my way through
> leaf-piles soaked by the night-rain;
> spaces between earth and sky
> cloud, field, and stone
> you too once entered.
>
> It is ten years since
> you last saw your breath,
> and these shadows
> moving with day
> across the base of this oak.
>
> Ten years ago
> I walked your dark stairway,
> water hissing on the stove,
> your orientals worn
> and beaten into deep
> reds and blues by your
> half-confessed past.
>
> When you took my head
> in your arms
> and kissed my hair

I stared as always
at the skin of your hands
still discolored by
the arid Turkish plain.

I called it "Words for My Grandmother." This early poem—
just some clear images—had come out like a quiet rush of something
pent-up, and that was not how I usually wrote. Looking back, I can
see that those words came out of guilt for not having gone to the
hokee hankisd. I don't think my grandmother would have cared; her
love for me was unconditional. But I had let the family down, and
from that feeling came my personal *hokee hankisd,* a poem in which
I could arrest time and freeze memory. My grandmother had come
back to me for the first time in years.

The poem was a surprise. Out of my head came things I did-
n't know I remembered. Images that focused and located forgotten
scenes. Those Friday afternoons at my grandmother's apartment in
East Orange when we baked *choereg.* The dark stairway, the apartment with its oriental rugs. The phrase that most startled me was
"half-confessed past." Not only didn't I know where it came from, I
wasn't even sure what it meant. The phrase was ahead of me, pointing to things I would come to know, things psychological, things historical.

The image of my grandmother kissing my hair as she
eenched me to death was no surprise, nor her discolored hands, but
the last image, "the arid Turkish plain," also seemed to come out of
nowhere. I was twenty-three and no one had spoken to me about the
Armenian Genocide. My grandmother's flashback had been a
strange set of surrealistic images that left an imprint on me, but she
never talked about her past in rational language. This poem, then,
was a tremor from the unconscious—the historical unconscious, the
deep, shared place of ancestral pain, the place in the soul where we
commune with those who have come before us. I had written this
poem for a personal reason only. I had no historical awareness, no
political ideas, but somehow out of the collision of language with
personal memory came something larger. It was the first time for me

that poetic language became a mode of historical exploration, the first time a poem became an act of commemoration.

The next day I typed it up and sent it to my mother, with a note of muted regret about having missed the *hokee hankisd*. With a bit of the poet's ego I suggested as well that the poem was its own *hokee hankisd*, and maybe even a better one than a church service. Mostly, I was happy about the poem, not because I thought it was great but because it had done what art can do: bring lost things back into your life. My poem brought my grandmother back to me, whose love, perhaps, meant more to me than anyone's. She was my friend and nurturer again, now in my adult life. And with the poem's final image I had placed her at last: in the old world, the arid Turkish plain, lost Armenia. Now I would have to go and find out what that lost place was.

PART V

BLOODY NEWS

BEFORE THE NAZIS

I came to find out more about the arid Turkish plain when I picked up a book at a time when I was prepared to read it.

Every summer after the last day of classes, I would head down to a summer job as a mail runner for a steamship terminal company. I delivered mail and picked up checks from shipping companies: $50,000, $100,000, $250,000. My aunt Lucille, who was one of the higher-ups in the company, had gotten this job for me when I was fifteen. The office was at 17 Battery Place, the tip of Manhattan.

I liked the freedom of running mail in the city in the summertime. The solitude amidst multitude. I walked in the shadows of buildings, snaked through crowds on the chopped, narrow streets of lower Manhattan. Broadway, Trinity, Greenwich, Coentis Slip, Maiden Lane, Wall, William, Pearl, Water. I ran through the blackened gravestones in the cemetery of Trinity Church, practiced pass patterns in an empty alley, got lost in niches of time and space. Hidden entrances, basement trapdoors, submerged steps off sidewalks, back alleys. I knew the network of freight elevators, too. I loved the heavy, black, accordionlike doors rolling open and shut with their clanking smoothness and the smell of Cuban cigars that lingered there.

The boss of the mail room was Jimmy Thompson, a light-skinned black man in his mid-seventies, a retired Pullman porter who said, "I've seen a million miles of this sweet country, and everything that people could do to each other in a single car." He spoke slowly and softly with a faint Southern lilt, and he liked to be talking. "Peeta, Peeta, Peeta," he said my name in a half whisper as he came in and out of the room. Every day Jimmy wore a white short-sleeved shirt and khaki chinos and walked in short bursts of energy. His soft, large hands, which could sort and shuffle hundreds of pieces of mail in a few minutes, took to a deck of playing cards as if he were a dealer at a casino. And on coffee break, if I hadn't disappeared into the stockroom to read or work on poems, Jimmy and I would play blackjack on the sorting table next to the mail-metering machine.

Jimmy was my protector. He covered for me. He knew how to manage people. He pretended to be deferential but he was cunning. "Peeta's having a little problem with his bladda, but I'll see to it that he gets out of the little boy's room soon as possible," or "That damn freight elevator at Chilean Line is always breaking down, but I know he's going as fast as can be," or "Peeta ate one of those Sabrette dogs–those things, Mr. Dominick, they're poison as bad pig, and that boy is retching down on the fifth floor 'cause he's feelin' too shamed to do it here." That got me out of trouble on a missed message at two o'clock, and when you miss messages at two o'clock the money doesn't make it to the bank on time, and a day's interest lost on $100,000 is not small. I did my best to look glazed the rest of the day, and later when the president passed me in the hall he winked and said, "Pack a brown bag."

A few days before I was to leave for my first year of graduate school at Brown, I decided to return to my old job to earn a few extra bucks. Over the weekend, I picked off the bookshelf in my parents' den a book whose spine I had stared at for years. *Ambassador Morgenthau's Story*, published by Doubleday & Page, 1919. It seemed like a book that would get me through the workweek. On Monday, as I stood under the big, arching copper beeches on Knickerbocker Road waiting for the bus to take me to work, I stared at the photograph of Morgenthau used for the frontispiece. A look from the era of Woodrow Wilson: the bifocals, the high forehead, serious eyes, the stylish mustache and goatee. The dignified face of a German Jew who came to America at the age of nine in 1865; who graduated from Columbia Law School at twenty-three and started his own law firm; a Democrat with an old mugwump's idealism. In his youth, Morgenthau worked for the Jewish settlement houses and cofounded the Free Synagogue. Instrumental in the International Red Cross, a passionate supporter of the League of Nations, in 1912 he campaigned for Wilson and later for FDR. By 1913, when Wilson appointed him Ambassador to Turkey, he was a seasoned statesman. An ambassador to a strategic zone of international politics on the eve of the Great War.

> It was an amazing fate that landed me in this great
> headquarters of intrigue at the very moment when
> the plans of the Kaiser for controlling Turkey, which
> he had carefully usurped for a quarter of a century,
> were about to achieve their final success.

By the time the bus came rattling over the potholes of Knickerbocker Road, I was lost in my father's birthplace. Ships moored along the Bosphorus. The water, green, tepid, caique-flecked, the glitter of silver. Terraced clumps of fig and olive trees. The dome of Hagia Sophia, golden, with minarets jutting up. Men in fezzes. Smells of shashlik and sewage in the streets.

The man first sent by the Kaiser to achieve the subjugation of Turkey to Germany was Baron Von Wangenheim, a Prussian autocrat whose ambition typified the new German Empire: "Pan-Germany filled all his waking hours and directed his every action. The deification of his emperor was the only religious instinct which impelled him." He believed Germany was destined to rule the world. Turkey was a strategic place to the European powers; influence in Turkey meant access to the Dardanelles and new commercial markets in the Middle East and central Asia. In the imperialist struggles for domination, a controlling alliance with Turkey also meant being able to check Russian access to the Mediterranean. Germany's Berlin to Baghdad Railway was one symbol of Germany's hope for hegemony in the Near East.

Morgenthau used the phrase of my eighth-grade social studies text–"the sick man of Europe"–to describe Turkey, a country that "was in a state of decrepitude that had left it an easy prey to German diplomacy." Abdul Hamid II, who was to be Turkey's last ruling sultan, was an unbenevolent despot. He watched his empire begin to crumble as Romania, Serbia, Montenegro, and Bulgaria became autonomous or independent, and the empire sank into further financial ruin. Gladstone called Abdul Hamid II the "bloody assassin," because during the last decade of the nineteenth century, the sultan took out his frustration over the diminishment of his empire on his Christian minorities, especially the Armenians.

Following the Russo-Turkish War of 1877–78, which the Russians won, the peace drawn up at San Stefano gave the Russians control of the Armenian provinces of northeast Anatolia and hence the ability to protect the Armenians there from Turkish misrule. But at the behest of Disraeli the lines were redrawn, and the 1878 Treaty of Berlin gave the European powers only a theoretical obligation to protect the Armenians. The very sultan who had been abusing the Armenians again had direct responsibility for protecting them. The setback of the Treaty of Berlin left Armenians frustrated and demoralized but determined to improve their deplorable condition as "infidels" in Turkish society. As the sultan's policy toward Armenians became even harsher in the 1880s and early 1890s, Armenians organized reform movements, most importantly the Hunchak and the Dashnak parties. These groups sought cultural freedom; equality before the law; freedom of speech, press, and assembly; freedom from the unjust tax system imposed on Christians; and the right to bear arms. In the wake of these demands, the sultan became further enraged.

After Armenians were massacred at Sassoun in 1894 for protesting the unequal tax laws for Christians, and more massacres of Armenians occurred throughout the empire, a small group of Armenians seized the Ottoman Bank in Constantinople in August 1896, staging a protest and demanding civil rights. No money was taken or bank property damaged, and after a thirteen-hour bloodless drama, the Armenians exiled themselves on a ship bound for Marseilles. The protest not only failed but resulted in Abdul Hamid accelerating his program of massacring Armenians with secret military forces; by the end of the 1896, more than 200,000 Armenians had been killed.

The intensified culture of massacre initiated by the sultan in the '90s went unchecked by the European powers and served as a prologue to what would happen to the Armenians in 1915. By 1908, Abdul Hamid's crumbling reign was brought to an end by a trio of upstarts, Talaat Pasha, Enver Pasha, and Djemal Pasha, who called themselves *Ittihad ve Terakki* (the Committee of Union and Progress) and were known as the Young Turks. The Young Turks overthrew the old theocracy and promised a new secular nationalism and reform for the empire and its Christian minorities. In 1908, Armenians, anticipating an era of liberty and justice, were celebrating the new regime.

Morgenthau's descriptions of Talaat, Enver, Djemal – the men who engineered the Armenian Genocide – fascinated me the way descriptions of Hitler did when I first read about the Holocaust. The leader of the triumvirate, Talaat Pasha, like Hitler, Napoleon, and Stalin, was an ethnic outsider – a Bulgarian gypsy whose peasant upbringing had not included the "use of a knife and fork." A former telegraph clerk in Edirne, he was forty-one when he came to power.

> [He] liked to sit at his desk, with his shoulders drawn up, his head thrown back, and his wrists, twice the size of an ordinary man's, planted firmly on the table ... his fierceness, his determination, his remorselessness – the whole life and nature of the man [took] form in those wrists.

As Minister of the Interior he was head of the secret police and he also administered the six Armenian provinces in the eastern part of the country.

Jemal Pasha, once a colonel in the Turkish Third Army, at forty-one became Minister of the Marine. In a photo from the *Illustrated London News* of 1913, he is pictured in his decorated uniform, looking bemused.

Enver Pasha, age thirty-two, had been a major in the Turkish Third Army, "a Europeanized dandy," with delusions of Napoleonic grandeur. He had "a clean-cut face, a slightly curled up mustache, a small but sturdy figure, with pleasing manners." He hung pictures of Napoleon and Frederick the Great in his parlor, and "his friends commonly referred to him as 'Napoleonik.'" Enver spoke German fluently, worshipped Prussian militarism, and believed he was divinely chosen to reestablish the glory of Turkey. Having spent years as a military attaché in Berlin, Enver was the bridge between Turkey and Germany and a tool for Baron Von Wangenheim and the Kaiser, who cultivated him as a possible instrument for their plans in the Orient.

For more than a decade, Morgenthau noted, the Kaiser and Von Wangenheim had advocated the evacuation of all the Greeks of Smyrna and the surrounding region; the Turks referred to the city as *giaour Ismir,* or infidel Smyrna. Morgenthau wrote that Pan-Germanism of this period advocated the virtues of deportation, "the shifting of whole peoples as though they were so many herds of cattle." The Germans would practice this in Belgium, Poland, and Serbia during the Great War, but its "most hideous manifestation" would be inspired by Germany and practiced by Turkey on its Armenian population. How prophetic that Morgenthau, a Jew who emigrated from Germany to America in the middle of the nineteenth century, wrote this less than two decades before the next German empire would subject his own people to a "deportation" that would claim more lives than any other in history.

In 1913, Talaat ordered boycotts against all Greek merchants, and demanded that all foreign establishments dismiss their Greek employees. Morgenthau wrote:

> I did not have the slightest suspicions at that time
> that the Germans had instigated these deportations,

but I looked upon them merely as an outburst of
Turkish chauvinism.... By this time I knew Talaat
well; I saw him nearly every day, and he used to discuss practically every phase of international relations with me. I objected vigorously to his treatment
of the Greeks; I told him that it would make the
worst possible impression abroad and that it would
affect American interests.... Talaat explained his
national policy ... if what was left of Turkey was to
survive, he must get rid of these alien peoples.
"Turkey for the Turks" was now Talaat's controlling
idea.

My hands were sweating on the faded brown cloth binding. I
ran out of the empty bus, down the escalator, down two more flights
of stairs, through the turnstile and onto the platform to see an A
Train sitting with its doors open and aisles packed with strap-hang-
ing commuters. I read standing as the train cut through Manhattan.

The common term applied by the Turk to the Christian is "dog," and in his [the Turk's] estimation this is
no mere rhetorical figure; he actually looks upon his
European neighbors as far less worthy of consideration than his own domestic animals.... "My son," an
old Turk once said, "do you see that herd of swine?
Some are white, some are black, some are large,
some are small—they differ from each other in some
respects, but they're all swine. So it is with Christians."

In Turkey,

[T]he mechanism of business and industry had
always rested in the hands of the subject peoples,
Greeks, Jews, Armenians, and Arabs. The Turks
have learned little of European art or science, they

> have established very few educational institutions,
> and illiteracy is the prevailing rule.

I sat sucking the air off the bottom of a Tropicana carton and thinking that the parallels in history are frightening; it was the same with the Third Reich and the Jews. The paradox of dependency and power that existed between Armenians and Turks was a tinderbox.

Under Islamic Ottoman rule, the "infidel" Christians were excluded from military and civil service and government. They had no civil or legal rights; the Koran was the basis of justice. The Turks

> erected the several peoples, such as the Greeks and
> the Armenians into separate "millets," or provinces.
> And, they did this not to promote their independence
> and welfare, but because they regarded them as ver-
> min, and thus not fit for membership in the Ottoman
> state.

In such a culture, a Christian was forever vulnerable to the arbitrary violence of any Turk: "And for centuries the Turks simply lived like parasites upon these overburdened and industrious people. They taxed them to economic extinction, stole their most beautiful daughters and forced them into their harems."

In Armenia, Greece, and Albania, as well as the areas now comprising Bosnia and Herzegovina and the former Yugoslav province of Macedonia, Turkish officials came each year and took to Constantinople the brightest and strongest male children between the ages of eleven and thirteen, where in the cruelest of ironies they taught them to beat down the cross and die for the crescent as Janissaries of the sultan's personal army.

After my morning pickups at Peralta, Cunard, M.O.S.K., and Norton-Lily, I took a coffee break. I bought a carton of Tropicana orange juice from the woman who wheeled the coffee cart around the eleventh floor at 10:30 and I went to the storage room, a dimly lit bowling alley of a place in which I often wrote poems. It was lined with brown boxes of Xerox paper, manila envelopes, stationery,

Scotch tape, mimeograph paper, binders, and all the other things that made offices run in those days before computers. In the narrow space between the stacks of boxes, the silence settled on me.

And then Armenian church came back to me—not what I learned from the lessons of the Gospels and the Nicene Creed—but the theater of it all. The haunting minor keys of the hymns I could still sing in Armenian. The echoes of the deacons and altar boys chanting. The ashy, resinous smell of incense spreading in clouds as the deacon walked into the aisle swinging the silver censer with its chains and bells, and the sound of acolytes shaking gold scepters ringed with tiny bells as the altar curtain opened and closed and we sat and kneeled and stood. When the priest in the high-collared, gold-and-red embroidered robe raised his jewel-studded cross to the congregation we crossed ourselves, and then he disappeared behind the curtain.

What I had learned in Sunday School was this. Armenia emerged from Urartian civilization sometime around the sixth century B.C. For a short time Armenia held the status of a world power. (Our Sunday School teachers made sure we knew this.) Under King Dikran II, known as Dikran the Great, who ruled from 95 to 55 B.C., Armenia reached the height of its empire, extending north to Transcaucasia, east to the Caspian Sea, west to central Anatolia, and south to Cilicia on the Mediterranean Sea. The Romans under Pompey feared Armenia's power, and Pompey sent the general Lucullus to conquer King Dikran and subjugate Armenia. We were told that the final battle between the Romans and the Armenians was a close one, decided by something like a blocked field goal. Dikran's son, Artavazd II, who wrote plays in Greek and founded a Greek theater in his court, was kidnapped by the soldiers of Mark Antony, who put Artavazd and his family to death.

At the turn of the fourth century, about A.D. 301, the Armenian nation officially adopted Christianity, thus making Armenia the first nation to become Christian. Armenian Christianity developed independently from that of Rome and Byzantium. To consummate its cultural identity, in the early part of the fifth century, King Vramshapuh commissioned a monk, Mesrob Mashtots (later sainted), to invent an alphabet, enabling Armenians to read scripture in Armenian which, until then, had been a spoken language. The Armenians thus were freed from their dependency on Greek and Persian for written language.

When Persian King Yezdegrid tried to force Armenia to adopt Zoroastrianism in the fifth century, promising them gifts and honors in return, the Armenian leaders replied: "From this faith none ever can shake us, neither angels, nor men, neither sword, fire, water, nor any bitter torturers." So the Persians invaded Armenia with an army of close to a quarter of a million men and teams of elephants, attacking an Armenian army of about 60,000 men, led by Vartan Mamikonian. Saint Vartan–who I pictured then like Vince Lombardi but with a beard and a sword and a shield–was killed, but after a long, exhausting war, the Persians, seeing that the beleaguered Armenians refused to give up, finally withdrew. This was 451, and Armenia remained Christian. Armenia's neighbors on the ancient map–the Cappodocians, Chaldeans, Sumerians, Babylonians, Scythians, Parthians, Hittites–were gone, but the Armenians had survived, their religion and their alphabet keeping them unassimilated by their neighbors.

I pictured those wind-bitten stone churches built out of the Armenian highlands of Anatolia, with their wooden belfries prescribed by Ottoman law so that no bell could be heard. I could hear those wooden clappers making a thump like a muffled throat. Then I thought of St. Thomas' Armenian Church in Tenafly, where women in coifed hair and mink coats sat in mahogany pews, their perfume mingling with the incense, as the morning light came through the pale colors of the flat, modern images of Jesus, the Virgin, and the Apostles in the stained-glass windows. The store-bought carpet glowed with the colored light, and the large windows in the Sunday School rooms looked out to the split-level and ranch houses with swimming pools and tennis courts on Tenafly's east hill.

In order to mobilize Turkish racism into a political movement, ideology was necessary. Between 1908 and 1915, the Young Turks were developing their own version of Hitler's racial nationalism, called

Pan-Turkism, and their Himmler was the Turkish propagandist, Zia Gökalp. Pan-Turkism advocated the revival of a Turkish nation based on racial purity, "Turkey for the Turks." Gökalp's racist theories were predicated on reviving a pre-Ottoman ideology of glory, when Turkic warriors like Ghengis Kahn, Timur Babur, and Attila pillaged and conquered. His hope was to create a Turkic empire that spanned from Anatolia into Transcaucasia and on into central Asia. Gökalp's racialist romanticism was based on eradicating Christians and other minorities so that the "Pan-Turkish ideal" could be realized. Just as the Third Reich would isolate the Jews by increments to obliterate Jewish life, the Turks began to level anything that wasn't Turkish – in particular, everything that was Armenian.

> They attempted to make all foreign business houses employ only Turkish labour, insisting that they should discharge their Greek, Armenian, and Jewish employees. The Turks developed a mania for suppressing all languages except Turkish. For decades French had been the accepted language of foreigners in Constantinople; most street signs were printed in both French and Turkish. One morning the astonished foreign residents discovered that all these French signs had been removed and that the names of streets, the directions on street cars, and public notices appeared only in those strange Turkish characters, which very few of them understood.

Implementing Pan-Turkism so that the Turkish people would act on it not only meant demonizing Armenians, Greeks, and Zionist Jews (the Young Turks already had taken care of this); now it was important to make a formal and political accusation that Armenians were a security threat to the nation. The Young Turks and successive regimes used the rhetoric of "provocation." Any act of civilized protest, self-defense, or resistance to massacre was seen as an act of provocation. For centuries the Armenians had been called the loyal millet; now they were demonized as traitors. Hitler, who learned things from the Young Turks, would use the same rhetoric to demonize the Jews.

What happened in the province of Van (pronounced *Vahn*) became crucial to the Turkish rationale for commencing the Armenian Genocide. As Turkey was entering World War I, Enver Pasha replaced the governor of Van with his brother-in-law, Djevdet Bey, a devotee of Pan-Turkism and a hater of Armenians. When Djevdet Bey "returned to Van from a disastrous military expedition in northeast Persia, he demanded 4,000 Armenian soldiers for the Ottoman army." Fearing this was a pretext for slaughtering the men, a tactic the Turks had employed regularly, the Armenian leaders of Van responded by offering 400 soldiers and to pay for the rest with an exemption fee, which as Christians they were legally allowed to do. When Djevdet Bey insisted on the 4,000 soldiers, four Armenian leaders went to negotiate with him; on the way to the meeting they were murdered. That was April 16, 1915. On Monday, April 19, Djevdet Bay issued the following: "The Armenians must be exterminated. If any Muslim protect a Christian, first, his house shall be burned; then the Christian killed before his eyes, then his [the Muslim's] family and himself."

On April 19, in Akantz, a village close to the Russian border, the entire male population of 2,500 was murdered. The next day, as the Turkish army began to bomb the city of Van, an Armenian resistance of 300 men with pistols fought back. Two extraordinary things happened. By the middle of May, the Armenians were under siege but had beaten back the Turkish army until the Russian army arrived to help them repel the Turks. Talaat called this resistance to massacre treason, and used the event as a provocation for implementing what the Young Turks had been planning: race extermination. An entire stateless and defenseless Christian minority—constituting six percent of the population of a country with one of the world's largest standing armies—had been defined as seditious.

I heard the metallic crunching of a key in the door handle. "You were supposed to pick up a check at Chilean Line a half hour ago," Jimmy said.

"I will not leave a single Armenian standing," Djevdet Bey said, "not one so high," and he pointed to his knee.

THE MURDER OF A NATION

I RAN OFF TO GET THE CHECK, AND RETURNED TO THE OFFICE BEFORE the bank closed. I went back outside and sat sweating on a bench in Battery Park a few feet from a steel band and two jugglers flipping balls and bowling pins.

> Most of us believe that torture has long ceased to be an administrative and judicial measure, yet I do not believe that the darkest ages ever presented scenes more horrible than those which now took place all over Turkey. Nothing was sacred to the Turkish gendarmes; under the plea of searching for hidden arms, they ransacked churches, treated the altars and sacred utensils with utmost indignity, and even held mock ceremonies in imitation of the Christian sacraments. They would beat the priests into insensibility, under the pretense that they were the centers of sedition. When they could discover no weapons in the churches, they would sometimes

arm the bishops and priests with guns, pistols, and swords, then try them before courts-martial for possessing weapons against the law, and march them in this condition through the streets, merely to arouse the fanatical wrath of the mobs. The gendarmes treated women with the same cruelty and indecency as the men.

The Jehovah's Witnesses were passing out leaflets. The barefoot Hare Krishnas paced in front of me. I could smell the drunk under a fly-ridden raincoat a foot away.

A common practice was to place the prisoner in a room, with two Turks stationed at each side ... and then begin with the bastinado, a form of torture ... which consists of beating the soles of the feet with a thin rod ... until the feet swell and burst, and not infrequently ... they have to be amputated. The gendarmes would bastinado their Armenian victim until he fainted; they would then revive him by sprinkling water on his face and begin again. If this did not succeed in bringing their victims to terms, they had numerous other methods of persuasion. They would pull out his eyebrows and beard almost hair by hair; they would extract his finger nails and toe nails; they would apply red-hot irons to his breast, tear off his flesh with red-hot pincers, and then pour boiled butter into the wounds. In some cases the gendarmes would nail hands and feet to pieces of wood—evidently in imitation of the Crucifixion, and then while the sufferer writhes in his agony, they would cry: "Now let your Christ come help you!"

One day I was discussing these proceedings with a responsible Turkish official, who was describing the tortures inflicted. He made no secret of the fact that the Government had instigated them and, like all Turks of the official classes, he enthusiastically approved this treatment of the detested race. This official told me that all these details were matters of nightly discussion at the headquarters of the Union and Progress Committee. He told me that they even delved into the records of the Spanish Inquisition and other historic institutions of torture and adopted all the suggestions found there. . . .

If the Young Turks displayed greater ingenuity than their predecessor, Abdul Hamid, in killing Armenians, they did not have the Zyklon gas and large ovens the Nazis would, and so the business of genocide was carried out by hand.

The Central Government now announced its intention of gathering the two million or more Armenians living in the several sections of the empire and transporting them to this desolate and inhospitable region [the Syrian desert]. . . . The real purpose of the deportation was robbery and destruction; it really represented a new method of massacre. When the Turkish authorities gave the orders for these deportations, they were merely giving the death warrant to a whole race; they understood this well, and in their conversations with me, they made no particular attempt to conceal the fact.

All through the spring and summer of 1915 the deportations took place. Scarcely a single Armenian, whatever his education or wealth, or whatever the social class to which he belonged, was exempted from the order.

The police fell upon them just as the eruption of Vesuvius fell upon Pompeii; women were taken from the wash-tubs, children were snatched out of bed, the bread was left half baked in the oven, the family meal was abandoned partly eaten, the children were

taken from the schoolroom, leaving their books open
at the daily task, and the men were forced to abandon their plough in the fields and their cattle on the
mountain side. Even women who had just given
birth to children would be forced to leave their beds
and join the panic-stricken throng, their sleeping
babies in their arms. Such things as they hurriedly
snatched up–a shawl, a blanket, perhaps a few
scraps of food–were all that they could take of their
household belongings. To their frantic questions
"Where are we going?" the gendarmes would vouch-
safe only one reply: "To the interior."

I sat on the bench sipping hot coffee out of a styrofoam cup
and recalled something my grandmother told me when I was ten, as
we sat alone on the patio after Sunday dinner. It was late summer
because I remember the sound of the cicadas in the maples, and how
the whole yard sounded like a great shaking rattle. My grandmother
sat reclined in a green-and-white chaise lounge, drinking a glass of
tahn. She wore sunglasses, and all I could see was the hedge of rhododendrons reflected in the dark plastic of her glasses. As usual, she just
started in, as if she were talking to herself. "You know the one about
the man who went to Constantinople to seek his fortune?" she said.

"Nope," I said, hoping to indicate that I didn't want to know
about the man who went to Con-stan-tin-o-ple.

"After he had been in Constantinople for a while, he heard
about a man from his village who had also arrived, and because he
had left behind his father, mother, brother, sister, and his dog named
Manook, he went to find the man from his village. He was led to a
pastry shop where he noticed his fellow villager eating *kadayif* and
drinking coffee. 'Hadji Ovan' (that is, John who has made a pilgrimage to the Holy Land), he cried as he walked into the pastry shop,
'have you come from Bitlis?'

'Yes,' Hadji Ovan said, cutting his *kadayif.*

'What's the news there?'

'What news do you want?'

'How is my dear Manook?' For he missed his dog more than anything.

'I'm sorry, my friend, but Manook is dead.'

'Are you telling me that Manook is dead?' the man asked, because he couldn't believe it.

'Yes, my friend, he ate the meat of your mule and died.'

'Does that mean the mule is dead?'

'Yes my friend, the mule died while hauling your father's gravestone.'

'Are you trying to tell me, Hadji Ovan, that my father is dead?'

'Yes, he lived two weeks after your mother's death. She died of a broken heart when she heard how your brother died trying to save your sister.'

'Are you telling me that my mother and brother and sister are dead? Why don't you just come out and say it: my family is all dead, my home ruined!'

'I don't know if your home is ruined,' Hadji Ovan said, 'but when I left the village, the Turks were tilling the soil where your house once stood.'"

It was one of those bizarre stories my grandmother came out with occasionally that left me bewildered and speechless. As I watched the sun glare off her dark glasses, I sat there in silence picking at the nylon bands of the chaise lounge until my mother appeared with a tray of watermelon and cheese, and everyone came out and started in on dessert, and I was relieved.

The government officials would also inform the Armenians that, since their deportation was only temporary, they would not be permitted to sell their houses. Scarcely had the former possessors left the village, when Mohammedan mohadjirs–immigrants from other parts of Turkey–would be moved into the Armenian quarters. Similarly all their valuables–money, rings, watches, and jewelry–would be taken to the police stations for "safe keeping," pending their return, and then parceled out among the Turks.

Before the caravans were started, it became the
regular practice to separate the young men from the
families, tie them together in groups of four, lead
them to the outskirts, and shoot them. Public hang-
ings without trial – the only offense being that the victims were Armenians – were taking place constantly.
The gendarmes showed a particular desire to annihi-
late the educated and the influential. From American
consuls and missionaries I was constantly receiving
reports of such executions, and many of the events
which they described will never fade from my memory. At Angora [Ankara] all Armenian men from fifteen to seventy were arrested, bound together in
groups of four, and sent on the road in the direction
of Caesarea. When they had traveled five or six hours
and had reached a secluded valley, a mob of Turkish
peasants fell upon them with clubs, hammers, axes,
scythes, spades, and saws. Such instruments not only
caused more agonizing death than guns and pistols,
but, as the Turks themselves boasted, they were more
economical, since they did not involve the waste of
powder and shell. In this way they exterminated the
whole male population of Angora!

The elevator shot up six floors, stopped, and shot up to the
eleventh, where I got out with a check for a hundred grand, which I
stuffed in Morgenthau's book like a bookmark. I rushed to Auntie
Lu's office and handed it to her, and saw her do a double take when
she noticed the book in my hand. I returned to the mail room and sat
by the postage-meter machine sorting mail and spot reading.

A guard of gendarmerie accompanied each convoy,
ostensibly to guide and protect it. From thousands of
Armenian cities and villages these despairing caravans now set forth; they filled all the roads leading
southward. When the caravans first started, the indi-

viduals bore some resemblance to human beings; in a few hours, however, the dust of the road plastered their faces and clothes, the mud caked their lower members, and the slowly advancing mobs, frequently bent with fatigue and crazed by the brutality of their "protectors," resembled some new and strange animal species. Yet for the better part of six months, from April to October, 1915, practically all the highways in Asia Minor were crowded with these unearthly bands of exiles. They could be seen winding in and out of every valley and climbing up the sides of nearly every mountain—moving on and on, they scarcely knew whither, except that every road led to death. Village after village and town after town was evacuated of its Armenian population, under the distressing circumstances already detailed. In these six months, as far as can be ascertained, about 1,200,000 people started on this journey to the Syrian desert.

Detachments of gendarmes would go ahead, notifying the Kurdish tribes that their victims were approaching, and Turkish peasants were also informed that their long-waited opportunity had arrived. The Government even opened the prisons and set free the convicts, on the understanding that they should behave like good Moslems to the approaching Armenians. Thus every caravan had a continuous battle for existence with several classes of enemies—their accompanying gendarmes, the Turkish peasants and villagers, the Kurdish tribes and bands of Chetes and brigands.

Those who escaped these attacks in the open would find new terrors awaiting them in the Moslem villages. Here the Turkish roughs would fall upon the women, leaving them sometimes dead from their experiences or sometimes ravingly insane. After

spending a night in a hideous encampment of this
kind, the exiles, or such as had survived, would start
again the next morning.

At lunch I returned to the park and watched the smog burn
off and the Statue of Liberty become visible. In a brown bag, I had
two Sabrette hot dogs with everything on them, and after an hour of
reading in which I had forgotten to eat them, I threw them in the
trash can and jogged back to the elevator. When I returned to the
mail room, Jimmy Thompson was sitting at the desk, with a white
visor on, licking stamps.

"Jimmy," I said, needing to say something to someone, "did
you know what happened to my ancestors?"

Jimmy squinted at me through his thick lenses. "Your ancestors?"

"You know, Armenian, Jimmy, I'm Armenian."

"Peeta, Peeta, Peeta. The starving Armenians." Jimmy said it
smoothly, like it was an old campaign slogan. "When I was growing
up in Charleston, if we left a green or some gravy on the plate, my
mother would say, 'Remember the starving Armenians.'"

"How old were you? When your mother said that."

"During the Great War, because I left home before the war
was over."

"Did you know what 'starving Armenians' meant?"

"I knew the Armenians were massacred, starved to death,
almost wiped out." Jimmy made a broad X sign with his index finger.
"By the Turks. They don't fool around, those Turks. Like the whites
in the Old South."

"Remember the starving Armenians" was a disturbing
phrase that had floated in a gray zone of my mind where rhetoric
drifts without cognition. I didn't realize it was a snippet of popular
culture during and after World War I. I had heard older people use it,
a friend's uncle at a bar mitzvah, a social studies teacher as I pushed
through the cafeteria line, my friend's grandmother the first time she
met me. It made me uncomfortable. Others used it, but I never
recalled it uttered at home or among my family. No one ever told me

that the image of Armenians starving to death was, for Americans, a slogan for the most dramatic human rights issue of its day.

"I've got a pickup at Cunard," I said to Jimmy, and went back to the park to read.

> And thus, as the exiles moved, they left behind them another caravan – that of the dead and unburied bodies, of old men and of women dying in the last stages of typhus, dysentery, and cholera, of little children lying on their backs and setting up their last piteous wails for food and water. . . .
>
> The most terrible scenes took place at the rivers, especially the Euphrates. Sometimes, when crossing this stream, the gendarmes would push the women into the water, shooting all who attempted to save themselves by swimming. Frequently the women themselves would save their honour by jumping into the river, their children in their arms. . . . In a loop of the river near Erzinghan . . . the thousands of dead bodies created such a barge that the Euphrates changed its course for about a hundred yards.
>
> At another place, where there were wells, some women threw themselves into them, as there was no rope or pail to draw up the water. These women were drowned and, in spite of that, the rest of the people drank from that well, the dead bodies still remaining there and polluting the water. Sometimes, when the wells were shallow and the women could go down into them and come out again, the other people would run to lick or suck their wet, dirty clothes, in the effort to quench their thirst.

Of one particular death march, Morgenthau wrote,

> On the seventieth day a few creatures reached Aleppo. Out of the consigned convoy of 18,000 souls just 150

women and children reached their destination. A few of the rest, the most attractive, were still living as captives of the Kurds and Turks; all the rest were dead.

I have by no means told the most terrible details, for a complete narration of the sadistic orgies of which these Armenian men and women were the victims can never be printed in an American publication. Whatever crimes the most perverted instincts of the human mind can devise, and whatever refinements of persecution and injustice the most debased imagination can conceive, became the daily misfortunes of this devoted people. I am confident that the whole history of the human race contains no such horrible episode as this.

· · · · ·

Morgenthau's interview with Pasha Talaat was illuminating.

"Why are you so interested in the Armenians?" Talaat asked. "You are a Jew; these people are Christians. Why can't you let us do with these Christians as we please?"

"You don't seem to realize," I replied, "that I am not here as a Jew but as American Ambassador. The way you are treating the Armenians puts you in the class of backward, reactionary peoples."

"We treat the Americans all right," said Talaat. "I don't see why you should complain."

"But Americans are outraged by your persecutions of the Armenians."

"It is no use for you to argue," Talaat answered, "we have already disposed of three quarters of the Armenians; there are none at all left in Bitlis, Van, Erzeroum. The hatred between the Turks and the Armenians is now so intense that we have got to finish with them. If we don't, they will plan their revenge."

"If you are not influenced by humane considerations," I replied, "think of the material loss. These are your business men. They control many of your industries. They are very large tax payers."

"We care nothing about the commercial loss," replied Talaat. "We have figured all that out and we know that it will not exceed five million pounds."

"You are making a terrible mistake," I said, and I repeated the statement three times.

"Yes, we may make mistakes," he replied, "but"– and he firmly closed his lips and shook his head– "we never regret."

One day Talaat made what was perhaps the most astonishing request I had ever heard.

"I wish that you would get the American life insurance companies to send us a complete list of their Armenian policy holders. They are practically all dead now and have left no heirs to collect the money. It of course all escheats to the State. The Government is the beneficiary now. Will you do so?"

This was almost too much, and I lost my temper.

Talaat's attitude toward the Armenians was summed up in the proud boast which he made to his friends: "I have accomplished more toward solving the Armenian problem in three months than Abdul Hamid accomplished in thirty years."

The sun had burned the sky clean of clouds. It was afternoon, and from the shadow the sycamores threw, it occurred to me that I had missed the Cunard pickup, a big one–a quarter million.

· · · · ·

In the years following my reading of Morgenthau's memoir, I read about the Armenian Genocide in thousands of eyewitness testimonies from diplomats, missionaries, survivors, travelers, perpetrators, and state archives.

A telegram from Talaat Pasha, dated September 16, 1915:

> Instructions to the government of Aleppo: It was at first communicated to you that by order of the Jemiet, "The Ittihad Committee" had decided to destroy all the Armenians living in Turkey. Those who oppose this order and decision cannot remain on the official staff of the Empire. An end must be put to their existence however criminal the measures taken may be, and no regard must be paid to either age or sex or to conscientious scruples.

From J. B. Jackson, Consul, American Consulate, Aleppo, Syria, August 19, 1915, to The Honorable Henry Morgenthau, American Ambassador, Constantinople:

> The city of Aintab is being rapidly depopulated of Armenians.... It is a gigantic plundering scheme as well as a final blow to extinguish the race.

From Leslie A. Davis, American Consulate, Mamouret-ul-Aziz (Harput), Turkey, December 30, 1915:

> The term of "Slaughterhouse Vilayet [province]" which I applied to this Vilayet in my last report upon this subject (that of September 7th) has been fully justified by what I have learned and actually seen since that time. It appears that all those in the parties mentioned on page 15 of that report, men, women and children, were massacred about five hours distance from here.

From Arnold J. Toynbee, *The Treatment of the Armenians in the Ottoman Empire:*

All this horror ... was inflicted upon the Armenians without a shadow of provocation. "We are at war," the Turkish government will probably reply; "we are fighting for our existence. The Armenians were hoping for the victory of our enemies; they were traitors at large in a war-zone, and we were compelled to proceed against them with military severity." But such excuses are entirely contradicted by the facts. These Armenians were not inhabitants of a war-zone. None of the towns and villages from which they were systematically deported to their death were anywhere near the seat of hostilities.... Civil and military power were safely in Turkish hands, and the Armenians were particularly unlikely to attempt a coup de main. It must be repeated that these Armenian townsfolk were essentially peace-able, industrious people, as unpractised in arms and as unfamiliar with the idea of violence ... the Ottoman Government cannot disguise its crime as a preventive measure."

From Third Army Commander General Vehib's Written Deposition submitted to the Turkish Military Tribunal for the Prosecution of the organizers of the Armenian Genocide, December 5, 1918, Constantinople:

The massacre and annihilation of the Armenians, and the looting and plunder of their properties were the result of the decision of the Central Committee of Ittihad and Terakki.... All the tragedies, the incitements and acts of depravity in the Third Army zone were enacted under the guidance of Behaeddin Sakir. Traveling with a special automobile, he stopped by at all major centers where he orally transmitted his instructions to the party's local bodies and to the governmental authorities. On one

hand he organized gallowsbirds and, on the other,
gendarmes and policemen with blood on their
hands and blood in their eyes who, with the knowledge and under the auspices to the state, perpetrated
the known crimes. Their victims involved human
multitudes, which lent themselves to being easily
rounded up, were defenseless, and which were set
upon. The atrocities were carried out under a program that ... represented a definite case of premedi-
tation.

From the "Narrative of Miss AA., A Foreign Traveller in
Turkey" (from the Bryce–Toynbee report):

In Angora (Ankara) I learned that the tanners and
the butchers of the city had been called to Asi Yoz-
gad, and the Armenians committed to them for murder. The tanner's knife is a circular affair, while the
butcher's knife is a small axe, and they killed people
by using the instruments which they knew best how
to use.

From a Report by Fraulein M. (Swiss resident in Turkey),
November 16, 1915:

I have just returned from a ride on horseback
through the Baghtche-Osmania plain, where thousands of exiles are lying out in the fields and on the
roads, without any shelter and completely at the
mercy of all manner of brigands. Last night about
twelve o'clock, a little camp was suddenly attacked.
There were about fifty to sixty persons in it. I found
men and women badly wounded–bodies slashed
open, broken skulls and terrible knife wounds.... In
another camp we found thirty or forty thousand
Armenians. I was able to distribute bread among

them. Desperate and half-starved, they fell upon it. I often saw them break down under their burden, but the soldiers kept on driving them forward with the butt-ends of their rifles, even sometimes with their bayonets. I have dressed bleeding wounds on the bodies of women that had been caused by these bayonet thrusts.

From "Narrative of the Montenegrin Kavass of the local Branch of the Ottoman Bank," Trebizond, October 2, 1915:

At the present moment there is not a single Armenian left at Trebizond except two employees of the Ottoman Bank, who will also be deported as soon as other persons arrive from Constantinople to take their place.

FALL FROM THE CLOUDS

I FINISHED MORGENTHAU'S MEMOIR AND THEN DISAPPEARED INTO THE whirlwind of my first year of graduate school. When I came up for air the following spring, my Auntie Gladys and Auntie Lu had invited me to join them on a trip to France. We flew to Aix-en-Provence to see my brother Jim, who was finishing a year of study abroad, and then drove to Paris to visit our relatives there. By the 1920s, thousands of Armenians, fleeing the Turks, had settled in France, including members of both sides of my family.

In Paris we spent our days at the Louvre, the Jeu de Paum, and the Grand Palais. We visited the tomb of King Leo V in the basilica of St. Denis, where the French kings are buried. Although King Leo was French, a Lusignan, he held the distinction of being the last King of Armenia when he assumed the throne of Lesser or Cilician Armenia in 1374, after the Third Crusade. His defeat by the Mamulukes the following year marked the end of Armenia's independent rule until the twentieth century. At night we visited with our cousins: my father's cousin, Micheline Lanoote, and her family, and my grandfather Bedros Aroosian's sister, Gadar, and her three daughters, Vergine, Astrig, and Nevart, and their families.

Every night we sat in their swank apartments and ate paté and *midiya, yalanchees* and Camembert, roast duckling and dolma, pilaf and pommes frites, cheese *kadayif* and melons and strawberries and chocolate. We drank good wine and Perrier and brandy. We spoke in a crisscross of languages. French, English, Armenian. Phrases of one language turning into phrases of another. Everyone kissing each other on each cheek. My great-aunts and cousins patting my head, *eenching* me with their affection. But because most of the speaking was in Armenian, all I could do was interpret gestures and faces, pick up a word here and there, as I watched from the outside.

One morning after a week of this I knocked on the door of my aunts' hotel room, a room with high ceilings, long shuttered windows, and Louis Quatorze revival furniture. My aunts were sitting in their robes and slippers, sipping coffee. A silver tray of bread and croissants, butter and strawberry preserves in front of them. I poured a cup of coffee and sank into a big, soft armchair, reading Theodore White's *The Making of the President: 1964.* We were all reading and sipping coffee when my aunt Gladys looked over at my book and said, "Oh that crook, you can be sure if he didn't have Kennedy killed, he knew about it."

"LBJ kill Kennedy, you think so?"

"Oh, they're all so crooked," Auntie Gladys said.

"What a crime to pull off," I said, "and then get yourself right into the head honcho job."

"Well, that's the way they do it. The world is full of crimes."

My aunt's voice was getting louder each time she spoke. "Look at what they did to Armenia."

The words hung in the air of that nineteenth-century hotel room, up around the ceiling, and then I felt them drop on the table.

I was stunned to hear my aunt's indignation and her language. Perhaps it was the week of being in Paris with her aunt and cousins. Perhaps it was being away from home, out of context, so to speak. But I had never heard her say anything like this.

I knew she had been a small child at the outbreak of the Genocide, and that she had survived; still, no one had talked about it, and I felt this might be a moment to talk. A peaceful morning over coffee in a hotel room in Paris on Boulevard St. Germaine. We picked at croissants a little longer, then I said, "What do you remember, Auntie Gladys?"

"About what?"

"About how you and Granny and Auntie Alice got out of Turkey."

My aunt poured more coffee.

"We had been at the country house, where the family went every summer. Mind you, I don't recall this, it was told to me years later. It was midsummer, and we were returning from our country house where we had been on vacation. We traveled by horse. The country around Diarbekir is a little like the southwest–open space, dry plateaus, and mountains. The Tigris runs north of the city and the Euphrates southwest of it. My mother's family had been silk merchants, and they were wealthy, so wealthy that when my father married my mother, they moved into my mother's house." My aunt paused and poured some warm milk into her coffee.

"Once in a while, Mama would mention that she had a house with many servants and a pasture of Arabian horses. My mother's father, Karnig Shekerlemedjian, traded as far west as Greece and as far east as Ispahan, maybe even India. And the story goes that after he returned from one of his business trips to Athens, mother was born. Her father, who had been charmed by a friend's little girl named Athena, named your grandmother after her. It became Nafina.

"We were riding back to the city house–my father, mother, Alice and me, and some servants, and we were stopped by friends and told our house had been burned down and that everyone in the family had been killed. Before long we were rounded up and put on a deportation march."

I was surprised by my aunt's openness.

"Do you remember anything from the march?"

"No," Aunt Gladys said, as she settled into the pink silk divan, holding her coffee cup very firmly. "I was two and Alice was an infant."

"Did Granny ever talk about that period in her life?"

"Not really—not in any specific way. But I remember in 1940 she gave a commemorative speech. The Armenian General Benevolent Union asked her to talk on the twenty-fifth anniversary of the Genocide. We didn't use the term *genocide* then, we said The Massacres. Mama invited all the Armenians in the area to our house. It was still the Depression, really, in April 1940, and about fifty men and women squeezed into our living room. We were living in a Victorian house on Oraton Parkway in East Orange, not far from the apartment you used to visit us in. It was around Easter, because she had baked Easter *choereg* and we put colored eggs in each loaf. We loved dyeing eggs. Sometimes we'd blow out the insides and then paint them. We'd keep them for months after. In Armenian life there's nothing more important than Easter.

"The Armenians who came were American citizens, but the Old World wasn't far behind them. They were lawyers and doctors and merchants and factory workers, and they were all dressed in three-piece suits and evening dresses. I don't remember a thing Mama said. She spoke in Armenian. She used the dictionary stand as a podium and read a speech she had written. Her hair in a bun, horn-rimmed glasses on a chain around her neck, she looked like a schoolteacher.

"I remember that when she finished there was silence, then awkwardness. People looking at their laps. Then, some people weeping, some even sobbing, and then some talking, and then people began talking loudly, and the evening turned into laughter and storytelling, and the brandy poured. I wasn't really in on the whole thing. I watched from a distance, coming and going. I don't know, it was strange. People stayed, I think till the middle of the night. Your grandmother was always a great hostess."

"Was this the first time people in your community talked about the Genocide?"

"As I'm thinking about it now, I imagine that most of those people had been silent for all those years. They were proud new citizens of FDR's America. They just wanted to be left alone to raise families, do business in peace. The events of the past were not only too painful, they were beyond words."

"Did that evening lead to anything? I mean, did people go public in any way?"

"No, it wasn't a world where people went public about such things."

I was staring at flakes of croissant floating in my coffee, and my aunt paused for a second, then said, "But then something did happen."

She paused again, took a sip of coffee, and looked out the window. "The Japanese attacked Pearl Harbor, and the roof caved in on Mama."

"Meaning?"

"Mama had a breakdown."

"A breakdown?" I repeated incredulously.

My aunt paused again and buttered a piece of baguette. I looked over at Auntie Lu, who was sitting behind the *Herald-Tribune*.

"The news of Pearl Harbor, the news of war, set her off. She thought it was happening again. Her house burned down; her family killed; death marches into the desert. She thought the *zaptieh*, the Turkish military police, were coming."

Auntie Gladys got up and opened the shutters, and the morning light streamed into the room.

"She became paranoid. For the first time I heard her use the word *Turk*. One day I was coming home from my job at the *Newark Star-Ledger*. I was sitting on the bus in downtown Newark, the windows wide open, the humidity terrible. I was staring into the crowd on the street, when I saw mother's face. I thought I was hallucinating, but there was Mama's face, floating in the crowd. Her eyes glaring through her glasses. I got off the bus, and she noticed me and began shouting 'Where are you?' And I answered, 'I'm here, Mama.' And she kept repeating, 'Where are you?' and I kept repeating 'I'm here Mama,' until I realized it was no use. She wasn't reachable. I took her by the hand and I got a cab.

"That night she got worse. She lay on the living room couch under a shawl and stared at the ceiling, and she babbled and cried in English, Armenian, Arabic, Turkish. I remember this:

> There is a cloud in the air—
> Is it smoke?
> Over there is Moush
> And the road is lumpy
> Whoever goes is not coming back—
> What's going on?

"Moush was a big Armenian city, a mountain city on a plateau, where thousands of Armenians were slaughtered. It was a death-march lyric. It sent chills through me."

Little did I know then about the holocaust of Moush and its surrounding villages, in which the entire Armenian population of about 90,000 was killed.

"That night, Mama ranted from the *badarak*, prayers, hymns. *Der Voghormya, Sourp Asdvadz, Hayr Mer*. I remember thinking then how strange it was that we never went to Armenian church. We went to Presbyterian church, you know, but still Mama thought of God in Armenian."

"How did Mom take all this?"

"Your mother was just in high school, about fourteen. If she was frightened you wouldn't have known it because she just sat there and watched and said nothing."

My aunt paused to open the other shutter, and the light poured in.

"Then what happened?" I was beginning to feel like a greedy journalist.

"Mama went about her chores. She cooked. She went to the store to work. When she came home, she sat in a chair and cried. It was the first time she ever mentioned the past. She kept saying, 'They're coming again, they're coming again.' 'Who is coming, Mama?' I would say, 'Who is coming?' 'The Turks are coming. It doesn't matter what you do, we'll all be gone soon.'

" 'Mama, that's crazy,' I would tell her. 'We're in America, Mama. This is East Orange, New Jersey. This is Oraton Parkway.' She just shook her head and kept crying.

" 'Do anything you want,' she said every morning. 'Doesn't matter, we'll be dead soon. They're coming.'

"Every day she said: 'Nothing matters anymore. Nothing matters anymore.'

"She practically stopped eating. She cooked beautiful dinners, served them, and sat in a chair, repeating lines and praying. For the first time, she mentioned her brothers and sisters, her mother and father, her nieces and nephews, who had all been murdered by the Turks. 'They were so beautiful,' she said, 'I was the plain one in the family. They should have lived. Why me? Why me?'

"She left the house less and less. She didn't want to answer the phone or the door. One day an FBI agent came to the door to ask Mama about a friend of hers who was applying for a job with the government. Her name had been given as a reference for an oral recommendation. But, when she saw his badge and his official papers, she became frozen with terror. The FBI man stood there for a few minutes asking questions, but Mama stood speechless. The figure of a government official at her front door brought back her terror of the *zaptieh* and the gendarmes coming to the houses of Armenians to round them up. You can imagine that her friend never got the job.

"All during this time father wouldn't acknowledge any of this. When I protested to him that we had to get help, he said nothing."

"How bad did it get?"

"One day I read about electroshock treatment in a magazine, and I wrote the Mayo Clinic for advice. They answered me immediately and recommended a doctor in New York who specialized in this new treatment. I took her by the hand to the doctor. She underwent the treatment and by winter she was fine. And nothing like that ever happened again. No one ever mentioned this moment in your grandmother's life. I never heard her mention the Turks again. It was as if it never happened. We say in Armenian: *When the past is behind you, keep it there.*"

"Did you ask her about the past, after she reovered? Did it open things up?"

"No. We just didn't. Perhaps we were afraid of stirring more things up. Perhaps we were afraid to know. We just didn't ask questions. And Mama had no interest in talking. In fact, she never wanted to think about the past. Everything was always focused on the future. Buying stocks. Expanding the business.

Auntie Lu looked out from behind the paper and gave Gladys a cross look, one of those enough's-enough looks, but Gladys pursed her lips at Lu and went on.

"But you see, Peter, Mama was always filled with fear. Fear and anxiety. Always. Even after the treatment worked and she returned to her normal rhythms, she was full of fear. When your mother was about to go off to Bucknell in '44, Mama was terrified. She cried every day for weeks before your mother left for college. The war was still going strong. The news of Jews being murdered in concentration camps was being reported. Hitler's troops were on the Russian front. The Marines were taking Guadalcanal, and the Japanese had attacked Alaska, and Mama was still translating it into the Turks massacring the Armenians.

"Your mother would sit in the living room drinking pop and playing Artie Shaw records. She loved Artie Shaw because Cousin George played first trombone in his band. Anyway, Mama would sit in her chair and cry and say, 'If you go you'll never come back.'

"She never lost that fear. Even when we went to Europe that first time in '52, and Mama had her passport ready and her tickets. At the last minute she said no. She never wanted to leave this country. She said, 'I'm safe here. This is the only place I'm safe.' Dear God," my aunt said in a low voice.

"But what happened was that during Mama's breakdown I began to remember things."

"Like what?"

"First, just some images and sensations. Mama, Alice, and me in a hot, dry place. People and dust and smells of vomit and feces. Tents here and there. People wandering around. Voices. Crying.

"Then, we were standing in a bare room on a mud floor inside a house, and there was a wooden box on top of a table. A man dressed in black with a beard was swinging a censer and the room was filling up with incense. When I looked in the box I saw a man."

My aunt stopped for a second and exhaled.

"Lying in the box." She looked away and I could see she was trying to keep herself composed. "It was my father.

"The third image is of a city. Aleppo. Minarets and stone churches. A blue mosque. Goats and camels clomping. A *souk* with stalls of hanging things. Smells of sour milk, urine, dung. A man with elephantiasis begging coins.

"Alice and I were escorted by an Assyrian woman. The Assyrians are Christian, and in Diarbekir they lived side by side with us, suffering dearly at the hands of the Turks. The woman took us to a large building, where we were walked down a corridor where there were dozens of people lying in cots. Mother was on one of them. She was pale, thin, her eyes shut. She looked like a doll under a white sheet. We were told she would not live through the night. 'Say your prayers for her,' the Assyrian woman said."

Aunt Gladys was straining to stay composed. Her eyes glassed over, making her irises shine like teal stones. Her voice was clear and hard.

"They told us she had cholera. That meant nothing to us, but we began to cry, and they led us down a long hallway. A few days later Mama walked into the apartment where we were living with a few of father's remaining relatives. She was pale but fine."

My hands were cold from the caffeine. Auntie Lu now had put down her paper and was staring slack-jawed at Gladys. It seemed that she too was hearing this for the first time.

"Then what?"

"Mother worked as a seamstress to support us. She had no practical training, but she was good with her hands. She'd been raised as a rich girl with servants, and she'd spent most of her youth in a missionary school, until she married.

"One day when she went to the house of a wealthy family to drop off a wedding dress she had made, she noticed a large carpet in the living room. A Tabriz, one of those huge blue fields with animals and birds. Mama got hysterical and told the servants to get the master of the house, and when he appeared she told him that the carpet was stolen from her house and sold by Turks. She asks for the carpet back. Naturally, the family refuses to give it up. So Mama proceeds to take the family to court. This was a Christian family, and this was Aleppo and not Diarbekir. In court she was awarded the carpet, and then she went to the bazaar and sold it. With that money and money sent by her brother Thomas she bought tickets for our passage to America."

"So a rug got us here."

"It helped."

Aunt Gladys was talking as if she had unlocked some box in herself, and each thing she pulled out was hooked onto something else.

"Is that it?"

My aunt looked at me quizzically.

"Of your memories?"

"My last memory is of Marseilles. We took a ship from Beirut to Marseilles. A wonderful steamship. All of us Armenian children ran on the decks day and night. It was exciting to be on that ship and going somewhere. When we got seasick our mothers gave us *tourshi* [sour pickled vegetables], to settle the stomach. Whenever I smell *tourshi*, I think of that ship. We stopped in Marseilles for a week or so before taking a train to Paris. We were all women and children with hardly any money, and at night we were permitted to sleep in a Catholic church near the harbor. A big baroque church, with fancy carving and an enormous statue of the Virgin Mary. The ceilings were big vaults with cherubs, clouds, sun rays. The church was damp and you could smell the harbor—the dirty salt water mixed with petroleum. I loved that smell because it meant that we were going somewhere. We slept on woolen blankets and most of us slept in the pews, which were smooth from years of use. But the women didn't sleep. I would wake in the middle of the night and find all the mothers awake.

"After a few nights, I asked Mama why nobody ever slept, and she said: 'If we go to sleep the ceiling will open and dead bodies will fall from the clouds.' I remember just closing my eyes and trying hard as I could to go to sleep."

"In Paris, we were put up by a wealthy Armenian family. They had a lovely country house, and the wife had fallen in love with Alice, who was about four then, and the family begged my mother to let them adopt her. 'She'll live like a princess with us here in Paris,' they told Mama. But my mother was outraged by the idea. Two days later we boarded the S.S. *New York* for America."

I looked over and saw Auntie Lu listening at the edge of her seat. She had not said a word. I was holding back tears, as I asked her if she knew about Diarbekir, the death march, Aleppo. She looked at me, said nothing, and went back to her paper.

"Auntie Gladys," I said, "why haven't you ever talked about this before now?"

"I just haven't."

I felt stunned and overwhelmed. I had nothing to say. I just wanted to get out of the room, into the bright day.

．　．　．　．　．

I took a chair and sat under the lovely red awning and chestnut trees at a café on Boulevard St. Germain. I sat staring at the people walking by. I thought about my grandmother and how little I knew about what was behind her stories and dreams. How could the woman who loved the Yankees and Elvis, who seemed so poised and solid, have endured this cruelty, this devastation? My grandmother? I took out my notebook and began to write.

>Last night
>my grandmother returned
>in the brown dress
>standing on Oraton Parkway
>where we used to walk
>and watch the highway
>being dug out.
>She stood against
>a backdrop of steam hammers
>and bulldozers,
>a bag of fruit
>in her hand,

the wind blowing
through her eyes.

I was running
toward her
in a drizzle
with the morning paper.
When I told her
I was hungry –
she said,

in the grocery store
a man is standing
to his ankles in blood.
the babies in East Orange
have disappeared
maybe eaten by
the machinery
on this long road.

When I asked for my mother –
she said gone,
all gone.
The girls went for soda,
maybe the Coke was bad
the candy sour.
This morning the beds
are empty, water off,
the toilets dry.
When I went to the garden
for squash
only stump was there,
when I went to clip
parsley
only a hole.

We walked past piles
of gray cinder and cement
trucks, there were no men.
She said, Grandpa left
in the morning
in the dark;
he had pants to press
for the firemen of
East Orange.
They called him
in the middle of night,
West Orange was burning
Montclair was burning
Bloomfield and Newark
were gone.

One woman carried
the arms of her child
to West Orange last night
and fell on her uncle's
stoop, two boys came
with the skin
of their legs
in their pockets
and turned themselves in
to local officials;
this morning sun
is red and spreading.

If I go to sleep
tonight, she said,
the ceiling will open
and bodies will fall
from clouds. *Yavrey*
where is the angel
without six fingers

and a missing leg,
where is the angel
with the news that the river
is coming back,
the angel with the word
that the water will be clear
and have fish.

Grandpa is pressing
pants, they came for him
before the birds were up—
he left without shoes
or tie, without shirt
or suspenders.
It was quiet.
The birds, the birds
were still sleeping.

I called the poem "The History of Armenia." Later, when my
head had returned to the ordinary world and could think about the
poem, I realized that in order to touch the woman behind the grandmother I knew, the one who never spoke in a direct way about her
past, I had to bring the pain of the past into the landscape of the
present. The poem can be a headstone in a world of unmarked
graves. I wanted the language of the poem to be bare-boned. I
wanted the lines to convey fragmentation and shock, and also the
broken rhythms of immigrant speech. "The History of Armenia" let
me into the past, and allowed me to feel my grandmother again. In
the poem I returned to Oraton Parkway in East Orange, New Jersey,
where I first knew my grandmother, and where after our chores she
would take me to watch the Garden State Parkway being built.
There, I could bring the two of us together again and create what she
had in her encoded way told me. I realized that she was my beloved
witness, and I the receiver of her story. When I was a boy, she had
showered me with love; now as a man, I could return that love.

A THOUSAND SHOES

Auntie Lu kept saying, "We can't leave until you eat at the Brasserie Lipp." So the next evening we were there eating hefty portions of choucroute and drinking Stella Artois, and Auntie Lu said, "I want you to know this about your grandfather. He"–she said it emphatically–"saw the writing on the wall. After Abdul Hamid massacred the Armenians in the 1890s, he decided to leave. All Armenians lived in terror then, especially in the interior, and tax burdens for Christians had gotten even worse, and the military tax was so severe, it could sink you."

"What do you mean?"

"Until 1910, Christians were forbidden to serve in the Ottoman army. They were forced to pay a large military tax each year instead. We were too inferior to serve in the army, but we had to pay through the teeth for it. That's how that sick society worked.

"Papa left Diarbekir in 1903 and arrived in New Jersey later that year. Because our family had been in the silk business back in Diarbekir, he went to work in the silk mills of Paterson. He used most of his earnings to bring his brother Harry and nephew Haig to

New Jersey in 1911, and his sister Azniv later in 1920. It was Azniv who met Mama and fell in love with her on the ship to America, and made the match between Mama and her brother. Later Papa brought his sister Gadar as far as France but one of her daughters had an infectious eye disease and they weren't allowed into the United States. He planned to bring his parents as well, but they were killed in the Genocide.

"With the little money he had left, he began buying shoes with the idea that he would return to Turkey, sell the shoes for a good profit, and come back to New Jersey and start his own oriental rug business. By 1918 he had bought about five hundred pairs of shoes, and his Armenian friend in Constantinople was going to buy the whole lot at a handsome profit for Papa."

"He crated five hundred pairs of shoes, and lugged them to Turkey?"

"I want you to know that he never told any of us this story. I heard it only a couple years ago from a good friend of his, who was on the boat with him. She told me, he had packed ten large wooden crates of shoes, about fifty pairs in a crate. She was quite precise about it.

"After the war, he boarded the *Black Arrow*, a German war-ship which had been captured and refitted for commercial use. When the *Black Arrow* docked in Constantinople, the *hamals* unloaded the ship, and Papa was told to wait for a few minutes on board until his packages could be properly unloaded.

"After an hour of standing in the hold, he was let off the ship by the Turkish police. He went to the baggage area to get his crates of shoes, and he stood waiting for a while. But nothing happened. There were no officials, no hamals, no dock-unloading. Everyone was gone. He realized that the shoes had been stolen, that he had been duped. He turned around and walked back to the *Black Arrow* and stayed there until the ship left the next day for New York."

"He never mentioned this to anyone? To Granny?"

"Not to any of us, at least." Then there was silence, and I felt a kind of blankness as if the exhaustion of listening for the past two days had short-circuited my mind. I sat there looking at the waiters dressed in red and white, the carafes of wine on the tables, the beautiful color of the room. People eating and drinking and laughing.

"His friend said that it broke him. The shoes for which he had scrimped and saved all those years while he was bringing his family out of that miserable place. Those shoes which represented new hope in life. The damn evil of those Turks stealing those shoes." My aunt's voice was hard with anger now.

I kept picturing my grandfather on the *Black Arrow*, with his Yul Brenner bald head and big handsome face—the jokester and wit of the family—staring into the sky over the Bosphorus as the ship pulled out of the harbor. Staring back at Constantinople as it faded into the Turkish blue and then out of sight. Knowing that the Armenians of Anatolia had been murdered or deported, that Anatolian Armenia no longer existed. So what. So what was a thousand shoes anyway?

A DOCUMENT AND A PHOTOGRAPH

Oₙₑ EVENING NOT LONG AFTER WE HAD RETURNED FROM EUROPE, Auntie Lu invited me over for some cheese *kadayif* she had bought at a Turkish bakery. I remember it was midsummer because the sweetness of the privet was piercing as I walked through the apartment courtyard, and the scent of dolma was lingering in the air-conditioned air when I opened the door.

While the syrup for the *kadayif* was heating up, Auntie Gladys pulled a brittle manila envelope out of the drawer of the secretary, one of those ball-and-claw-foot Chippendale mahogany ones, and handed it to me. I pulled out a thick, legal-sized pile of papers stapled in the upper left-hand corner, stared at the strange typefaces and markings, and kept turning the pages. Auntie Gladys said nothing, and by now Auntie Lu was cutting the large pie of *kadayif* into wedges on the coffee table. When I sorted it all out, I realized that it was a legal document, filed by my grandmother against the Turkish government. I came back to page one and began reading.

DEPARTMENT OF STATE
WASHINGTON, D.C.,
May 15, 1919.

LAW OFFICES
JOSEPH J. DURNA
1169 FIREMEN'S BLDG., NEWARK, N.J.

APPLICATION
FOR THE SUPPORT OF
CLAIMS AGAINST FOREIGN GOVERNMENTS.

GENERAL INSTRUCTIONS FOR CLAIMANTS.

1. General Statement.—The great number and variety of international claims arising out of the recent war and the considerable difficulty heretofore experienced by the Department of State in obtaining adequate reports as to the nationality of claimants and the facts regarding their claims, have made it imperative, by the use of an Application form, to standardize the manner of reporting claims to the Department of State and to specify the particulars about which the Department desires to have information, in order that claims may be readily examined and classified and properly prepared for presentation to a foreign Government or to an Arbitration Commission or other tribunal. [...]

4. International Claims.—Claims presented by the Government of the United States against a foreign government are based fundamentally, among other things, upon loss or injury (1) which was suffered by the United States or by its citizens or those entitled to its protection, and (2) for which a foreign Government, including its officials, branches, or agencies, was responsible.

Had my grandmother been a U.S. citizen? Her husband? Could my grandmother make a claim to U.S. citizenship?

Q. 1. Give the (*a*) name, (*b*) residence, and (*c*) occupation or business of *each* individual

A.1.:(*a*) N̶a̶f̶i̶n̶a̶ ̶H̶a̶g̶o̶p̶ ̶C̶h̶i̶l̶i̶n̶g̶u̶i̶r̶i̶a̶n̶ (b)(B̶o̶r̶n̶ ̶S̶h̶e̶k̶e̶r̶l̶e̶m̶e̶d̶j̶i̶a̶n̶)

(a) (b) G̶h̶u̶r̶i̶ ̶S̶t̶.̶ ̶A̶l̶e̶p̶p̶o̶,̶ ̶S̶y̶r̶i̶a̶.̶ (c) T̶a̶i̶l̶o̶r̶e̶s̶s̶

My mother saying: "I don't care how long it takes, we're waiting in line until the tailor is done; you will not go out without a suit that fits. My mother made everything from scratch."

My grandmother's hands. Blotched. Streaked white. Raw-looking. They had sewn my torn trousers. They kneaded dough, flew like birds when she told her dreams. White-knuckled on her cane. Stirring the *lokma* batter. Clapping in the Little League stands. Nimble with a silver needle. Like wings in my mind the night she died.

Q. 2. Give the (*a*) nature and extent (such as complete ownership or extent of partial ownership, of life interest, of lien, mortgage, etc.) and (*b*) duration (giving inclusive dates), of the right, title, or interest in this claim held by *each* individual, *each* member of a partnership, and *each* joint-stock company or corporation mentioned in *Answer 1*, (*c*) name and residence of the person, partnership, company or corporation from which such right, title, or interest was acquired, (*d*) manner of acquisition (such as purchase, inheritance, mortgage, assignment, etc.) and date thereof; (*e*) the consideration, if any, given upon such acquisition; and attach (*f*) documentary evidence of such acquisition (such as deed, will, contract, bill of sale, affidavits as to personal injuries or as to relationship to the decedent, birth, death, or marriage certificate, letters of administration, etc.) If it is impossible to obtain this information, so state under each heading *giving reasons.*

A.2. __Complete_ownership.___ Since_1_August_1915._(c)____
(Nature and extent.)   (Give dates.)   (Name.)

From_my_husband_Hagop_Chilinguirian,_the_original_____
(Residence.)   (Manner.)   (Date.)   (Consideration.)

_claimant,_who_was_a_citizen_____of_U.S.A.,_residing_in__
(List papers attached.)

U.S.A._beginning_his_minority_till_the_year_1909_____
(Nature and extent.)   (Give dates.)   (Name.)

A.D.,_when_he_returned_to_Diarbekir_in_order_to_arrange_
(Residence.)   (Manner.)   (Date.)   (Consideration.)

his_affairs_but_he_died_during_our_deportation_from_____
(List papers attached.)

Diarbekir_at_1_August_1915,_____being_a_citizen_of_____
(Nature and extent.)   (Give dates.)   (Name.)

U.S.A.,_as_it_will_be_written_in_detail_in_the_answers__
(Residence.)   (Manner.)   (Date.)   (Consideration.)

_of_the_questions_concerning_Naturalization.(d)_By_mar-__
(List papers attached.)

riage_at_15_Dec._1910,_in_Diarbekir,_Turkey._(e)_____
(Nature and extent.)   (Give dates.)   (Name.)

_____Attached_the_affidavit_for_my_marriage._____
(Residence.)   (Manner.)   (Date.)   (Consideration.)

__Partial_ownership____Since_1_August_1915_(c)From_
(Nature and extent.)   (Give dates.)   (Name.)

my_husband_named_above,_and_from_my_brothers_and_other__
(Residence.)   (Manner.)   (Date.)   (Consideration.)

_relatives_who_are_perished_on_account_of_the_deporta-___
(List papers attached.)

tion,_leaving_me_and_my_living_brother_Thomas_Sheker-___
(Nature and extent.)   (Give dates.)   (Name.)

lemedjian,_now_residing_at_U.S.A._by_this_address._Mr.___
(Residence.)   (Manner.)   (Date.)   (Consideration.)

Thomas_Shekerlemedjian_____Box_125_West_Hoboken,_New____
(List papers attached.)

Jersey_U.S.A._____as_the_only_legal_heirs._Details_in__
(Nature and extent.)   (Give dates.)   (Name.)

the_answer_Question_55_(d)By_inheritance_since_1915_(e).
(Residence.)   (Manner.)   (Date.)   (Consideration.)

_____(f)_Attached_the_affidavit_for,_in_the_answer____
(List papers attached.)

Question_55._____
(Nature and extent.)   (Give dates.)   (Name.)

I, Nafina Hagop Chilinguirian, the undersigned of this
procuration, do hereby declare that I have appointed
attorney Abdullah Fatalian, Lawyer, of Aleppo, residing
in Khan Harir, Aleppo, Syria, to make the appeal and
pursuits, to prepare and present the papers necessary
concerning my losses and injuries caused by the war
(1914-1919) and the deportation, near the Hon. Department of State, Washington D.C., U.S.A., and to receive
and return me the sum given as compensation and indemni-
fication.

Nafina Hagop Chilinguirian
nafine hagop chilinguirian

22nd Jan. 1920

    Aleppo, Syria.

    I, Pere Harutiun Yessayan, the Prelate of Armenians
in Aleppo, Syria, do hereby certify that I have no
interest in the claim to which the foregoing procuration
relates; that I am not the agent or attorney of any person having interest in such claim; that this copy of
procuration is conformable to its original.

31st Jan. 1920

    Aleppo, Syria.

A first husband? He was a dark secret, an absent ghost. To talk about him would have been to tell the whole story. I had never thought of my mother and her sisters Gladys and Alice as half sisters, or Lucille and my mother as having a different father.

Affidavits. A word from "Perry Mason." Sworn statements in writing made before a magistrate. A signature required. Testimonies. The Armenian Prelate of Aleppo, Father Yessayan. A notarized seal in Armenian and French. Voices of ordinary people. Not lawyers, poets, or journalists, but people of daily life. Clean, basic words. My grandmother walking the streets of Aleppo. She had begun her suit in Aleppo before leaving for America.

Q. 14. State race to which claimant (whether an individual claimant or a member of a partnership claimant) belongs —A. 14.

    Armenian, white.

(White, Negro, Oriental, native tribes, i.e., American Indian or other native tribes of American possessions.)

Q. 15. Give (*a*) date and (*b*) place of birth of claimant and (*c*) attach documentary evidence thereof unless submitted with answer to some other question.—A. 15. (*a*) 22 Oct., 1890.

((Date.))

(*b*)Diarbekir   Turkey

(City or town.)   (State or Province.)   (Country.)

(*c*)My birth certificate was lost; attached the affidavit for.

(List papers attached or refer to question where attached.)

Note.—Documentary evidence may consist of a birth certificate or affidavits of persons acquainted with claimant since birth.

Q. 16. Has claimant resided in the United States all of his life?—A. 16.

    No.

(Yes or no.)

Q. 17. If not, give *in detail* the (*a*) dates (inclusive dates), places (town, state or province, country), and *causes* or *purposes* of residence *abroad* since birth; and (*b*) dates (inclusive dates), and places of residence *in the United States* since birth. — A. 17. (*a*) My husband and I were about to depart for U.S.A.; but the roads were closed on account of the war, so I was obliged to rest in Aleppo, Syria, after the deportation, my husband Hagop Chilinguirian being dead on the way.

Deportation: a concentration camp in perpetual movement, caravan of death, the Turkish government's term, Orwellian double-speak. Morgenthau wrote, "On the seventieth day a few creatures reached Aleppo. Out of the combined convoy of 18,000 souls just 150 women and children reached their destination." Which convoy was that? *Hagop Chilinguirian being dead on the way.* His name in the drawer of the mahogany secretary for sixty years. His name like a floodgate, holding things back.

How had he died? I thought of Morgenthau's words, the "sadistic orgies" Armenians endured, "whatever crimes the most perverted instincts of the human mind can devise."

SECTION V.

FACTS REGARDING CLAIM.

Note.—All questions in Section V. must be answered.

Special attention is called to the necessity of making the answers to these questions *full, complete,* and *accurate,* as they will be thoroughly examined before any claim based upon them will be supported by the United States Government.

Q. 55. Give an *itemized* statement of the claim covering: (*a*) The kind, amount, and description of property *entirely* lost or destroyed, (*b*) the extent and description of damage to property *not entirely* lost or destroyed, (*c*) the particulars regarding death or personal injuries (accompanied by an affidavit of a reputable physician in case of death or injuries to the person), and (*d*) value in American dollars of the losses or injuries suffered.

Note. This question calls for a mere itemized statement of losses or injuries, and should not be confused with *Question 63* as to *how* these losses or injuries occurred.

A. 55.(a)_Given_as_martial_tax_to_the_Turk._Gov._____
in_Diarbekir_at_different_dates_against_bills_____
which_have_been_lost_during_the_deportation,_____
25000_kg._of_sugar,_a_3_p._gold_____750_Ltq.
Household_furniture_____250_____

```
-----The goods left at my husband's shop in Diarbekir:
1000 kg. of sugar-----a 5 p. gold_____500_____
-500 " " coffee_____a p. 15 gold_____750_____
2000 " " hemp-cords___a 5 p. gold_____100_____
1000 parcels of sacks a 25 p. gold_____250_____
1000 curry combs_____a 5 p. gold_____50_____
25000 kg. of rice_____a 3 p. gold_____750_____
6000 " "_____gall-nut_a_____100_____
------Ready money robbed on the way by_____
------the Turks_____400_____
------The money necessary to rear my two_____
------orphan daughters, Zivart, 7 years_____
------old, and Arshalois, 5 years old,_____
------till their marriage_____2000_____
```

The things of a dry goods store. Walnuts? Gall nuts. Her daughters: on the death march; Auntie Gladys, named Zivart, meaning Joy, would have been two, and Auntie Alice, named Arshaluis, meaning morning light, an infant.

```
-------TOTAL IN GOLD_____5900 Ltq.
(b).....(c) My husband Hagop Chilinguirian_____
died of sufferings on the way_____350____
-------TOTAL IN GOLD_____6250 Ltq.
(d) Changed into American dollars at the rate_____
of that time when the deportation happened_____
in 1915 A.D.: 6250 11 68750 dollars._____
(Sixty eight thousand seven hundred fifty_____
American dollars)._____
```

(If more space is needed use sheets of paper marked *"Question 55"* and insert them at this point.)

(continued the answer question 55)

My and my living brother Thomas Shekerlemedjian's

list of the losses and injuries come down by

inheritance from our relatives as indicated below

a) My brother Harutin Shekerlemedjian, merchant
in Diarbekir, had at Karadja Hagh, a village in
Diarbekir, 150 tons of rice kept in three wells,
which have been captured by the government   3500 Lt
He had in his shop at the market-place
Bastadjilar in Diarbekir, goods: calicoes,
clothes, silken clothes, etc.   2000
In the shop at the st. Iz-ed-din, Diarbekir,
goods as cotton-clothes, calicoes, leathers, etc.   3000
He had 500 sheep by Kehya Ismael of the village
Talavli in Diarbekir, which were captured by the
government   700
The jewels and money possessed by my relatives,
mentioned below, were kept under the ground in a
box at the house of my sister Hadji Anna, in
Diarbekir which were captured by a Turk named
Hadji Bakkar of Diarbekir, residing at the st.
Oulou Djam'i in Diarbekir; –
My brother Harutiun's ready money   1000
" aunt Gadar Keshishian's money and jewels   500
" sister Hadji Anna's jewels (Der Hovsepian's)   200
" " Arusyag Berberian's jewels   150
" brother Harutiun's deceased wife Lucia's jewels   350

TOTAL IN GOLD   11400

(b) . . . . c) My father Hagop Shekerlemedjian,
               75 years old, killed by Turks   350
My mother Lucia Shekerlemedjian, 50 years old,
                    killed by Turks   350
" brother Dikran   " 35 years old "   "   "   350
His son Karnig   " 7   "   "   "   "   "   350
"   " Diran   " 4   "   "   "   "   "   350
My brother Harutiun " 30   "   "   "   "   "   350
His son Levon   " 2   "   "   "   "   "   350
" daughter Azniv   " 5   "   "   "   "   "   350
My sister Hadji   28   "   "   "   "   "   350
      Anna Derhovsepian
"   " Arusyag Berberian 25 "   "   "   "   "   350
" aunt Gadar Keshishian 55 "   "   "   "   "   350

TOTAL IN GOLD. 15250

```
(d) Changed into American Dollars at the rate of that
time when the deportation happened in 1915 A.D. : 15250
11 167750 dollars. (One hundred sixty seven thousand
seven hundred fifty American dollars.
     According to the Turkish inheritance law, the sister
receives the half of what the brother receives. Hence,
167750  3                               55916.66 dollars.
Then my whole claim is:
     My individual claim on the page 12,  68750     dollars,
     My partial claim as above           55916.66      "

     Total American dollars . . . . . .  124666.66
```

The names of villages. Real places. Dry soil and plateaus. Northern Mesopotamia. Southern Armenia. Kurdish bandits in colorful garb in the mountains. North of Nineveh. South of Ararat. The Tigris and Euphrates running through. History and myth flowing. Cloth. Calicoes, silken clothes, cotton, leather. Jewels. Ready money and jewels. All her sister's jewels. My aunts and grandmother always in pearls and colorful stones in their hair clips and bracelets.

The names of the dead. A generation. Not a passing allusion to them in our family, ever. Was I dumb enough to think my grandmother was an only child—in an Armenian family? Did I never think to ask? Nieces and nephews. Dikran. Harutiun (Harry). Anna who was Hadji because she had made the pilgrimage to Jerusalem. Arusyag. Aunt Gadar. Her father Hagop (Jacob) and mother Lucia. And the little ones. Karnig, 7; Diran, 4; Levon, 2; Azniv, 5. Second grade. Kindergarten. Nursery School. A toddler. Her blood and flesh vanished. A place they lived. A black hole. No graveyard.

The word Shek-er-le-med-jian. *Sheker* meaning "sugar" in Turkish. Shortened to Shakarjian by her brother after he arrived in New Jersey. The name in bright bold letters on the real estate signs which spot the lawns of the beautiful houses of Bergen County.

We the undersigned of this affidavit, Thomas
Alchikian, 50 years old, Armenian, Shoemaker, and Yervant
Ekmekdjian, 35 years old, Armenian blacksmith, both of
us born in Diarbekir, Turkey, residing in Djideide St.
Aleppo, Syria, before the deportation in Diarbekir, do
solemnly affirm that Nafina Hagop Chilinguirian is the
very owner and proprietor of the goods enumerated in the
Answer 55 of this Application; that she and her living
brother Thomas Shekerlemedjian, Box 125 West Hoboken,
New Jersey, U.S.A. are the only legal heirs of their
killed relatives mentioned in the same Answer; that the
Turk functionaries of the Turkish government and by
their allowance the Turk people plundered and captured
the goods mentioned; that the persons whose degree of
relation is mentioned are just the same persons relating
in the same degree; that they are all killed by the
Turks during our deportation from Diarbekir, except Mrs.
Nafina's husband who died of violent sufferings caused
by the unhuman cruelties of the deporter gendarmes.

Thomas Alchikian

Yervant Ekmekdjian

Subscribed and sworn before me this *Thirty first* day of
January 1920 in the city of Aleppo, Syria.

And the statement: *Mrs. Nafina's husband who died of violent sufferings caused by the unhuman cruelties of the deporter gendarmes.* I kept imagining. How had he been killed, and the others? Could a human being torture a two-year-old? A second grader?

Q. 63 State *in detail* the facts or circumstances attending the losses or
injuries enumerated in *Answer 55,*

—A. 63. At 1 August 1915, our parish in Diarbekir was
besieged by the gendarmes under the command of the
Vali of Diarbekir. The same day with the menace of
death they removed us, the Armenians. We could take
by us only our ready money, if it was easy to take,
our birth and marriage certificates; my husband
Hagop Chilinguirian's Naturalization Paper and Passport; all our other goods were left behind. The Turk
officers of the Turkish Government and by their
allowance the Turk people plundered and captured our
goods left behind. The deporter gendarmes separated
the men from the women, and binding them to each
other, they carried all of us to an unknown direction. After three days journey, they killed one by
one the man deportees of whom only a few were saved.
So were killed mercilessly my brothers and sisters,
and other relatives mentioned in the Answer 55. My
husband in spite of that he was a citizen of U.S.A.,
was forced to be deported with us, his Naturalization paper and Passport being taken of him by the
gendarmes. As he was feeble and indisposed, being
subjected to such conditions, and seeing our relatives killed unhumanly, he could not support the
life, and died, leaving me a widow with my two
orphan daughters named Zivart 7 years old and
Arshalois 5 years old. We, the remaining of the
deportees, women and children, were forced to walk
without being allowed even to buy some bread to eat.
Frequently we were robbed by Turks and the gendarmes, as if they would carry us safely to our destiny which was entirely unknown to us. So for thirty
two days we were obliged to wander through mountains
and valleys. Fatigue and hunger enforced by the whip
of the cruel gendarmes, diminished the number of the
deportees. After many dangers whose description

would take much time, a few women and children,
included I myself, arrived at Aleppo, Syria, in the
beginning of September 1915. Since then I am supported by the Hon. Consulate of U.S.A. in Aleppo,
Syria. The deportation itself and the fiendish steps
taken against the Armenians in general being well
known by the civilized world, I do not mention other
evidence concerning this matter. Only I assert that
1) The Turkish government is responsible for the
losses and injuries happened to, because I am a
human being and a citizen of U.S.A., I am under the
support of human and International law. 2) That the
circumstances being very extraordinary, and our
deportation unawares, it was impossible to have by
me the documentary evidences concerning my losses
and injuries; but my co-deportees, saved of death by
any way, witness that I am the very owner and proprietor of the said losses and injuries occurred.
Herewith I attach their affidavit.

I didn't want to break down in front of my aunt. I clenched
my jaw for a long time until it felt sore. My grandmother's words
now like a taste. Nafina Hagop Chilinguirian, born Shekerlemedjian,
remarried in the United States, in New Jersey, Aroosian. My grandmother at twenty-five.

*My husband . . . feeble and indisposed, being subjected to such
conditions, and seeing our relatives killed unhumanly, he could not
support the life. . . .*

The spice closet flew open. *Mahleb,* cinnamon, cardamom,
ginger, the roots of small plants dried in paper bags; behind the
candy store, the empty lot—with high straw grass, with the monarchs and dragonflies and cicadas, smells of dog shit, rusted-out
bikes, the crown of *Canada Dry* in red script and the crows and we
raced and she got to the store before me. I was pissed and laughing
and she bought me red licorice and we sat on the stools of the soda

fountain while she had tea and we ate red licorice her dentures painful

And faster down the sidewalk to the great pit where the bull-dozers and steam hammers were digging, putting down asphalt; like buildings on wheels and the noise was everywhere and we were free and it was what she called a parkway, the Garden State Parkway, going up, and President Eisenhower was going to build roads that would take us fast to California, where Auntie Alice and Uncle Ed and Lynn and Karen lived.

"*I am come into my garden, my sister, my spouse: I have gathered my myrrh with my spice; honey; I have drunk my wine with my milk; I sleep, but my heart waketh: it is the voice of my beloved that knocketh,* saying, *Open to me, my sister, my love, my dove, my undefiled:* Then the oven got hot and the *choereg* swelled into rings and braids and the black seeds seemed like they would burst. So for thirty two days we were obliged to wander through mountains and valleys. Fatigue and hunger enforced by the whip of the cruel gendarmes, diminished the number of the deportees. After many dangers whose description would take much time, a few women and children, included I myself, arrived at Aleppo, Syria, in the beginning of September 1915.

–*witness* Only I assert that 1) The Turkish Government is responsible for the losses and injuries happened to, because I am a human being . . . I am under the support of human and international law.

Q. 68. If no steps were taken to obtain redress, or if the remedies sought were not exhausted, state the reasons therefor. — A. 68. Because there has not been yet created any executional or judicial body to consider such matter.

Q. 69. State what set-off against this claim or what defense against its recovery, in whole or in part, might in the opinion of the claimant be interposed by the foreign government concerned. —A. 69. The foreign government concerned attributes these losses and injuries to the committee of "Union and Progress", and does not undertake any responsibility thereof; but it is an admitted principle that any acting government is responsible for the actions taken by the former one.

SECTION VI.

APPLICATION FOR SUPPORT OF CLAIM BY THE UNITED STATES

Application is hereby made for the support of the Government of the United States of this claim (herein before set forth) against the Government of _____Turkey_____ with a view to obtaining a settlement
(Name of country.)
thereof by diplomatic interposition, or otherwise.

This business of mass extermination, state planned, in great concentration, was something new, something that would be done again.

Then she signed in the careful script of her new language.

SIGNATURE AND OATH OF CLAIMANT.

nafina hagop chilinguirean
(Witness in cross-mark signature.)

Subscribed and sworn before me this 27th day of *march*, 1920

I slumped in the chair and stared at my aunt.

"Why hasn't anyone said anything about this all these years?" I was sounding uncontrollably angry. "This happened to you! To Granny. To our family."

"What good would it have done you, when you were a boy, to know this?"

"It's the truth. It's important." I was shouting. "Not just to us, but to the history of this whole horrible century."

"Maybe so," she said, sounding dismissive, "but children shouldn't know this."

"It would have helped if I had known some of this."

"How?"

"I would've understood things about how our family is."

"You only understand things in life when you are ready to understand them. Maybe it would have been worse for you to know all this."

"How much did you know about the past?" I was sounding petulant now.

"Not too much. Your grandmother's silence about the Genocide was nearly total. And we respected that."

"You never asked about her life before August 1915? About the death march? About your own childhood?"

"No. We had a different kind of relationship with our parents. What was private was private. It's not like today when everything is discussed by everyone to anyone in any place. You see parents on TV discussing their sex lives and their children are in the audience while their husbands watch from work with their friends. What kind of world is this? Maybe some mystery to life isn't so bad. Why does everyone these days feel they have to know everything from the time they are born?"

I could see how upset my questions were making her. I realized that silence had played some role in my grandmother's life. But still I did not understand it. How could one not talk? We sat staring at the document in silence. The story in it so clear and palpable, and the words had stayed in the drawer of the mahogany secretary for almost sixty years.

I got up, wrapped a wedge of *kadayif* in a napkin and stuffed it in my pocket and said good-night with a stiff hug. As I walked toward the stairs, Auntie Gladys said, "You know," and then she stopped, and I waited, and she said nothing, and I began walking down the stairs, and she said:

"Don't forget, Peter, after World War I, in the Treaty of Sèvres President Wilson advocated a strong, free Armenia, which would have included a good portion of our homeland in what is eastern Turkey today–Van, Bitlis, Moush, Erzeroum, and some of the Black Sea Coast. That would have made a difference. But that treaty was nullified by the Treaty of Lausanne in 1923, and all was taken back at the request of Ataturk. Had the Treaty of Sèvres passed, it would have said: the civilized world cares about the most ancient Christian nation of the Near East. It would have said: the martyrdom and suffering of Armenians will not go unheeded. Armenia had built a beautiful civilization for three thousand years, and we had to watch it be destroyed. Even Harding said he would stand behind Wilson's mandate for Armenia. We deserved some justice, and we got nothing. We were left to the perverted barbarism of the Turks, and only Russia came to our aid to help save the little bit of Armenia that was left in the Caucasus. And then after 1923, no one cared about Armenia. For Armenians it was a pill too bitter to swallow. A pain too bad to feel."

"And one more thing," she said, and I walked back up the stairs to see her crouching at the bottom secretary drawer. She opened a white envelope and took out a sepia photograph. A studio photograph of the Shekerlemedjians dressed in formal attire, in a formal pose. The men in high white collars, ties, and jackets. The women in dark dresses. Two young girls in what looked like school uniforms, with Armenian writing stitched on the neckline. They were all looking seriously into the camera. The young men must have been in their late twenties, or early thirties. Their hair was parted, fairly short. The young woman was thin, statuesque, quite stunning: high forehead, beautiful cheekbones, and dark long hair pulled back in a bun. A half smile, serious and somehow connected to the dark languidness of the eyes.

The little girls had big eyes and high, broad cheeks. The elder of the two—she must have been six or so—bore a resemblance to my mother in pictures I had seen of her as a young girl.

"It's the only picture she brought with her."

The elderly couple, my great-grandparents. He was in a three-piece suit, a gold watch chain draped from a vest pocket, a little portly. She wore one of those complicated Victorian dresses that had several layers of lace and collar. Her hair was in a bun, and her countenance appeared a bit entitled. I pointed to the young beautiful woman.

"Who's she?"

"My Aunt Anna, Mama's oldest sister. I don't remember her. She was killed by the Turks in Diarbekir. They were all killed."

I stared at her face, a frozen image in a photographer's studio somewhere near the Tigris River. Southeast Anatolia—place of Arabian horses and flat-roofed stone houses. Once Armenia.

DOVEY'S STORY

MY AUNT POURED COFFEE FROM THE *JEZVEH* INTO A DEMITASSE AND
it frothed to a creamy tan head. Thick like mud and sweet, and I
could almost chew it. Ever since our conversation that morning in
Paris, Auntie Gladys had wanted to talk about the past. She had
opened up in a new way and she seemed to evince a kind of authority in talking about these things that had been kept secret for so long.

"I want to tell you Dovey's story. Dovey [Aghavni in Armen-
ian] was my mother's cousin, and she lived nearby in Diarbekir.
They were like sisters. You remember her, don't you?"

"Yup. I always thought it was strange that she was blonde,
with blue eyes," and as the words came out, I looked at my aunt's
blue eyes and still-blondish hair.

"Do you remember when her daughter Margaret died?"

"I remember that she had a brain tumor and we visited her
in their apartment in East Orange. I remember Dad saying afterward
that the X ray showed a tumor the size of a tangerine."

"Dovey's husband Setrak died of a brain tumor too, five years
before Margaret. Now we think it was caused by the toxic fumes

from the dry cleaning fluids they used in their business. Father sent almost all of his customers' clothes to their plant. Margaret worked in the plant with her father from the time she was twelve. At thirty-eight she was dead. She was Dovey's only child." Aunt Gladys paused. "Last year in the hospital when she thought she was dying, Dovey told me about some things that happened to her. This is what she said.

· · · · ·

In Diarbekir in July the wind hardly ruffled a scarf. The sky was blue and cloudless, and the high massif to the north seemed closer than it was—a misshapen pyramid, treeless and brown. South toward Edessa and Nineveh the ridges were gullied and gray-white like polished granite. From up on the flat roof of the house, you could tell the vultures from the hawks, and when the vultures swoop, their thick necks unscroll, and the late sun glares on the obsidian houses. Beyond the iron gates and the black stone walls of the city, irrigation ditches crossed terraced fields, and the vineyards and the melon fields fanned out. The mulberry orchards were like green islands beyond which the desert spread, and only the shadows of rocks darkened the clay. The Tigris was blue and then brown, blue and then green, and the watermelons that grew along the banks were giant. Between the olive trees, black partridges ruffled, and sometimes their blunt spurs caught on the wire loosely wound around the stakes and they made a horrible cry.

After dinner we used to come up to the roof. In the summer we enclosed the roof with white sheets and at night we slept there. For miles the closed courtyards of sheets on the rooftops sparkle in the evening light like the sails of the *dhows* on the river. The roof dust is like sifted flour on the mud-brick dirt up there. In July we would winnow and wash the *bulghur* and *hadig,* hull and beat and grind it up there, and we'd lug baskets of *Mairazdvadzadzni-gorgod* (Mother-of-God pods) up to the roof to hull. Hulling on the roof in the evening when the sun was gone, but the clear evening light lingered on us, and we sang and told stories.

In the summer of 1915 in Diarbekir, every day you heard about Armenians disappearing. Shopkeepers disappearing from their shops in the middle of the day. Children not returning from school. Men not coming back from the melon fields. Women, especially young ones, disappearing as they returned from the bath. Shops had been looted by Turks more frequently that year. The pastry shop on Albak Street had been robbed and burned. The carpet store near the mosque had been broken into and cleaned out. Farms in the outlying valley had been stripped of their goats and sheep by Kurdish bandits, and everyone knew this had been sanctioned by the Vali. In the middle of the day a teacher at the Armenian school, Kanjian, was shot to death by the son of the *mudir.* No reasons given. No action taken. Mr. Kanjian's body was thrown in a wagon by the *zaptieh* and driven around the market square.

People were using the word *deportation* now. It was a word I kept hearing in the streets, in church, at the *souk.* We heard that in the cities east of us, in Harpert, in Aintab, in Sivas, Kasieri, Yozgut, the town crier had come through the streets in the morning and the Armenian men were ordered to appear at the city hall. They were led out of the city, not to be heard from again. We heard stories of Armenian soldiers being shot by their officers in training camp and at the front. There were stories of men, of the most prominent men—physicians, teachers, priests, and merchants—being hung in the gallows of the town squares of Van, Bitlis, Moush and Erzeroum, and Harpert, and Sivas, and Malataya, in Tokat, and Angora, and in Constantinople. They were called traitors and they were strung up in front of crowds in the middle of day. We heard that Armenians were being arrested and rounded up and sent out into the countryside under armed supervision of the *zaptiehs* or the gendarmes, and we were told that they would return when conditions got better. This was what we heard. These were stories, rumors of the unbelievable, of the things we said could not happen to us here in Diarbekir. We did not want to think about it or talk about it.

We went about our work inside. It was late July and we were busy, baking, cleaning, sewing, and packing for the coming month at our house in the highlands near Karadja Hagh. I slept well, but that is because I sleep well. Everyone else I knew was not sleeping well. Now because we were afraid, we stopped going up on the roof at night, stopped hulling wheat and pods in the evening. The heat in the house at night was very bad. Armenians in Diarbekir did not sleep well that July. People looked tired when you saw them in church.

And then the Turkish gendarmes and *zaptieh* went from Armenian house to Armenian house confiscating weapons or anything they thought might be one. If possible, the priest would come to warn each family that the gendarmes or the *zaptieh* were coming so they could prepare. The *zaptieh* knocked on Armenian doors any time of day or night, and they preferred coming at night. They came to the Kazanjians, and the Arslanians, and the Meugerditchians, and to the Hovsepians and Haroutiunians and to the Shekerlemedjians. And finally, they came to our house in the evening after dinner. Three men in dark brown uniforms walked into the foyer and through the courtyard and said to my mother that if she did not hand over every gun in the house, we would be killed. My father was away, and my mother went to the sideboard and took out the one pistol my father kept, and handed it over. They pulled out and dumped every drawer in our kitchen, leaving utensils and silverware on the floor, and they took a butcher knife and a meat cleaver too.

One morning I woke to the smell of something foul burning. It came through the curtains like wind, and I got out of bed and saw that it was shortly after sunrise. From my balcony, I saw the Arab halvah maker setting up his stand and the Assyrian women going to morning service. I dressed fast and put on my *charshaff,* because if you look Muslim they might ignore you. I began walking down the street past our church, and I kept pulling the *charshaff* around my face as the odor got worse, and in the distance I could hear women's voices screaming. I was breathing deeply into the *charshaff,* almost sucking on the silk. There was nobody out on the street except for a few vendors, and I began to walk faster.

The sun was already hot, and I felt foolish in the black *charshaff* but it kept some of the odor out. Near the Citadel Gardens the screaming got louder, and I could see a crowd of people, and I was walking faster now when a group of Turkish men came out of a side street and began to throw stones at me. "Armenian. Whore. *Giaur.*" They chanted it, and they ripped my *charshaff* off and began spitting at me. I backed up and then I fell by the wall of the Assyrian cemetery. As I tried to regain my balance, the men stood around me and began chanting. "*Giaur.* Whore. Dirty Armenian," and they began throwing stones at me. We were stoned often, and mostly on Sundays when we walked to and from church, but this time it was worse. I tried to shield my face with my arms, but the stones kept coming, and then my one eye shut. I could see little and I could feel the wetness of the blood rising through my dress. I held myself against the wall until I could regain my balance and then I stumbled back the half-mile to my house.

Inside our courtyard I passed out. When I came to, my mother was sobbing and saying "I wish I were blind so I would not see you like this." My eyes were swollen shut, and my face a mass of wounds. My mother rubbed me with beeswax and covered my eyes with gauze soaked in *hohdehd* milk. In the morning she dipped a cloth in egg yolk and put it on my worst wounds. In a week my face was almost normal. But when I looked in the mirror I looked at the big space where my front tooth had been. By then father was back from his trip.

One morning, shortly after that, my father said that we would be leaving for our summer house in Karadja Hagh the next day, and so I worked all day wrapping walnuts to make *bastik* and baking bread and ironing. I went to bed early and was ready to get up at dawn. My riding dress was hanging on the coatrack in my room. I was going to ride a new mare up front and my brother Hagop promised he would hold up the rear and tend to the donkeys. In the middle of the night there was a knock on the door. Everyone in the house woke up. It was a loud knock, and I heard the voice of a Turkish soldier who was shouting loudly. "Effendi Kassabian." He kept repeating it, in a slightly ingratiating way. Finally my father answered the door. The soldiers entered the foyer and I could hear their boots click on the tiles. I stood by the inside of my bedroom door and listened. Nobody else budged. My mother, my brother, my sister stayed in their rooms.

I could not hear what was being said. Because my father was a spice merchant, he spoke many languages—Turkish, Arabic, Kurdish, French, and English. He was a soft-spoken man who had gone to Euphrates College before he returned to Diarbekir to marry mother and start his business. They talked for several minutes. I heard my father shout: 'I was born a Christian and I will die a Christian.' Then I heard some footsteps and some clicking of boots on the tiles and the front door closed. It was a big door made of walnut and it had a round silver knocker, and when it closed the knocker slapped the door. I heard the clomping of horses on the cobblestone as they rode away with my father. Then there was silence, and not one of us—my brother Hagop or my sister Takooi or my mother or our servant Dikran—made a move. I went back to bed and lay watching the candlelight flicker against the wall, watching the wall turn to purple as the dawn hit it, and the next thing I knew I was wakened by a scream. A scream that was my mother's voice. I noticed that my candle had burned down and left a messy puddle of wax on my nightstand. There was a knock at the door and it was Dikran saying, "You must stay in your room."

I put on my riding dress and hurried downstairs. I ran through the courtyard to the foyer and found mother lying unconscious on the green-and-black tiles. Then I saw an object sticking through the door and something that looked like a horseshoe. I walked over to the door and pushed it open. I saw that two horseshoes were nailed to two feet, and my eye followed the feet to the ankles, which were covered in blood, and then to the knees which looked disjointed. I looked up to the genitals, which were just a mound of blood, above which long snake-like lacerations rose up the abdomen to the chest. The hands were nailed horizontally on a board, which was meant to resemble a cross. The hands were clenched like claws around big spikes of iron driven into the board. The shoulders were remarkably clean and white, and the throat had a fringe of beard along the last inch of the body. There was nothing else on the cross. They had left the head near the steps to our house, just at the edge of the street. I could see his nose propped on the step. I could see the beard trimmed neatly along the cheekbones. I could see it was my father.

For a week no one left the house except for the burial. We sent Dikran to get water and food, and the Shekerlemedjians came to check on mother. But mother would not leave her room. She would not speak to anyone. Takooi and Hagop and I spoke very little too. We stayed in our rooms. We helped Dikran around the house. We walked around in silence, and in the camphor-smelling rooms of death, we sat and ate and got up and walked around and went to sleep. At night I heard screaming from the direction of the Citadel Gardens. Sometimes I smelled smoke and a bitter odor. On the sixth day of staying inside the house I found I could not stand the silence anymore, and none of us would go up to the roof even to look out on the city. The quince and apricot trees looked dead.

I walked out of our courtyard through the doorway where my father's crucified body had been left, and into the street. The sun was high and bright and the sky cloudless, and I decided not to put on my *charshaff.* It did not matter anymore. Everyone seemed to know who was Armenian. We were marked, and I felt for the first time how false our names were. How the Turks had stripped us of that, too. None of us had Armenian names anymore, only patronymics that were attached to Turkish designations. Topal-ian, son of a lame man. Hamal-ian, son of a porter. Sarraf-ian, son of a money lender; Charshaf-ian, son of the veil. They were names of manipulation and control. Names of hatred and domination, and we who had lived on this land since the beginning of time were stripped of our true names, by the Turks who had come from the Gobi Desert. They had stolen our genes, too. They had raped us for centuries. They stole our cooking, our art, our buildings, our bodies. Their whole culture was a theft. I walked out into the street on that day in late July hating my name.

I walked past Saint Giragos, past the Assyrian church and the Mosque, past the archway with the tiled courtyard, and the walls of the city looked even blacker in the heat. Through the doorway of the New Gate I could see how brown the plain was, and in the sun the Tigris looked like floating mud. In the Citadel Gardens nothing was green except the cypress trees. As I passed the Gardens I began to smell the foul odor again. The shops were open, and the rugs and dresses and belts were hanging, and the awnings were stretched out, but there was no one around. The streets were empty. The shops were empty, and the crowd in the southeast corner of the market was growing. I was self-conscious without my charshaff, but no one noticed me as I slipped into the crowd that was making such a commotion in the square.

The crowd lined the square, some people were sitting in chairs, some Arabs selling quinces, people burning incense, the Turkish women in *burugs* were sitting on hassocks eating *simits*. The sun was terribly hot, and on the black walls some cranes were perched. In the middle of the crowd there were fifteen or twenty Armenian women, some a little older than me, some my mother's age. They were dressed in their daily clothes. Some in long fine dresses, others, who were peasants, in simple black. They were holding hands and walking in a circle slowly, tentatively, as if they were afraid to move. About six Turkish soldiers stood behind them. They had whips and each had a gun. They were shouting, "Dance. *Giaur.* Slut." The soldiers cracked the whips on the women's backs and faces, and across their breasts. "Dance. *Giaur.* Slut."

Many of the women were praying while they moved in this slow circle. *Der Voghormya, Der Voghormya.* (Lord have mercy). *Krisdos bada raqyal bashkhi i miji meroom.* (Christ is sacrificed and shared amongst us), and occasionally they would drop the hand next to them and quickly make the sign of the cross. Their hair had come undone and their faces were wrapped up in the blood-stuck tangles of hair, so they looked like corpses of Medusa. Their clothes were now turning red. Some of them were half naked, others tried to hold their clothes together. They began to fall down and when they did they were whipped until they stood and continued their dance. Each crack of the whip and more of their clothing came off.

Around them stood their children and some other Armenian children who had been rounded up from the nearby Armenian school. They were forced into a circle, and several Turkish soldiers stood behind them with whips and shouted "Clap, clap." And the children clapped. And when the soldiers said "Clap, clap, clap," the children were supposed to clap faster, and if they didn't, the whip was used on them. Some of the children were two and three years old, barely able to stand up. They were all crying uncontrollably. Crying in a terrible, pitiful, hopeless way. I stood next to women in *burugs* and men in red fezzes and business suits, and they too were clapping like little cockroaches.

Then two soldiers pushed through the crowd swinging wooden buckets and began to douse the women with the fluid in the buckets, and, in a second, I could smell that it was kerosene. And the women screamed because the kerosene was burning their lacerations and cuts. Another soldier came forward with a torch and lit each woman by the hair. At first all I could see was smoke, and the smell grew sickening, and then I could see the fire growing off the women's bodies, and their screaming became unbearable. The children were being whipped now furiously, as if the sight of the burning mothers had excited the soldiers, and they admonished the children to clap "faster, faster, faster," telling them that if they stopped they too would be lit on fire. As the women began to collapse in burning heaps, oozing and black, the smell of burnt flesh made me sick. I fainted and your mother's brother Haroutiun found me and took me home.

The next day, Mother, Hagop, Takooi, and Dikran and I were arrested, as were all the Armenians of Diarbekir. Turkish gendarmes came to our house in the morning and told us that we were going to be put on a deportation march. We were given a little time to gather a few things that we could pack on a donkey. We gathered silverware, some clothes, two rugs, a Bible, soap, some family photographs. We packed as much food and water as we could, but we expected to be able to buy food when we needed more. We hid some jewels on our bodies, and each had an allotment of money. Dikran packed several saddlebags and bundles on the donkey. By noon we joined a long line of Armenians and were marched down the streets to the Citadel Gardens, where we met up with thousands of Armenians. Some had donkeys, some had ox-drawn carts, and most were on foot carrying packs and small children and infants.

The gendarmes began cracking the whip and we began to move in a big mass toward the New Gate from where I could see a long snakish line of Armenians moving around the city walls going south. We were marched out past the Citadel and around the black city walls wavering in the heat. By the end of the day, we were sleeping on the ground somewhere on the flat, hard plateau. The tributaries of the Tigris cut ravines into the limestone ridges, and in their flanks were occasional huts built out of the rock, where Kurds lived. There was nothing but dry ground and sky and limestone ridges. Nothing.

Our food did not last long, maybe two days, and we hated ourselves for not bringing more. We ate the apricots and walnuts sparingly. But the bread was gone and the cheese was gone. We walked about sixteen hours a day. At sunrise we were waked by the whips and gunshots, and at sunset we fell to the ground wherever we were. I put my *charshaff* over my face at night to keep the scorpions and camel-spiders off. It was impossible not be eaten by flies and scarabs, and our sores grew worse in the sun. By the third day, we had broken up into smaller caravans, each directed by a dozen gendarmes. After our food and water ran out, we spent our energy trying to find things to eat or drink. Sometimes when we approached a brook or a well, the gendarmes would drink in front of us and laugh in our faces. By the third day, people were dropping by the way from starvation. At night and in the morning we sucked the dew from our clothes. I even chewed the sweat off my *charshaff.*

By the end of the fifth day, mother became delirious. She fell to the ground and told us to go on. We told her we would not leave her. She looked at us and said, "Children, I have lived my life." We stayed with her for half the day, when the gendarmes from the next caravan spotted us and began to use the whip on us. I began to bleed badly and I saw it was no use. Hagop was hit repeatedly with gunbutts and cut with a bayonet across the face. We left mother there on the hard ground under the sun in the middle of nowhere to die. For weeks after I dreamed about her. I dreamed she had joined the next caravan. I believed that we would see her again when we reached our destination. For days I heard her calling me. I looked back over my shoulder, and I heard her calling *Aghavni, Aghavni.*

All the time on the march, the gendarmes would harass us. Often they wanted money, and we had to give them coins, always protesting that this was all we had, and always they would whip us and demand more. We had to hold on to some money, for we knew we would need it, if not for the gendarmes, then for the Kurds and other nomads who came out of their villages to rape and rob us. The Kurds came down from the ravines on horses, with axes and rakes and other objects, attacking us and robbing us. By the fifth or sixth day, all our possessions were gone, including our donkey. The gendarmes had shot our donkey one afternoon, and then roasted it and ate it in front of us while they got drunk. The only things I had left were my silk baptismal cloth and a small kilim. And some coins that I kept in my private place. I put as much dirt on my face as I could, so the gendarmes and the irregulars (the convicts and Kurds) would think I was old and unattractive. Hagop and Dikran dressed as women, because there was less chance of being shot if you were a woman. By the end of the first week, most of the men had been shot. Usually, the gendarmes would just shoot a man in the back of the head while he walked. It was as if the men's heads were just there for target practice, and as we walked we would hear a shot and watch a man drop to the ground. We didn't stop to look. Everyone just kept marching.

Women were tortured. If a woman would not readily submit to sex with a gendarme, she was whipped, and if she tried to run away, she was shot. Once when a young girl tried to run, the gendarme took out his sword and slashed her dress open, and she stood there with her young breasts naked, and he slashed each breast off her body, and they fell to the ground. I stared at the two small breasts lying on the ground. I stood frozen, then I just walked away. The girl bled to death next to her breasts.

At night I lay on the ground and heard women screaming as they were raped. I listened to their voices echo in the immense dark desert air. There was no one, absolutely no one anywhere to help us. Takooi, Hagop, Dikran, and I slept on the ground together, almost as if we were attached to each other, as if we were one lump of a body. We hoped this would discourage the gendarmes from raping us, or from killing Hagop and Dikran.

Every time someone squatted to relieve themselves, a gendarme came over and with his bayonet and sometimes with his hand inspected the feces to make sure there were no coins in it, because many people began swallowing their last coins for safe-keeping. Sometimes the gendarmes would threaten us with a bayo-net and say "shit," and we were forced to squat so they could see if there were any coins to be had.

Whenever we passed near a eucalyptus tree I gathered some leaves so that at night I could suck on them to get water in my mouth. I lay on the desert ground at night, sucking a eucalyptus leaf and staring at the moon. The moon is terribly bright in August in the desert around the Euphrates. All that month it grew each night. It followed us. It was a wolf's eye. It was the opal charm of a Turkish sorceress. Some nights it was a damask seal and some it was a Per-sian charger stripped of its blue. It was scouring and harsh on the weeds and rocks, and the few animals that darted through looked like unreal silvery creatures. I lay on my back and felt the grooves of my cuts made by the Turkish whips ease onto the hard ground, and I stared at the moon. Often I unfolded the piece of the kilim. It was the piece I used under the lamp on my nightstand in my bedroom. I held it up to the moonlight and looked at the colors and thought of my bedroom windows, one looking out to the street and the other into the fruit trees of our courtyard. It was just a simple kilim of aubergine and saffron medallions. In one latch-hook medallion there was a green scorpion, in the other a red scarab. In the moon-light the colors were eerie, and after a while they seemed to float in the black air and then drip like roman candles.

One night as I sucked on a eucalyptus leaf and stared at my kilim in the moonlight, I felt the boot of a gendarme against the side of my neck. I rolled over so as to hide my face in the ground. But the boot continued to kick me and then to step on my head. As I buried my head more fiercely in the ground, the boot hooked me under the chin and pried me up, and the next thing I knew I was looking up at a man whose mustache looked silver in the moonlight. I watched him unbuckle his pants and I shut my eyes and the next thing I knew a stream of hot piss shot into my nose and over my face. The cuts on my neck and cheeks began to sting and my eyes burned. Soon my hair was like a sticky mess of rancid flax. When he finished he kicked some dirt onto my face, and I lay there squeezing my kilim, which was also wet, and I felt a small breeze blow over my face. For a long time I did not open my eyes.

When I did, I took a eucalyptus leaf I had saved and wiped my eyes. When I looked up, the moonlight had turned the sky white and I could see my mother's face as if it floated on the white lace of our dining table. She was saying to me: *Let them take you, let them take you, we will bring you back at Easter.* Then the moon turned red as my taffeta dress, and my love had come in green velvet gloves and the scarf that hung in the walnut tree.

Run, run run the little chicken said. Your cheeks are like apples, and the wind takes your golden hair and sends it to the mountains.

From seven stores, I gathered silver and made a ring. And put it on pearl's finger.

The moon stared at me all night. In the morning I woke inside the piss-gummed web of my hair, and I sucked on the eucalyptus leaf to make some saliva to clean off my face. Later I found some weeds, and I ground them up and spread them in the wounds enflamed by the piss.

One night I was raped. I prayed every night to the Virgin Mary and to Jesus and to God. And they answered my prayers. After this I felt some mindless will to survive.

I remember how the Euphrates wound down the descending plateau as we approached it from a distance. It was brown and muddy and thick. Now and then I saw some Kurds out by the banks hawking gazelles, and searching piles of feces for coins. Along the valley paths of the tributaries, corpses began to appear in piles, and as we got closer to the bank near nightfall bloated bodies covered with worms were everywhere. The smell was horrible. Many people began to vomit. Many people passed out. Many of the bodies were black from the sun, black tongues hanging out. Emaciated bodies showing a whole skeleton through the decaying skin. The stomachs of pregnant women had been slit open, and their unborn children had been placed in their hands like a bunch of clotted black grapes. Children were crying next to dead parents. Women were delirious.

The corpses of the elderly were shriveled. For miles and miles you saw nothing but corpses, and the brown water sloshing up on the banks. When I reached the bank, I found corpses washed up, half-deteriorated, headless, limbless, body parts floating. On the mud shoals that often cropped up like crocodiles, hundreds of rotting bodies were piled in a heap and the black terns were feeding on them. The bodies were melting into the mud.

Many women and girls threw themselves into the river rather than be abducted or raped. At several spots there were clusters of girls who had tied their hands together and drowned themselves. On the bank they were washed up and their blue bodies were still tied to each other's. Their tongues were black, half-eaten, and their hair was muddy and dry like old grass. There were dead babies along the riverbank too, and when Dikran, who was delirious now, began to pick the bodies of the babies out of the water, the gendarmes whipped him and told him to put them back. Later the geese and the wildcats came down from the valley to eat them.

As the plateau gave way to the desert, the sun grew worse and the ground was harder. We were delirious from hunger and thirst. We picked seeds out of the camel dung and we cleaned them off the best we could and put them on the rocks to dry them out in the sun before we ate them. Wherever there was grass, we sucked the dew off it and ate it. Occasionally we passed a well and one of us went to it to bring up a bucket of water. But often the gendarmes would push the woman with the bucket down into the well and if she did not die, they shot her at the bottom of the well, and the water became bloody and ruined. In the dried-up irrigation canals the Romans had built near Ourfa (see map), we found some locusts and we crushed them with our fingers and made a dinner of them. We had no shoes now and our feet had become swollen and infected. As the calluses formed we found we could walk faster. South of Ourfa we passed a circle of rocks where Armenian babies had been abandoned. Many of them had just been born, and their mothers had left them to die. They had been cooked in the sun. They were black and many of them had turned to skeletons, because the vultures had eaten them quickly.

By the time we were marched into the desert, there were

very few of us left. Almost everyone had died. Many had been thrown into the caves at the Euphrates and been set fire to. Dikran died there. But when we reached the desert, Takooi and Hagop and I were still together. On the second night in the desert, I lay on that hot ground to sleep. I never had trouble falling asleep. My dress was shredded and my cuts were festering. At night I dropped into numbness, thinking always that the next day we would arrive somewhere where someone would help us. Shortly after I dropped to sleep one night, I felt myself floating out on the air and the ground was vibrating, shifting, and moving, as if a terrible hiatus had opened under me. I looked up and the sky was clear and black and the Milky Way was swirling like muslin in the wind. I was on the back of a horse— the horse of a Kurd nomad. I spent the next five years in the house of this Kurd. I bore him two children.

· · · · ·

One day in the spring of 1925 I was shopping at Saks. I was at the cash register in the lingerie department, and as I stood in line to pay I heard a voice with a Dickranagertsi accent at the next cash register. When I finished paying, I walked out in front of the register, so I could see who was in line. I stared for a while at the woman who had been speaking and looked right into her big eyes. She stared back at me with my hands full of packages, and then she said "Aghavni?" And I said "Nafina!" And we fell into each other's arms crying.

Of my life with the Kurdish nomad all I can say is this. I escaped. I had a good mare, and when we came to the mountains, I squeezed her sides so tight that the milk of my mother came out of her nostrils, and the two mountains parted.

THE CEMETERY OF OUR ANCESTORS

I WAS GIVING A READING FROM MY NEW BOOK OF POEMS, *SAD DAYS OF Light*, at a library in a fashionable town on Long Island. Writing "The History of Armenia" was the beginning of a new book, one that dealt with family history. Between poems, I found myself talking about Armenia, the Genocide, my family, and feeling a good rapport with the audience. It was all strange and new to me, because I had never thought of myself as a voice for things Armenian, and my first book of poems had been quite different from this.

About halfway through the reading, I heard a rumble of noise in the room and recognized the voice of my aunt Anna. I looked over at her and could see her face grimacing with disapproval. Startled and disoriented, I kept reading, and then I heard her saying to those around her, "That's wrong, he has the wrong dates. Why is he writing about Armenia?" I was working hard now. Sweat coming down my temples. I couldn't believe that my aunt was attacking me from the audience. I got through the last few poems, then fielded questions from the audience. Although I had read poems about things unrelated to Armenia, my audience was intensely interested in talking about Armenia, and the questions kept coming until my host announced that some wine and cheese were being served in the foyer, and that the questions could continue there.

In the foyer, Auntie Anna was standing, not looking at me, but waiting as if she expected me to go up to her. I didn't. I watched her as she tried not to watch me, then I was ushered over to the men and women sipping wine out of plastic cups and cutting brie.

The next time I saw Auntie Anna was late summer. We were sitting around her dinner table, and she started in again.

"Why are you writing about Armenia?" she asked, her voice welling up with anger. "Why?"

I felt stuck. I really wanted to say: If the extermination of a million and a half people and the erasure of a three-thousand-year-old civilization isn't important enough to write about, what the fuck is?

"What else is there?" I said, hoping to be witty and end the conversation.

"This is not what poetry is for!" She was shouting now, and I saw Auntie Nona throw her a dagger look.

"What is poetry for?"

"You can't be circumstantial in poetry," she said, her voice shrill.

"Aren't Dante and Homer circumstantial?"

"That was a long time ago." Her voice was shaking.

"You can't have the circumstances of history in a poem?"

"Not after Mallarmé," she said.

"What about Neruda?"

"Please. Spare me," she said. "He's just political."

"*Residence on Earth?*" I was shouting now, and then Auntie Nona broke in and said, "Listen, Anna, Peter is writing wonderful poems. Why do you care *what* he writes about? Do you dislike Saroyan because he uses Armenia?"

And with that my two aunts were off on a discussion of their own. But Nona had succeeded in terminating the conversation and separating Anna and me. I felt more than anger. I wanted to know why my aunt had such a view of poetry. And why such anger about what I was writing about?

No conversation about poetry or anything else, for that matter, passed between us for the rest of the day. We poured scotch, ate steaks, corn on the cob, chocolate cake. When we kissed good-bye, we pretended the conversation hadn't happened, and indeed years later my aunt would even deny having attacked me for writing about Armenia.

My aunt was upset with me not only because I wasn't following her aesthetic program for poetry but also because I was delving into the Armenian past. "Why does this Armenian thing interest you?" she had asked me when my book first appeared. "How did you learn about Armenia?" she asked in disbelief. All week I thought about her reaction to my poems.

To understand my aunt, I felt I needed to go back to her books again; needed to get the gist of her message in cold, clear type. I happened to open her first book, *Literary Origins of Surrealism*, a book I had thumbed through as a schoolboy. Staring at the book flap, which read "Born in Constantinople of Armenian parents." It hit me in a certain way now. My aunt was born in Constantinople in 1915, the year the Turkish government commenced the Genocide. The Balakians in Constantinople in 1915. The real Byzantium in a real year of history. Whoever my aunt Anna was couldn't be dissociated from that place and that year.

Writing from Constantinople during those years, Gostan Zarian says:

"We have always been victims. Victims of unfavorable circumstances, elemental forces and events over whose evolutions we have had no control.

"We wait, our tattered clothes spread before the triumphal arches of other nations. We wait for what? For whom?"

．　．　．　．　．

What little I knew about Anna's father, my paternal grandfather Diran Balakian, I knew from a few fragments of stories and three pieces of paper. An entry written about him by my father in 1954 in something called *The National Cyclopedia of American Biography;* a copy of my grandfather's letter of application for a job at the American Hospital of Chicago dated November 1924; an affidavit dated

July 1923 and signed by his brother George, living in West Hartford, Connecticut.

Diran Balakian. Who was he? His dapper image hung on my wall in an old sepia photograph from his medical school days in Leipzig. Dressed in an overcoat with silk lapels, a vest buttoned up to a high white collar, he holds a top hat in his clasped hands. His hair is neatly parted down the middle; there's a space between his mustache and goatee. With his serious gaze and fine features, he has a youthful D. H. Lawrence look. No one ever said much about him. He had died suddenly in 1939 of a heart attack. His children were still young, my father eighteen, the youngest.

My father seemed to suggest that his father was quiet, or rather distant, perhaps stern. He was always busy, always with patients. His patients loved him, it seems. My father's cousin Armine, who lived with the Balakians as a young child, said he was obsessed with hand washing. As soon as the children came into the apartment, he ordered them to wash their hands. He inspected the children's hands, to make sure they were washed and washed well. If they weren't, he sent you back to the sink to try again. I recalled what Freud said about hand washing–a compulsive reaction to death. A ritual to ward off death.

The Balakians were from Tokat, and Diran was born there in 1878. He was the eldest of the four children of Hovaness (John) Balakian and Elizabeth Semerjian. Tokat was a small city etched out of the north central highlands of Turkey, about seventy-five miles from the Black Sea. It looked over the mouth of a rocky valley that opens out to the Tozanli River. A walled city with one gate, with a population of about 25,000 at the time of his birth. A small, multicultural city of the Ottoman Empire with about 9,000 Armenians, 2,500 Greeks, 1,000 Jews, and 10,000 Muslims, mostly Turks, but some Tartars and Kurds as well. Light manufacturing and trade were done there, and colorful patterns printed on white Manchester cotton were its special export. French clothes, French furniture, French textiles were sold in the chic shops downtown. My father notes in the *Cyclopedia* that his father's father, Hovaness, was a merchant. No one knows what kind of merchant. Was he wealthy enough to send my grandfather and his broth-

ers Krikor and Levon to secondary school in Etchmiadzin? Or did
they go on scholarship? At least he was shrewd enough to send his
sons over the border to Russia, where Armenian schools flourished
without Turkish surveillance and intrusion. In the Ottoman Empire,
Armenian schools were often run by American missionaries and
were always answerable to Turkish authorities.

Etchmiadzin was an ancient city in Russian Armenia and
the seat of the Armenian church, and there at the Kevorkian Seminary my grandfather walked to class in a seminary robe, speaking
Armenian with his classmates along the narrow cobblestone streets.
He would have received the news from the other side of the border.
The news that Abdul Hamid was massacring Armenians throughout
the Ottoman Empire. My grandfather a teenage boy, protected by the
Russian border, no doubt as his father had planned. By the end of
1896, over 200,000 Armenians had been killed, and by that time my
grandfather had gone further west and north to Tiflis.

Along with Constantinople and Baku, Tiflis was one of the
three cosmopolitan centers of Armenian culture. A Georgian city,
with more Armenians than Georgians. The most beautiful city of the
Caucasus, with its Parisian-style architecture and its terraced hills
rising from the banks of the Kura River. Tiflis was the site of dozens
of medieval Armenian churches and a great cathedral from the fif-
teenth century. In 1823, Nersesian College was founded there; the
first secular Armenian college, it was the place where Armenian
elites were educated. There my grandfather hung around with
Socialists and Armenian progressives, Hunchaks and Dashnaks,
young students with idealistic hopes for reform and change for the
plight of working people, for the plight of Armenians in the Ottoman
Empire. By the time he graduated from Nersesian College in 1898 he
had been away from Tokat almost half his life. He had passed
through the best channels of Armenian education. He and his classmates had watched with fear and anxiety and helplessness the
atrocities committed against Armenians on the other side of the border. Surely he was not going home.

Diran Balakian now was rising in the world. He had far
more opportunities than most Ottoman Armenians from the interior

cities. It was best to go west, to Europe, and he went to medical school in Leipzig, Germany. In 1899, when he arrived there, Germany was the new, dynamic European country. Berlin, a center for avant-garde culture as well as émigrés and students from eastern Europe and Asia Minor and the Middle East. The Germans called Leipzig *Klein Paris*, "Paris in miniature," an epithet given the city by Goethe in *Faust*. A beautiful medieval Saxon city with Gothic buildings, narrow streets with high-pitched roofs of the sixteenth century, and the Königshaus, the palace of the Saxon monarchs. The city's market square was like a *souk*, with its labyrinth of narrow streets connected by covered courtyards. Leipzig was famous for its great fairs, which attracted merchants from "all parts of Europe, and from Persia, Armenia, and other Asiatic countries," the 1910 *Britannica* noted. Had Balakian, the merchant, traveled there?

At the turn of the century, the University of Leipzig was one of the most influential universities in the world. It was founded in 1409, and Goethe, Klopstock, Jean Paul Richter, Fichte, and Schelling were among its alumni. Its music conservatory drew students from all over Europe and the Middle East. Bach had been the organist at the famous *Thomaskirche*. Luther had held his momentous disputation at the Pleissenburg Citadel in 1519. Schiller, Gellert, and Mendelssohn had lived in Leipzig, Leibniz and Wagner were native sons. My grandfather at twenty-two in this city so heavy with high culture. What freedom to be in Europe. To be out of the "east," out of Russia, out of Armenia, out of Turkey, where life for Armenians was growing dimmer. Where the sultan's last days as ruler were marked by the upstart Young Turks.

Because the German government forced my grandfather to sign an agreement stating that he would not stay to practice medicine after he completed his degree, he left Germany in 1905. Under the Kaiser, immigrants were not really welcome. Perhaps my grandfather could have gone to another European country to begin his career, but decided instead to return east. Back to Russian Armenia, to join an archaeological excavation of Ani, a ruined ancient Armenian city in the highlands that in the tenth century had been the capital of the Bagratid kings of Armenia. It was called the city of one thousand and one churches, because the obsessive Armenian builders of Ani had covered that rocky terrain with churches. Although it was destroyed by the Turks and the Mongols and finally by an earthquake in 1319, the excavations directed by the famous linguist and Orientalist Nicholas Marr, beginning in 1892, revealed the walls and streets of the city. By 1906, when my father and his cousin, Krikor Balakian, then an ordained priest, joined Nicholas Marr's continuing excavation of Ani, many of the churches had been uncovered.

Ani, which was Russian in 1905, would be taken by the Turks after World War I. A city on the cusp of the two empires that divided Armenia. My grandfather must have found that an appropriate place to survey his future. A place to find out about lost Armenia. And an expedition, a romantic thing to do after studying all those years. A physician, quite handsome, worldly, twenty-eight, no strings attached. Was he there for weeks, months, a year? How many on the dig with him? Frescoes, tiles, *hatchgars* (stone crosses), odd artifacts popping up out of the rubble. I think of him in 1906 in some tenth-century church vestibule, in the cool vaults of the Armenian earth, joking around with his cousin Krikor. I imagine the two of them drinking some good Georgian wine, eating bread and goat cheese, some herbs they've pulled from a nearby field. Laughing in Armenian, not worrying about Turkish officials hearing their native tongue. Looking up at the blue sky over Ani from some hole in the ground.

The sequence of events is unknowable, but my grandfather wrote in his letter of application for a position at the American Hospital in Chicago: "I have been a general practitioner from 1907–1913 in Egypt and Constantinople." Sometime after the dig in Ani, my grandfather went to Egypt to set up a medical practice. Was he going to live in Egypt? I was sure it was Cairo, because somehow the word stays in my memory. *Cairo,* a word passed in low voices around the table now and then. *Yes, yes, Cairo.* It must have been to him they were referring. Where should an Armenian live after the Hamidian massacres? A good climate, some freedom from being the infidel, from massacre. What happened there? He practiced medicine for a while and left.

I was beginning to see the past as a worn rug. Some taut warp and weft here and there. Some good pile in spots where clear images appeared; then just frayed wool, then a big hole. So many were cut out of time, and the pain that ensued made it hard for anyone to talk about the past. My grandfather seems to have lost contact with his parents after he left Tokat. What happened? I once heard my father say that his father had a sister who died. "Oh, yes," Auntie Anna said, years later, "she was killed by the Turks."

"When?" I asked.

"1915."

One sister killed by the Turks in 1915. "And the rest of the family? In 1915? Killed?"

"I guess so."

"What did your father say about his family? About what happened in the Genocide?"

"He never once sat us down and said, 'let me tell you about my parents.' He never said, 'This is what my father did for a living. Wasn't it good that he sent me to school in Russian Armenia.'"

But still I kept going for those clear images on the rug.

In 1909, my grandfather was either in Cairo or in Constantinople. I'm guessing Constantinople. I imagine that he spent a couple of years in Cairo and didn't love it. It was too far from Europe and his sense of things familiar. When the Young Turks dethroned the sultan and the era of Abdul Hamid seemed to be over, my grandfather decided to return to Turkey, to the great city, Constantinople. The Greek presence in that historic Greek city was still very much alive. Armenians too had been instrumental in its founding and building, and now 161,000 of them were living there, making it a center of Armenian culture. The Young Turks were promising a new age of fraternity between Armenians and Turks, a new age of reform. Why not give it a shot? Why not come back to the empire? With his command of German and his Leipzig degree, he was able to have a private practice as well as a job as a physician for the German Railroad Co., a branch of the Berlin to Baghdad Railway in Constantinople.

I imagine life going nicely for him at the beginning of 1909. He was settling into a career in the big city, on his way to a good life. He had met Koharig Panosyan, a young teacher at the American College for Women. A very young teacher, just twenty and fresh out of college. An unmarried, Christian woman who commuted each day to work across the Bosphorus by ferry and carried a gun beneath her coat for protection. Very bright. Very progressive. Very strong-willed. Some even called her fierce. Everyone said she was warm and generous. A postcard photo taken in Constantinople in 1910 shows her face and the top of a white silk dress with a high collar. She is staring with intensity. Her lips full, her jaw clenched. Her eyes fiery. Her hair is long and tied back, but looks as if it's coming undone, as if she's just gotten off a horse or run a mile. It would be five years before they married.

Then, abruptly, things changed. Or rather, they didn't change. Although the Young Turks had promised equality for Christians and other minorities and had introduced some constitutional changes purporting to liberalize the regime, the changes were never enacted. The commitment to constitutional change provoked Islamic fundamentalists, Abdul Hamid loyalists, and a whole range of reactionary groups in Turkey, who staged a counterrevolution. The most bloody episodes were carried out against the Armenians of Adana in 1909. In Adana, Armenians had been celebrating their alleged new freedoms. How naive. How impolitic. Announcing that they were now equal to their fellow Turkish citizens. For such celebration, the Armenians were massacred.

By the middle of April 1909, Armenians defending themselves against the Turkish counterrevolutionary forces in Adana put down their weapons, believing that the British Consul in the nearby city of Mersin would help restore peace and order. What followed has been called one of the most gruesome and savage bloodbaths ever recorded in history. The British Consulate did not get involved, and to make matters worse, the Turkish army arrived and joined the counterrevolutionaries, descending upon a defenseless Armenian population, butchering and burning them alive by the thousands per day. Schools, hospitals, and churches were favorite targets. By the end of April, the Adana holocaust had taken more than 30,000 lives.

My grandfather must have been in Constantinople when news of the Adana massacres came, and he went immediately to Adana with a group of Armenian physicians, where he worked for months, perhaps longer, treating the maimed survivors and helping to bury the dead. Traveling back again to the hinterlands of Turkey, far south and slightly west of his home city. Down to another ancient part of Armenia known as Cilicia, or Lesser Armenia. That last Armenian kingdom governed by King Leo V, before it fell to Egypt in 1375. Since the hospitals had been destroyed by the Turks, they must have worked as doctors on battlefields, using what they could. In the city of Adana and in the fields, villages, and towns for miles. A landscape of corpses. Thousands of murdered children. Thousands of mangled, raped, and murdered women. Everything burned. Stink of rotting flesh. Stink of hair and clothes and shit. Blood hardening and darkening earth, stone, clothes, objects, cobblestone streets. Adana, 1909.

In Constantinople, after the Genocide, after Turkey had gone down to defeat in World War I with Germany and the other Central Powers, Gostan Zarian wrote:

> The struggle for existence. From one school to another. I sell a little knowledge for a piece of bread. It is terrible to be a writer and belong to a small nation. It is even worse being an Armenian writer.
>
> Our generation has more friends in the next world than in this one. There are places where I walk with anguish as if I were crossing a graveyard of memories.
>
> I want to understand this city.... It is not a city but a collection of districts and panoramas. A jumble of worlds. It is a passage; its inhabitants, perpetual travelers. Nothing is stable....

To be an Armenian writer, Zarian wrote. Some of my grandparents' good friends were writers, and most of them were executed by the Turkish government in April 1915. One friend in particular was a poet, Adom Yarjanian, who used the pen name Siamanto. In the years before the Genocide, the house of my grandmother's family had become a sort of salon where writers and painters came to talk and eat and hang out. Painters Sarkis and Vava Katchadourian, poets Daniel Varoujan, Vahan Tekeyan, and Siamanto, the novelist Krikor Zorhab, the playwright Levon Shant, a young professor of philosophy, Armen Barseghian, who would marry my grandmother's sister Arusyag, the composer and priest Gomidas, Gostan Zarian, and others. My great-grandparents' Victorian clapboard house overlooking the Bosphorus was a place where writers read their poems and stories, artists showed new paintings. My grandfather, the doctor, treated his artist friends for free or in exchange for a book or painting.

On the eve of the Genocide, Armenian literature was in the midst of a renaissance. Armenian writers had brought their own ancient traditions in literature and the plastic arts together with the European Enlightenment and Romanticism. Voltaire, Racine, Hugo, Byron, Shelley, Swift, Milton, Manzoni, and Leopardi had been important to them, and by the turn of the century so had Zola, Balzac, Chekhov, and Dostoyevsky. In Constantinople, the Mehian literary movement included Siamanto, Varoujan, Zarian, and others. It was Armenian modernism and it mingled with Italian futurism and German expressionism. Armenians were also rediscovering their own cultural past: the epic "David of Sasoon"; the poems of Sayat Nova and Gregory of Nareg; the illuminated manuscript painting of Sarkis Pidzak and Toros Roslin. A new interest in architecture emerged in the wake of archeological digs like the one my grandfather had been part of with Nicholas Marr in Ani. The squinch domes, niche buttresses, and blind arcades with which Armenian architects had revolutionized building in the late Middle Ages were being rediscovered by Europeans, Armenians, and Russians.

Like Osip Mandelstam, Bertolt Brecht, and Nazim Hikmet in their own times and places, the poets Siamanto, Daniel Varoujan, and Vahan Tekeyan were among many Armenian writers targeted by the Turkish government as enemies of the state. As Mandelstam said, because totalitarian regimes always find poets the most dangerous of people, they are often the first to be executed. The Young

Turk government began its plan of genocide by arresting a group of 250 prominent Armenian leaders and intellectuals on April 24, 1915. They were taken away in the middle of the night to small towns in the interior and executed. It haunts me to think about how a whole generation of writers was silenced in 1915, just as they were maturing and beginning to create something dynamic and new. With the destruction of the Armenians of Anatolia, Western Armenian literature was strangled. Diasporan Armenian writers would continue to write in the Western Armenian dialects; but once snuffed out on its native soil, it was ostensibly extinguished. How many literatures on the planet had perished this way, how many cultures annihilated?

I am wondering if my grandfather aspired to become a writer, a poet, even. His experiences in the killing fields of Adana pushed him as close to poetry as he would come. In Adana, he not only was an eyewitness to atrocities as only a physician could be but was compelled to write what he saw, in letters sent to his family. I imagine these letters spared little detail. I imagine they helped him release some of his outrage. I imagine they were vehicles for grief. I imagine they helped him to comprehend the world he left behind at the age of ten. I hear him saying to himself in Adana, it is important to get this down on paper.

The poet Siamanto lived near the Balakians, and when he learned that Diran was sending letters about the massacres, he came by regularly to read them. The letters have not survived, but they became the source for Siamanto's next book of poems, *Bloody News From My Friend.* In his entry for the *Cyclopedia,* my father wrote,

> During 1909, he served with a group of Armenian doctors in Adana, Turkey, aiding stricken refugees of the Turkish massacres of those years. During that time he wrote a series of letters to his friend, the poet, Siamanto, describing the conditions in Adana and the plight of the refugees, and these were published by the poet in 1911 [*sic*] under the name *Sanguinous News from My Friend.*

My father never spoke to me about this directly. Only once or twice do I remember my father and aunts referring to Siamanto and the title of a book of poems, about which they said nothing. My father's translation of the title suggests his own queasiness about the title, and his description is inaccurate. Siamanto didn't publish my grandfather's letters verbatim. But writing the entry as he did, my father was acknowledging how profoundly a joint venture this book of poems was. A physician and a poet collaborating to tell some truths.

THE DANCE

In a field of cinders where Armenian life
was still dying,
a German woman, trying not to cry
told me the horror she witnessed:

"This thing I'm telling you about,
I saw with my own eyes.
From my window of hell
I clenched my teeth
and watched the town of Bardez turn
into a heap of ashes.
The corpses were piled high as trees,
and from the springs, from the streams and the road,
the blood was a stubborn murmur
and still calls revenge in my ear.

Don't be afraid. I must tell you what I saw,
so people will understand
the crimes men do to men.
For two days, by the road to the graveyard . . .

Let the hearts of the world understand.
It was Sunday morning,
the first useless Sunday dawning on the corpses.
From dusk to dawn in my room,

with a stabbed woman –
my tears wetting her death –
When I heard from afar
a dark crowd standing in a vineyard
lashing twenty brides
and singing filthy songs.

Leaving the half-dead girl on the straw mattress,
I went to the balcony of my window
and the crowd seemed to thicken like a forest.
An animal of a man shouted, 'You must dance,
dance when the drum beats.'
With fury the whips cracked
on the flesh of the women.
Hand in hand the brides began their circle dance.
Now, I envied my wounded neighbor
because with a calm snore she cursed
the universe and gave her soul up to the stars ...

In vain I shook my fists at the crowd.
'Dance,' they raved,
'dance till you die, infidel beauties.
With your flapping tits, dance!
Smile for us. You're abandoned now,
you're naked slaves,
so dance like a bunch of fuckin' sluts.
We're hot for your dead bodies.'
Twenty graceful brides collapsed.
'Get up,' the crowd screamed,
brandishing their swords.
Then someone brought a jug of kerosene.
Human justice, I spit in your face.
The brides were anointed.
'Dance,' they thundered –
'here's a fragrance you can't get in Arabia.'

With a torch, they set
the naked brides on fire.
And the charred corpses rolled
and tumbled to their deaths ...

I slammed my shutters
sat down next to my dead girl
and asked: 'How can I dig out my eyes?' "

·　·　·　·　·

In 1913 my grandfather returned to Europe, first to Berlin and then to Vienna. This time, he was doing specialty work in ophthalmology with Ernst Fuchs, the preeminent ophthalmologist of his day. Did he uproot once more to be by Dr. Fuchs's side? Just to study the human eye? He was going back to Europe to study the nerve paths and tracts that convey visual impulses – a journey to the interior, a way to focus deep, to blot out the large chaotic world of politics and death?

Or did he leave the Ottoman Empire once more finally to propose to my grandmother, who had left Constantinople for a graduate degree at the École Normal in Chartres? Why did she leave Constantinople? Wasn't one university degree enough for a young woman in 1910? Was she tired of waiting for this evasive, restless, talented man? Was she too fleeing the bloody news of Adana?

They came back to Constantinople to get married in 1913. Cousin Krikor, who was my grandmother's uncle as well (my grandparents were cousins once removed), performed the wedding. Then they returned immediately to Vienna, the capital of the Austro-Hungarian Empire, only eleven months before the Archduke was assassinated in Sarajevo and World War I began. Vienna was a fitting place for this rebellious, now exiled, couple. Although the families were not wild about the marriage, nothing was going to get in the way of these two strong-willed people. These romantics. Vienna: city of Baroque churches and parks, and its legacy of Mozart, Beethoven, Schubert, Brahms, and Mahler. Vienna: the last buttress against the

Turkish invasions of Europe in the seventeenth century. As late as 1683 the Austrians, with the help of the Saxons, Bavarians, and Poles, held off the Turks, who were so determined to sack Vienna that they drilled tunnels under the bastions of the city. A fitting place for my grandparents to start out together. But then the war came, and, my grandfather writes, "I returned to Constantinople and during the World War served in the Turkish army in the Dardanelles and other parts of the country with the rank of captain."

Why go back to Turkey? Was my grandfather conscripted into the Turkish army while he was in Vienna? (After 1910, Christians were conscripted.) Were they forced to leave the Austro-Hungarian Empire because of the war? Did my grandmother want to give birth to her first child back in Constantinople? Did they return before or after April 1915, when many of their friends, the intellectuals and leaders, were being rounded up for execution, including Cousin Krikor? Because Turkey entered the war in the fall of 1914 and Anna was born in Constantinople in July 1915, I'm guessing that they arrived around Christmas of 1914. The young couple reuniting with the family for the first time since their marriage. My grandmother pregnant on this trip back to Constantinople. It was a quite a time to start a family. Quite a time to think of the future.

A captain in the Turkish army, my grandfather was sent to an army base near the Aegean coast. Sometime after July 1915, my grandparents arrived at Soma with their new infant. In my father's dresser drawer I found a picture of my grandfather in a Turkish army uniform. He is posing in front of a studio backdrop tapestry with a rococo garden scene. The uniform looks dark brown. A belt across the tuniclike top, fastened to a broader belt around his waist. Two buttoned pockets and some stars on the epaulets. The pants look like jodhpurs, bunching around his knee near the top of the high black boots. On his head, a peaked cap bearing an insignia.

I'm imagining this scene. Outside Soma are some tents, some cottages—shacks really—built quickly for the doctors, and a primitive barrack for a hospital. Soma: an ancient Greek town not far from Troy, meaning "body" in Greek, *the physical entity of an organism, as distinguished from the germ cells.* Having taken the Hippocratic Oath in 1905, my grandfather was now in Soma in the Turkish army, which was allied with Germany and the Austro-Hungarian Empire in World War I. In the fall of 1916 it rained a great deal, and the tobacco plantations flooded. The smell of rotting tobacco is like a blanket over the base, and from the porch of the hospital the once green valley looks like a mudslide. Smells of carbolic, urine, rubbing alcohol, raki, and mastic in the air of the big square courtyard of the base. Turkish casualties are many and increasing. Every day the wounded arrive in trucks and ambulances, from the western front and the Balkans, from the eastern front along the Russian border. On the field is a huge Turkish flag, white with a red crescent, spread on the ground to warn aviators not to bomb the hospital.

Mustafa Jelal is a lieutenant, and he arrives at Soma delirious with fever. He is unpacked from a truck, wrapped in a wool blanket. His face is round, his hair black, and his eyes slightly slanted upward. A long, thin scar runs from his cheekbone to his jaw, and his mustache is trim. The shrapnel in his body has created an infection, and my grandfather hopes to save his life by amputating his leg to stem the gangrene. Because ether is not available at Soma, my grandfather uses a combination of raki and opium to drug his patient. As my grandfather asks his assistant, a Turkish private, for the saw and the scalpel, Lieutenant Jelal lifts his head and says: "Effendi, save me."

"You will be fine," my grandfather says.

The evening is slate gray over Soma and it is drizzling. The smell of sodden tobacco is oppressive in the wet air. My grandparents and their daughter Anna live in a small, pine shotgun house a few hundred yards from the hospital. From the window of the room where they eat, they can see the red crescent floating on the field. At night my grandfather returns to the hospital to check on Lieutenant Jelal. He checks the stitches along the back of the flap of skin that covers the stub of bone. When he arrives the lieutenant is sitting up and talking in a slurred way. My grandfather pours him half a tumbler of raki.

"Effendi, Effendi, in my pocket is my home address. Please write my wife, if anything happens."

My grandfather nods that he will, that he promises.

"You understand, Effendi?"

My grandfather says, "Yes, lieutenant."

In the morning, when my grandfather returns to the hospital he finds Lieutenant Jelal dead. He reaches into the lieutenant's breast pocket looking for his home address and finds a small book, a wallet, and a watch. A ticking, gold pocket watch, monogrammed on the back in Armenian writing: "To Armen, with love Satenik, October 3, 1892." My grandfather puts the watch in his pocket, then opens the booklet and reads: Mustafa Jelal, Fatma Jelal, Siyat Street, Erzeroum.

An Armenian physician in the Turkish army. To be scissored between the Hippocratic Oath and the knowledge that those you were saving might be committing genocide. To be an Armenian doctor in the Turkish army during World War I was to try to save Lieutenant Jelal so that he could return to the field to rob and kill Armenians. My grandfather had no choice. Either he complied with his military conscription or he was executed for treason. To save his family and himself, he served at Soma.

"In 1922," my grandfather writes, "I returned to Vienna." My grandfather and grandmother and their three young children had stayed in Constantinople for four years after the war. Why? After more than a million Armenians had been murdered and the rest of them driven off their land. Why didn't they leave earlier? Who could bear to live in a place called Turkey? And to make life more complicated, my aunt Nona, who had been born in 1918 on the army base at Soma, had contracted a strain of tuberculosis at age two, which set into her spine.

Vienna in 1922. The Hapsburg Empire broken up, the mood of the city somber. If you are Armenian in 1922 and you've survived the Massacres, who are you? Zarian wrote: *Our generation has more friends in the next world than in this one. There are places where I walk with anguish as if I were crossing a graveyard of memories.*

My grandparents sought the best medical care they could for Nona. But also, my grandfather writes, "I returned to Vienna where I

worked in the clinics of Professor Dr. Hajek and Professor Dr. Neu-
mann for rhinolaryngology." The nose and larynx. More dark inward
spaces for my grandfather to study. With the calamity of their daughter's illness, the return to Vienna must have been one of mixed emo-
tions. They hadn't yet packed up their belongings in Constantinople.
They had come with a few suitcases and planned on returning to
Constantinople once Nona was well enough to travel.

Return to the Constantinople of the 1920s—to Mustafa
Kemal's new Republic of Turkey? To the culture that had exterminated the Armenians and wiped out the Greeks and Assyrians, and
the rest of the Christians of Anatolia? When they knew that Turkey's
plan was total race extermination? (By the spring of 1918, the Third
Turkish Army invaded Russian Armenia and confiscated substantial
portions of eastern Armenia, including the lost city of Ani. Major
General Otto von Lossow informed Berlin that spring that the Turks
were embarking on "the total extermination of the Armenians in
Transcaucasia.") When they knew that after the war the Turkish
army invaded the newly formed republic of Armenia, hoping to wipe
it out and annex the Caucasus, and that by 1920 another 200,000
Armenians in the Gumri and Leninakan regions had been annihilated? Why go back?

But they didn't go back. In the summer of 1922 my grandmother's father, Murat Panosyan, sent them a telegram that read
something like, "Smyrna has been burnt to the ground, the Greeks
and Armenians are being slaughtered again. The Greek forces are
being driven out of Anatolia. Don't return."

By 1924, my grandfather had left for the United States. Nona
was in a sanitarium in Geneva, but because the Swiss wouldn't give
them a visa, my grandmother pushed across the French border and
found her way to Collonges, a small village in the French Alps about
twelve miles from Geneva. By early 1923, my grandmother and her
sister Arusyag and their children, Anna, Gerard, and Armine, were
living together in a large house at the foot of Mt. Saleve. They were
being supported by their father, a wealthy merchant back in Constantinople. The mothers holding things together until they received
news from their husbands. Would Nona be cured? Would my grand-

father learn English quickly and pass his exam so that he could practice medicine in the United States? Would Armen find a job in America with his Ph.D. in continental philosophy?

They belonged to no country and were traveling on a passport that read République d'Arménienne, a passport from a country that no longer existed. (There had been a Republic of Armenia from 1918 to 1920, but after continued invasions by the Turks the failing new nation of famine-wasted refugees joined the new Union of Soviet Socialist Republics.) Two sisters from Constantinople in their early thirties in a small Alpine village. "*Sous Saleve*," my father's cousin Armine recalled. "When people in the village asked us where we lived, that's what we said, "*Sous Saleve*." Under Mt. Saleve.

For the children, it must have been a mythical time. My father recalled, "We didn't know whose mother was whose. We just called them the mothers." Three children living with the mothers in a house looking south to Mt. Blanc and north to Geneva. The herders in the meadows with their cows and goats. The great snow-fields in the winter. My father remembered the dreamy echoing of bells, bread and chocolate for breakfast. How could one do better? Anna and Armine in a Catholic school, learning the world in French. Armine remembers how tenaciously Anna embraced school in that small Alpine town. How quickly she excelled and embraced French.

My grandfather was able to enter the United States that year without a problem because his younger brother George, who had come to America in 1913, sponsored him. My great-uncle George had dropped the Armenian patronymic i-a-n and now went by the name Balak.

> I the undersigned, George Balak (Balakian), residing at 951 Farmington Avenue, West Hartford, Connecticut, being duly sworn, depose, and say:
>
> That I have resided in the United States since November, 1913: that I have known Doctor Diran Balakian was born at Tokat, Turkey; that my brother is about 43 years of age; that my brother, Doctor Diran Balakian is now living in Vienna, Austria.

That he desires to make America his permanent home, and to practice his profession in this country; that he is a physician by profession, and a specialist in the diseases of the eye, ear, nose, and throat (received the degree of M.D. at the University of Leipzig, Germany, and specialized later as an oculist at the University of Hugenklinic, Vienna Austria).

That he is in good health, without mental or physical defects, and in case he is permitted to land in this country, I do hereby guarantee that he shall in no way become a charge upon the Government of the United States, nor of any state or municipality therein.

That I am in business of my own, West Hartford Dye Works Company, West Hartford, Connecticut, and am financially able and willing in every way to be responsible for my brother should he be allowed to come to the United States.

George Balak (Balakian)

My grandfather's letter of application to Dr. Max Thorek at the American Hospital of Chicago, November 1924:

I am an Armenian by nationality, 46 years of age, married and father of three children, but my family is now remaining in Collognes (France) near Geneva (Switzerland) where they have to wait until I could bring them to this country.

Four months ago I landed in New York....I am devoting most of my time to learn English, which language I can understand fairly well and speak a little. Besides I can talk Armenian, Turkish, German, and French.

I have very good references, one from Prof. Meller, written to Dr. Vincent, President of The Rockefeller Foundation and another letter from Dr. Fuchs

to Dr. Landsteiner and another to Dr. Loeb both of
the Rockefeller Institute.

As to the salary I wish to tell frankly that I have no
idea of the work I am going to do, but I expect to
have my ticket to Chicago paid, have board and lodg-
ings in the hospital and I will be satisfied with any
reasonable honorarium for the work I do.

I hope that I will have some chance to perfect my
English and have some time for my examinations.

By the end of 1924, my grandfather was in Indianapolis. He
writes, "Four months ago I landed in New York." What deadpan
humor; my exiled grandfather, an Armenian man, searching for a
place to be safe, trying to outmaneuver the fate of Armenia. How
fantastic the unraveling routes of exile are. I think of my grandfather,
an Ottoman Armenian physician, in Indianapolis in 1924, in the
America of Sinclair Lewis in the middle of an affluent decade. A
physician who had witnessed this century's first racial mass murder,
who aided the victims in Adana in 1909 and served in the Turkish
army during the war. Finding himself in this pleasant middle-Ameri-
can city, with its ordered grid of streets and miles of railroad tracks
and terminals and stockyards and meat-packing plants. A city of
about a quarter of a million people, with sizable populations of German and Irish immigrants and blacks who had come north from the
South. What did they make of him?

I can see the name Balak printed on the mailbox of the slate-
blue rooming house, Queen Anne style, with a second-story front
porch and large, overbearing bay windows. At night he sits in a
rocker in a room with a bed and bureau, and works on translating
pages from *Great Expectations* and *David Copperfield* from German
into English, to "keep bettering myself," he wrote in scribbled English in the margins. His German editions of Dickens with his English
translations still lie in the family trunk; Armenian, German, and
English words floating in the yellowed margins. Some Dickens and
some street idioms. *Okeydoke, good to see you, so long, sullen, dispu-*
tatious, confounding.

It is 1924 and the Model T Ford is becoming a middle-class object in America, as are refrigerators, radios, and vacuum cleaners, yet the nation seemed more provincial. The legacy of the 1919 Red Scare is virulent. Prejudice against immigrants, blacks, Jews, Catholics is everywhere. The 1924 National Origins Act cuts back dramatically the number of immigrants allowed into the country. The Ku Klux Klan is cross burning, murdering, and kidnapping with a mission. Women are smoking cigarettes, bobbing their hair, showing their legs, voting. Mary Pickford, Clara Bow, and Charlie Chaplin are modern times. Babe Ruth is belting more homers than anyone ever has. Liquor is illegal, and certain Christian temperance groups believe whiskey and beer are Satan's tools and that new immigrants are prone to them. William Jennings Bryan is fighting Darwinism. My grandfather is writing letters to Collonges. Now, finally, he can tell them to come.

The Balakians arrived in New York in 1926. Because their papers were in such good order, they didn't have to come through Ellis Island–Aunt Anna was emphatic about that. My grandfather now had his own practice and was on the staffs of Lenox Hill and St. Luke's hospitals. By 1936 Anna had graduated from Hunter College. Her love of French literature led her on to a doctoral program at Columbia, where she studied with Horatio Smith and Paul Hazard, a Frenchman known for his book *The European Mind.* In a 1986 interview in *Ararat* magazine, Anna recalled that her father had been supportive of a career in academe, and that her parents didn't put any pressure on her to marry quickly, as was so often the case with Armenian fathers of that era. After her father died in 1939, she supported the family while working on a dissertation. "From the start," she said, "I had no notion of being a woman in a man's world."

But in the late 1930s, she was indeed a woman in a man's world. Only thirteen percent of all Ph.D.s in the early forties were women, about 350 out of 3,300. Half of those women were single, divorced, or separated, the pressures of marriage, motherhood, and career were that severe. Having set out in 1943 as an instructor of

Romance languages at Syracuse University with a book manuscript in hand, my aunt seems to have worried little about all that. And when I think of her in Syracuse, New York, in 1944, a single woman starting out a career in a provincial, wintry upstate city, leaving her Armenian family back in Manhattan, I think of my grandfather's voyaging spirit.

Was my aunt's passion for French vanguard poetry of the 1920s and '30s separable from the Balakian voyage out of Turkey, through Vienna, Geneva, and Collonges? "The Swiss wouldn't give us a visa, but the French took us in," she said. Heroic France, romantic France. The apogee of European poetics for her. Starting out her career at the end of the Depression, after her father's death. Why surrealism? She answered: "It demonstrated the transcendence of the spirit in a burgeoning materialistic world. It opened the doors of the imagination to expand reality beyond the bourgeois compromise. It channeled childlike qualities of wonder and innocence."

"I focused on literary figures who did not dwell on national elements but on universal issues. I felt that after World War II there was much too much national polarization and emphasis on ethnicity, whereas I had been reared in the spirit of one-world internationalism." I thought of my aunt at eight, in Collonges. I thought of the Balakians living on a mythical passport, belonging to no country, no nation, no social space. My aunt may not have been thinking of those days when she chose her career, but it was an interesting context to ponder now. My aunt went on, "The Futurist poet Marinetti said that we cannot carry the cemetery of our ancestors on our backs."

We cannot carry the cemetery of our ancestors on our backs.

Although my aunt Anna's ideas were very much a part of her generation, I felt the irony in her response as well. Notwithstanding the other realities entwined in her passion for such an idea of literature—a drive toward innocence, wonder, and transcendence—her view seemed to me also to have been affected by the Armenian Genocide. How could a critic be so hostile to the circumstantial world, to history and politics, were it not for some haunting specter? Hadn't she fled the real Byzantium of 1915–the year of her birth and the massacres—for the mythological Byzantium of romantic imagination?

The poetic embrace like the carnal/ While it endures/ Forbids all lapse into the miseries of the world. My aunt chose those lines from Breton as the book epigraph to *Surrealism: The Road to the Absolute,* and in so doing stated her own therapeutic notion of poetry as a form of personal salvation in the wake of trauma, dispersion, and exile. Among other things, the Surrealist poets of France embodied for her the zenith of European culture; they were a bridge from her parents' Europe and the magical bells of Collonges to her present.

But surely, one could love such an idea of poetry and also acknowledge history. How can one deny the cemetery of one's ancestors?

READING A SKELETON

ONE DAY AN ENVELOPE ARRIVED FROM MY FRIEND LEO HAMALIAN, the editor of *Ararat* magazine. A glossy page torn from a French magazine slipped out. Leo had scrawled on it, "Any relation?" My eye jumped to the headline: *Recueillement sur la tombe de Monseigneur Balakian*, then to a photo of people gathered around the archway of a church. *Recueillement:* meditation. At the tomb of Bishop Balakian.

There was only one Bishop Balakian. The bishop whose name came up now and then, the man who had married my grandparents in Vienna. The man who had written a book about the churches of Ani. That large man in the wedding photo with the Balakian eyes staring out from his clerical hood and robe.

The article was about a gathering in memory of Bishop Gregoire Balakian at his funeral chapel in the cemetery of Saint-Pierre in Marseilles, fifty years after his death.

But who still remembers Bishop Balakian? Very likely very few among us, for even the stone cross

which surmounts his tomb lies on the ground–this
cross which is the symbol of our national identity.

Bishop Balakian was, in the thirties, the bishop of
the Armenians of southern France, at a time when
the Armenian nation was still in a state of shock from
the first genocide of our century. A man of conviction, inspired beyond all doubt by the spirit of God,
he was truly modeled from the obsidian of Ararat.

To those without hope, he gave hope by showing
through his actions that to "well-born souls," the
word impossible was not in the Armenian language.
It was in this spirit that, destitute among the destitute,
he succeeded in an extraordinary task of building–in
Marseilles and its suburbs alone–six churches,
among them the Cathedral of Saint Mesrop. No one
more than he deserves the title, Gregoire the Builder.

But Bishop Balakian was not only the one through
whom the Armenians regained courage and became
themselves again. He was also a witness in the most
noble and most Christian sense of the term. He was in
fact one of the few survivors of the 250 martyrs arrested
in the night of 24 April 1915 in Constantinople.

The article then announced the reprinting of the "irreplaceable memoirs" of Bishop Balakian of the Armenian Genocide, and it
closed: "Bishop Gregoire Balakian, sleep in peace, those whom you
have loved so much will never forget you."

What were the irreplaceable memoirs of Bishop Balakian
about the Armenian Genocide? My father and aunts had mentioned
his book about the churches of Ani, but never a thing about memoirs.
Of the Genocide? That, too, a secret?

I sat in my office staring out at the red and yellow fall trees
on the hillside, feeling like I was reading a message in a bottle that
had floated into my life. A survivor of the 250 intellectuals and leaders who were dragged off to their deaths by the Turkish government.
A writer of a memoir about the Genocide. A builder of churches in

Europe. Wouldn't such a man be a hero in most families? Wouldn't
he be talked about?

I phoned the Diocese of the Armenian Church in New York
and asked them to fax me any information they had on Bishop Balakian. In an hour I received a two-page document, in Armenian, of
course. Only the dates 1873–1934 were legible. I faxed it to my friend
Nevart in Ithaca and she translated it and faxed it back later that day.
It was an obituary from the publication of St. James Seminary in
Jerusalem. "Bishop Krikoris Balakian (1873–1934)," November 1934.

> No one who met him even briefly could help but
> note his most remarkable attribute, which was his
> passion: passion of pathos, of thought, of word, and
> especially of deed.
>
> He spent his early years at Sanasarian in Karin,
> before he went to Nithvayday in Germany, where he
> lived for two years to study architecture. In Constan-
> tinople he served as secretary and member of the
> religious council and ... during the period of the
> Armenian massacres, he emerged as a primary
> "leader and organizer."
>
> Then, during the time of the massacres and his
> political deportation, he benefited most from his
> knowledge of German. He was then ordained by
> Bishop Gevork V and appointed representative of the
> Catholicos in Europe. He served successfully as pas-
> tor in Manchester, in London, and lastly as the Pri-
> mate in Marseilles. He was able to transform his
> initial impulses into the completion of large projects,
> such as the construction of two churches, one in
> Nice by Chankerbian and one in Marseilles by Kho-
> rasanjian, as well as in the building of seven chapels
> and an equal number of schools where true Arme-
> nian life could flourish again, and for which the
> Armenian nation and church are justly indebted to
> his blessed memory.

If disillusion followed each of his fine successes, it can be ascribed to a passion of mind, which often accompanies those souls who courageously pursue unexplored ideals.... This dynamic clergyman's qualities of being openhearted, fearless, genial, and spirited existed side by side with goodness, sincerity, devotion, and love of motherland.

Like pieces of a puzzle falling out of a box. My grandfather's cousin, my grandmother's uncle. I had to find the memoir he had written. Did it still exist? I called Nevart to see if she could locate a copy. An hour later she called to say she had tracked one down in Beirut and that it was on its way to a bookstore in Los Angeles, and that I could expect it in a week.

The book arrived in a large box. Titled *Armenian Golgotha.* A hardback, oversized two-volume edition. Reissued in 1977, it contained a frontispiece photograph of the Bishop, looking much like he did in my grandparents' wedding photo, only broader and stouter. I sat there never having wanted to read a book more urgently in my life, only to realize that it would be years before I could get it all translated into English. I sat staring at those Armenian characters that looked like strange flying birds in a white sky.

At least the table of contents could be translated. I Xeroxed those pages and faxed them to Nevart, and in an hour she faxed them back to me.

THE GENERAL CONDITION OF ARMENIANS AT THE
   BEGINNING OF 1915
THE FIRST BAD NEWS FROM CILICIA; THE SECRET
   MESSENGER
THE NIGHT OF GETHSEMANIE
THE BLOODY SUNDAY
TOWARD A PLACE OF EXILE
PLAN FOR THE EXTINCTION OF ARMENIANS IN TURKEY
THE CARAVAN OF DEATH TO ZOR, FEBRUARY 1916 —
   APRIL 1916

SECOND ARREST AND IMPRISONMENT
FROM YOZGAT TO BOGAZLIYAN, THE SKULLS
THE CONFESSIONS OF A SLAYER CAPTAIN
MEETING ANOTHER CARAVAN OF THE CONDEMNED

It was like reading a skeleton. A trail of places and phrases. Clues to a man's life. A man who had been sentenced to death by the Turkish government because he was an Armenian leader. A man who escaped his execution and spent four years in the killing fields. An eyewitness. Perhaps the only man of the famous 250 who survived, and survived to write down his story.

THE SWEET SMELL OF BREAD
THE REMNANTS OF THE ARMENIANS IN THE MOUNTAINS
    OF AMANOS
THE GHOSTS OF 10,000 ARMENIAN WOMEN IN THE
    DESERTS OF RAS-U-AYNE
SHEDDING OF BLOOD ON THE WAY FROM BORCHE TO
    MARASH; A GERMAN NURSE GOES INSANE
THE SUFFERING OF BRITISH PRISONERS AT KOUT-EL-
    AMARA
THE PROJECT OF FORCED ISLAMIZATION — ESCAPE TO
    INJIRLIE

Words like pieces of bone. I began to feel the presence of loss in a new way. What did it mean for a whole civilization to be expunged from the earth? What did it mean when a people who loved and worked and built a culture on the land where they had lived for three thousand years were destroyed? What did it mean for that culture's legacy? What did it mean for the human race? When a civilization is erased, there is a new darkness on the earth. I could feel dust blowing over dry land, where now blood is part of the rocks, where the water will never run clean again.

FRAGMENTS OF ARMENIANS IN THE TAURUS
    MOUNTAINS

IN ADANA, JANUARY 1917 — 1918

THE CONDITIONS OF THE REMNANT OF ARMENIANS IN
  ADANA

THE CURSE OF MURDERED ARMENIAN MOTHERS

THE DECLARATION OF THE ARMENIAN REPUBLIC

THE HOSPITAL/SLAUGHTER-HOUSE OF TURKISH SOLDIERS

THE NATIONAL VOW OF THE TURKS TO EXTERMINATE
  THE SURVIVING ARMENIANS; THE GENERAL
  MASSACRE IN DER ZOR

ESCAPE FROM THE LAND OF BLOOD

I could hear the piercing, wavering sound of a *douduk.* The hollow rasp of the dead blowing through the beautiful carved apricot wood of that instrument.

. . . . .

Soon after, a friend sent me another book, *The Case of Soghomon Tehlirian.* It included a transcript of the celebrated trial of Soghomon Tehlirian, a young Armenian refugee who had seen his family murdered and his town destroyed. On March 15, 1921, in Berlin, Tehlirian assassinated Talaat Pasha, the mastermind of the Armenian Genocide. Tehlirian was put on trial in the midst of outraged German public opinion, only to be acquitted by the jury when it heard the testimony of eyewitnesses of the Genocide. Among the witnesses at the trial: "Krikoris Balakian (Vicar from the Armenian-Apostolic Prelacy in Manchester, England, who has come to Berlin for the trial) takes oath. The witness speaks halting German. No interpreter is needed." Here is some of what he said:

WITNESS, BALAKIAN: I was in Berlin when the war broke out and in September 1914 I left to return to Constantinople. On April 21, 1915, I was arrested and deported along with another 250 Armenian intellectuals.

During the forced march to Deir-ez-Zor, we went through villages and cities where countless Armenians gave up their lives: Choroum, Boghazliyan, Kayseri, Tomarza, Jajin, Sis, Kars, Bozar, Osmaniye, Hassanbeylie, and Islahiye.

For example, 43,000 Armenian men, women, and children were massacred between Yozghat and Boghazliyan. We heard constant rumor that we were to be executed as well, even though the official word used was "displacement." In reality, displacement was a policy of extermination. Our group had money, altogether some 15,000–16,000 gold pieces, and we believed that this money would be our salvation. "Bakshish" [bribe] is a very strong inducement in Asia Minor. The reason I am still alive is because of "bakshish."

We were hungry and, whenever we came to a river, they would not allow us to quench our thirst. We stayed two days without any food whatsoever. They would not allow us to buy any food. They would never allow us to sleep, and yet we were content. We thought that we would be very fortunate if they did not kill us.

When we came to the bloodiest city, Yozghat, we saw a couple hundred skulls of women and young girls in a gorge located four hours' distance from town. With us was a police captain, Shukri, who had led us (we were 48 men and 16 police officers on horseback). I asked him whether it was true that only men were being killed and that women and children were being spared.

"If we only killed the men," he replied, "and not the women and children, then, 50 years from now, we would have a couple million Armenians. So we also have to kill the women and children; thus we will no longer have an external or an internal problem."

The captain explained to us calmly and in detail that 14,000 men had been taken from Yozghat and the surrounding villages and been killed, and their bodies had been put into wells. The surviving members of their families were told that the men were sent to Aleppo, Syria, that they were well and that the government had been asked to give orders for the members of their families to come and join them in

Aleppo. These families would find living quarters ready for them there. Furthermore, the government had decreed that anything that was moveable could be taken in carts with them to Syria.

On the basis of this order, families started packing everything they had of value, including carpets, silverware, gold, jewelry, and all other moveable possessions. They loaded these into their carts and set out for Syria in a caravan. On the road from Yozghat to Boghazliyan the captain told me that, as a commander of the gendarmes, he personally gave the orders for 40,000 Armenians to be killed. He went on to say, "Now the women were thinking that their husbands were alive and made preparations to join them." There were approximately 840 carts; of these 380 were oxcarts, and the rest horse drawn. Many women and children were forced to go on foot. There were some 6,400 women and children being deported to Aleppo.

I asked the captain why such things had been done. He explained that if the women and children were exterminated in the cities, then we would never be able to find out where they had hidden their gold and other valuable possessions. That is why we allowed them to pack all their valuables.

I asked the captain if he had any regrets. I asked him whether or not he felt responsible to answer to God, to mankind, and to what we call civilization.

The captain replied that he felt no responsibility whatsoever. He was only obeying orders given to him from Constantinople. He indicated that he was only a captain and had been ordered to kill everyone because a "Holy War" had been declared. When the massacre was over with, he told me he said a prayer and absolved his soul.

VON GORDON (defense attorney): When you were in Changre, did you go to the Vali with one of your professors and did you request him to do something on your behalf? Did he not show you a telegram that he had received from Talaat Pasha asking him a certain question?

WITNESS, BALAKIAN: One day when I was with Mr. Diran Kelekian, the editor of the Turkish newspaper *Sabah* and a professor at the Turkish University in Constantinople, he asked me, "Would you like to go with me and visit the Vice-governor, Assaf Bey?"

We then went to visit Assaf Bey.... He welcomed us very politely. We asked him what we could do to get to Constantinople. He said, "My dear professor, whatever you want to do, do it. Do it quickly; otherwise it will be too late."

We naturally asked him why it would be too late. Assaf Bey replied by saying that he could not say anything to others, but he said, "You are my teacher (Mr. Kelekian) and you (turning to me) are a clergyman, you can keep the secret. I trust you!" He showed us a telegram which I read. I have no reason to doubt the authenticity of a telegram shown to me by the Vice-governor. The telegram read: "Telegram us directly and immediately the exact figure of how many Armenians have been killed and how many are still alive. Minister of Interior Talaat."

At first, I was unable to comprehend the meaning of the telegram as I could not imagine that a whole nation would be massacred. No such thing had happened before in history. Mr. Kelekian asked the Bey the meaning of the telegram. He replied, "You are supposed to be intelligent. You are an editor-in-chief. The telegram means: Why are you waiting? Kill them all."

JUROR: What signature was on the telegram?

WITNESS, BALAKIAN: The telegram was signed "Talaat."

VON GORDON: Who helped you escape? Was it the Russians, British, Turks, or French? Who?

WITNESS, BALAKIAN: That is a disastrous story and the events that I endured for five years would take me weeks or even months to relate to you.

VON GORDON: We would appreciate it if you would summarize those events for us.

WITNESS, BALAKIAN: I fled from Islahiye to Ayran-Bagche. When I arrived at the Amanos mountain chain, I came across a group of German architects and engineers who were working on a tunnel. They were very polite toward me, especially when they discovered that I had done my studies in Germany and spoke German. They told me that I had to shave my beard, remove my frock and dress as a European. I stayed with them for four months. There were 8,000 Armenians working under the protection of these German engineers, but when the orders came to deport these Armenians as well, they were killed between Bagche and Marash. I fled again, this time to the Taurus mountains, where other German engineers were working on a tunnel, and I found refuge among them. The Chief Engineer, Leutenegger, was very good to me. However, as soon as the Turks discovered my identity, I fled to Adana. In Adana I found other Germans and again I remained with them for five months. I was in the main office under the protection of Chief Architect Winkler. I was given a German uniform and I passed as a German soldier.

With my German uniform, I joined other German soldiers and officers and went with them by train to Constantinople. I stayed in hiding in Constantinople until the Armistice was signed in 1918. In November 1918 I left Turkey and came to Paris to try to relate to the world the atrocities that were committed against the Armenians.

NEIMEYER (defense attorney): Are you aware that Talaat said, "I have done more in one day than Abdul Hamid did in 30 years to resolve the Armenian Question?"

WITNESS, BALAKIAN: What Talaat did had never happened, not only in the past 30 years but in the past 500.

JUROR EWALD: I would like to ask a question of witness Balakian. You said you went to see the Vali. Was he a governor or a mayor? Did you see the signature of Talaat on the telegram?

WITNESS, BALAKIAN: Yes, I saw it with my own eyes.

I wept as I typed out the words of my lost uncle. I felt his embrace, his beard on my face. Against odds, his words had reached me here in central New York near the end of the century.

PART VI

COMMEMORATION

TIMES SQUARE

If the Holocaust was a hoax, why not the Armenian catastrophe also? If Anne Frank's diary was faked, who is to say that certain documents signed by Talaat Pasha weren't forged as well? . . . The Turkish attack on truth exemplifies the new governing narrative, the one in which truth is fugitive.

— TERRENCE DES PRES,
*On Governing Narratives:
The Turkish-Armenian Case*

I LIVE IN THE CHENANGO VALLEY OF MADISON COUNTY, WEST OF Cooperstown, where James Fenimore Cooper once described the surface of a lake as glimmer glass, and east of the Finger Lakes, which are gouged out of glacial rock. The hills are soft in central New York, but there is nothing quaint about the silver and white silos, the flaking red barns, and the congregations of black-faced white heifers. It's a terrain of hard economies, a landscape of work. Route 20 is a two-lane highway, like old Route 66, and it runs four miles north of my house in Hamilton, cutting through towns and villages from Albany to Buffalo. Sagging Italianates, half-painted ladies, antique shops, diners and restaurants with faded neon signs mark the roadsides of even the smallest towns such as Bridgewater, East Springfield, Bouckville.

The April landscape is tawny. Corn stubble, hay-colored grass, muddy ruts bleeding through the snow. Red kernels on the trees barely visible. The thermometer rises to 70, drops to 10. There's frost on the windshield. From my window by the phone, pellets of hail assault the red tin roof of the side porch. Then rain and the smell of thawing, and in the afternoon the arms and legs remember July. Back to snow flurries at dusk. A month of false starts. The heart is a back tire spinning in mud.

I remember the phone call because it was my daughter's first birthday, and she was holding on to furniture as she made her way around the living room. Her hair was long and silky and fine and the color of Moroccan olives, like the hair of the Balakians of Constantinople and Tokat. Over the static of the cordless phone came broken phrases of Armenian English. A voice was asking if Dr. Balakian would agree to be part of the seventieth anniversary of the Armenian Genocide on April 24, the traditional day of commemoration. It was to be held at Times Square.

"Nine days from now?"

"Yes. You can come?"

Ever since *Sad Days of Light* had come out, I was getting invitations to read my poems. Not just at universities but at churches, town halls, human rights seminars, and genocide conferences. It came as a surprise, because I hadn't set out to write a book of social value or an "Armenian" book. I had little affection for nationalism, and I had been raised so outside of Armenian ethnic life that my life had become a hunt to find out about the past. I found myself pulled by the catastrophe that had happened to Armenia and to my family, and by the universal, moral issues the Genocide represented. And so I had written a book of poems about things I could

lay claim to. Armenia had become an Atlantis to my imagination.
Lost Armenia, where my family had lived only seventy years ago.
Armenia, whose misfortune had helped to define modernity, as
Michael Arlen noted, because "the harnessing of modern technology
for mass murder began with the genocide of the Armenians" and
was the source of "the bloody river linking the great murderous
events of our century."

I had come to believe that a poet had something in common
with the Japanese violin maker who worked for fifty years to create
his delicate wooden instrument. When a buyer came into his shop,
fell in love with the instrument, and offered the violin maker more
money than he had ever been offered, the violin maker smiled and
said, "This violin is for my great-grandchild; it can't be played for
fifty years." Perhaps the past had to settle for a while before music
could be made of it.

I had come to feel the significance of Armenia for its sheer
duration on the planet, and that duration in a place that we in the
West thought of as the *cradle of civilization*. The Tigris River flowed
past my grandmother's house in Diarbekir. No doubt she had bathed
in it. Her horse had lapped water from it. Her family had done laun-
dry in it. Sumerians, Chaldeans, Hittites, Cappadoccians, Babylonians were names in textbooks, but Armenia was still on the map. The
most eastern and oldest Christian nation in the world.

When the broken-English voice on the phone asked me to
come and speak on six days' notice, I said, "I need to check my
schedule," and hung up.

"It pisses me off," I said to my wife. "Damn Armenians,
expect you to come at the drop of a hat, as if you owe it to them. And
they never pay."

"You'll feel bad if you don't go," my wife said.

Bad meant guilty, and guilty is a mode of being in Armenian
culture, a way we check our individual egos against the collective will.

"Fuck it. I'm saying no." So I called the next morning and
said, "Okay, I can come."

"Noon at Times Square. You know where that is?"

"Yes," I said.

"Dr. Balakian," the broken-English voice said, "glad you can be there."

A damp wind and bright sun in late April. I was squinting in the noon glare. We sat in folding chairs on a plywood platform. There were mikes, cameras on tripods, video equipment from a TV station. The façades of buildings were familiar. The running lights of the SONY clock, the digital fragments of news wrapped around a sky-scraper, a huge bottle of Coke on a red sign. An American flag. Fuji Film. The letters carouseled around me. A movie marquee, eye-level ahead, *The Killing Fields.*

Times Square was cordoned off by light-blue sawhorses monogrammed NYPD. Policemen on large blindered horses moved slowly around them, creating a strange pageantry. I was introduced to my fellow speakers. Ambassador Morgenthau's grandson, Henry Morgenthau, III, Senator Al D'Amato, Elizabeth Holtzman, the Democrat who had lost to D'Amato in the Reagan landslide of 1980. I took a chair between Marjorie Housepian Dobkin, the novelist and historian, and a slight, Asian man named Dith Prahn, whose story of surviving Pol Pot's genocide in Cambodia, *The Killing Fields,* I had seen only days before.

As Times Square filled with people, Marjorie leaned over to say: "The Turks have come." I looked again at the light-blue sawhorses and the mounted cops on horses and realized that secu-rity had been tightened. Various Turkish organizations had come to protest our civic act of mourning. I sat watching, the rage I didn't want to feel coming at me.

On the other side of the sawhorses, Turkish people were pass-ing around pamphlets, one of which was *Setting the Record Straight: On Armenian Propaganda Against Turkey.* Published by the Assembly of Turkish American Associations, Washington, D.C., it said:

> In recent years claims have been made by some
> Armenians in Europe, America, and elsewhere that
> the Armenians suffered terrible misrule in the
> Ottoman Empire. Such claims are absurd.

Armenians were deported because they were a security threat and were massacring Muslims but great care was taken by the Ottoman government to prevent the Armenians from being harmed during these deportations. Thus orders were issued that: "when Armenians are transferred to their places of settlement and are on the road, their comfort is assured and their lives and property protected; that after their arrival ... their food should be paid for out of Refugees Appropriations; that property and land should be distributed to them in accordance with their previous financial situation."

The Turkish publication continued by attacking the Armenian survivors.

Carefully coached by their Armenian nationalist interviewers, these aged Armenians relate tales of horror which supposedly took place some 66 years ago in such detail as to astonish the imagination, considering that most of them already are aged eighty or more. Subjected to years of Armenian nationalist propaganda as well as the coaching of their interviewers, there is little doubt that their statements are of no use whatever for historical research.

Due to a variety of reasons, far more Turks than Armenians—about 3 million Turks—died in the same war. Very few of these fell dead on the battlefront. Consequently, one cannot conclude that the Armenians suffered any more terribly or that the Ottoman government attempted to exterminate them.

There was no genocide committed against the Armenians in the Ottoman Empire before or during World War I. No genocide was planned or ordered by the Ottoman government and no genocide was carried out.

My ancestors had been driven off the earth they had lived on for twenty-five hundred years, had been killed one by one, and the things they had built with care over centuries of tradition had been confiscated or destroyed, and now the grandchildren of those Turkish people were stalking the United States in order to prevent Armenians from telling their story. The perpetrators trying to silence the victims and their descendants. I stuffed the Turkish pamphlet in my briefcase.

From the time I'd learned about the Armenian Genocide until the previous year, I had known nothing about the Turkish government's campaign to silence the story of its crime against Armenia. But after *Sad Days of Light* came out, the New York State Department of Education asked me to be an advisor for a textbook on twentieth-century genocide that would be used in public schools. Not long after I and a group of scholars had begun putting together the chapter on the Armenian Genocide, the Turkish Embassy got wind of the project and began harassing the Department of Education, insisting that "this genocide business" was invented by Armenians, and if the chapter were included it would hurt U.S.–Turkish relations.

I traveled to Albany several times that fall, and sat in overheated offices imploring state bureaucrats, who were horrified by the Turkish assault, to hold firm on the chapter. The Turkish contingent was threatening to call President Reagan. Letters went back and forth. The Education Department grew increasingly befuddled. Before it was over, the Turkish government had succeeded in forcing changes to the textbook. One day, feeling the bile thicken, I called Elie Wiesel and filled him in on the mess in Albany, and he said, "I've talked to the President of Turkey about this. I said to him: 'Why can't you admit what you did to the Armenians? It would help your society. It would cleanse you of your guilt. You would gain something in the eyes of the world.'"

Wiesel told me his own Turkish story. In 1982, he was to chair a genocide symposium in Tel Aviv, where a group of scholars were giving papers on the Holocaust and the Armenian Genocide. It was a well-publicized event and was organized by Israel Charny, a distinguished Holocaust scholar and director of the Institute on Holocaust and Genocide. Shortly before the symposium was to convene, the Turkish government informed the Israeli government that if the conference included the Armenian Genocide, it would "threaten the lives and livelihood of Jews in Turkey." Wiesel decided he could not participate. The blackmail had worked, and the conference went on without Elie Wiesel and a majority of the scheduled Jewish participants. Papers on the Armenian Genocide were presented, but the conference lost its wind.

Perhaps the Turkish government's ability to poison American institutions for the purpose of covering up the truth began in the United States in 1934, when the Turkish ambassador, Munir Ertegun, filed a protest with the U.S. State Department because MGM had bought the film rights to Franz Werfel's best-selling novel, *The Forty Days of Musa Dagh*, which had been published in Germany in 1932. This novel about the Armenians of Musa Dagh, who had made a heroic resistance against great odds to stave off the Turkish invasion of their mountain town in 1915, was the first popular novel about the Genocide. In it, Werfel expressed a sense of apocalyptic foreboding about the fate of the Jews. A Jew himself, he fled Germany in 1938, three years after Hitler agreed to ban *The Forty Days of Musa Dagh*, at the request of the Turkish government.

If the film were released, the Turkish ambassador asserted, it would be taken as a hostile act on the part of the United States toward Turkey and would result in a Turkish ban on all U.S. films. After more than a year of exchanges between the two governments, the State Department acquiesced to Turkey's demand, MGM dropped the project, and the film was never made. This was 1935. How much did FDR's State Department know about what Hitler was doing to the Jews of Europe, and how much did it care? Why did the State Department care so little about artistic freedom? Why was MGM willing to go along? How ironic that on August 22, 1939, eight days before Hitler invaded Poland, he said to his inner circle, "Who today remembers the extermination of the Armenians?"

As I sat looking out at the crowd in Times Square, I kept thinking of Turkey's hypocritical posturing to the United States as a

civilized NATO ally. Turkey's greatest novelist, Yasar Kemal, wrote
from his jail cell recently:

> As a cultural mosaic, Anatolia has been a source of
> many modern societies. If Turkey's leaders had not
> tried to prohibit and destroy other languages and
> other cultures than those of the Turkish people, Ana-
> tolia would still be a fountainhead of civilization.
> Instead we are a country half-famished, its creative
> power draining away. The sole reason for this is that
> cancer of humanity: racism.

Not long after my experience in Albany I was invited to join
the writer's organization, PEN, and in the first *Pen Newsletter* I
received there was a feature story by Arthur Miller and Harold Pinter about a trip they took to Turkey in 1985 on behalf of PEN International. Miller and Pinter were representing the literary world in its
concern about censorship and human rights violations in Turkey.
There was widespread concern in Europe and the United States
about the imprisonment, torture, and execution of writers and journalists, and Amnesty International had defined "torture in Turkey"
as an international problem.

Miller and Pinter quickly discovered that Turkish society
"exists in a permanent state of McCarthyism," as Miller wrote. They
reported that the entire directorship of the Turkish Peace Party,
which comprised most of the country's intellectual elite, had been
arrested and sentenced to long prison terms for opposing NATO missile bases in Turkey and sponsoring a commemoration of the Marx-
ist poet Nazim Hikmet. After the trials, the lawyers who defended the
Peace Party were themselves arrested and tried, and their careers
subsequently ruined. Numerous painters, theater directors, and
writers were in jail for making "subversive" art. Almost twenty percent of the country's academics—that is, about 2,000 professors—had
been sacked or had resigned; about 7,000 teenagers and young
adults—mostly students between the ages of sixteen and twenty-
four—were in jail for being "terrorists." Miller defined censorship in

Turkey as "total," and both playwrights soon became recipients of this total repression. When it became clear why they had come to Turkey, they were smeared in the press and were declined interviews; their press conference, held at the Journalists' Association, was officially banned and a formal investigation was launched into their visit. They quickly left the country. When the *New York Times* reported in March 1996 that Turkey led the world in imprisoned journalists, ahead of China and Syria, who then could be surprised?

It has become clear to me that Turkey not only is a culture of profound human rights abuses but a place devoid of any mechanisms of critical self-evaluation. The aftermath of the Armenian Genocide is one example. In Turkish schools everyone is taught that in 1915 Armenians were traitors who attacked and killed Turks and deserved everything they got. There is no mention of Armenia, not on maps, in encyclopedias, in tourist pamphlets, or guidebooks, let alone in the telling of the history of Anatolia. A Turkish writer for the Encyclopedia Britannica had been sent to prison for letting the word *Armenia* appear on a map of ancient Anatolia. Tour guides and travel literature have expunged the word *Armenia* from their narratives. Armenian churches and buildings–many of them among the important and beautiful ancient structures in Anatolia–are not acknowledged as Armenian. Recently I checked a Fodor's guide to Turkey to find that the description of the great ruined Armenian city of Ani did not mention the word *Armenian*. When the permanent exhibit of the ancient Near East opened at the Metropolitan Museum of Art in New York, the word *Armenia* was removed from its historic place on the map. The chairman of the museum's board at that time was a former U.S. ambassador to Turkey. All this was a continuation of the genocidal program to wipe out Armenia.

I sat in Times Square thinking how important it is to have grown up in a society that believes in the ceaseless process of critical evaluation. To contemplate Turkey's denial of the Armenian Genocide is to contemplate a society that is not civilized. In the wind of late April, words issued from the mouths of public officials and people of conscience. I watched the police trot on horseback around the light-blue sawhorses, wishing I hadn't come.

When it was my turn, I stood at the mike distracted by rage, staring at a blur of people. As I looked at the front rows where proud survivors sat attentive and well-dressed, some holding up posters that read "Remember 1915," I read a short poem from my book, and then I was planning to sit down, but I didn't. I stood there for a few seconds and began speaking again.

"Seventy years ago, my grandmother was put on a death march with her two infant daughters. And so was every other Armenian living in their homeland in Anatolia. Innocent, unarmed, stateless people. More than a million of them, women and children alone. And today I have to stand here while Turkish people pass out propaganda which claims there was no genocide committed against the Armenians; that Armenians were responsible for their deaths; that Armenians had it coming to them anyway. What happened to the Armenians exceeds the UN's definition of genocide tenfold.

"After all that has happened we are forced to live with this kind of obscenity. The message the Turkish government sends us and the world is: We will say anything to absolve ourselves of this crime. We have no conscience. We just want to silence the victims and their descendants. I am asking good and decent American citizens to say no to Turkish attempts to cover up the Armenian Genocide."

• • • • •

My late friend, the scholar and critic Terrence Des Pres, saw the Turkish denial as an issue of power attempting to quash truth. In his essay "On Governing Narratives: The Turkish-Armenian Case," he writes,

> Knowledge is no longer honored for its utopian promise, but valued for the services it furnishes. A striking illustration comes from the conflict surrounding Turkey's determined effort to deny that the Armenian genocide of 1915 took place. And our own government, furthermore, sees fit to be involved.... Until recently the facts of the Armenian genocide

were beyond dispute ... our own official archives are
thick with first-hand evidence, but now we are hearing that there are two sides to the story, and we are
being told that we must hear what the Turkish government has to say. This is turning intellectual
debate into a gimmick for the use of the powerful.

The issue was power, and Turkey certainly had more of it
than Armenia, which until 1991 had no nation state. Turkey had
been a cold war ally and NATO partner, and used its power to coerce
the U.S. government on Armenian Genocide issues. "What does it
mean when a client-state like Turkey can persuade a superpower
like the United States to abandon its earlier stance toward the genocide of 1915?" Des Pres asks.

Des Pres was right, for it had come to this: by the 1980s, the
Turkish government was able to prevent the U.S. Congress from
passing a bill commemorating the seventieth and, later, the seventy-
fifth anniversary of the Armenian Genocide. A simple commemorative bill that would have had historical roots in President Wilson's
U.S foreign policy, which was dedicated to saving Armenia and
restoring its homeland for a modern republic. A bill that would
have echoed the American public's sentiment after 1918, when it
sent over 20 million dollars for relief to the Armenian refugees and
survivors.

In 1984, when the first genocide resolution came before the
U.S. House and Senate, the Turkish government threatened to close
down U.S. military bases in Turkey, built with millions of U.S. dollars, and to terminate defense contracts with U.S. firms. President
Reagan, who earlier that year went to Bitburg, Germany, to pay
homage to dead German S.S. officers—and in doing so conflated the
elite killing corps with its victims—had no difficulty acquiescing to
Turkish demands. In 1989, when Senate minority leader Bob Dole
proposed a bill to commemorate the seventy-fifth anniversary of the
Armenian Genocide, Turkey enlisted Senator Robert Byrd to fight for
the Turkish denial. Once again "intellectual debate was turned into a
gimmick," and the bill lost by twelve votes. What would happen if

such a scenario were to have unfolded against a Holocaust commemorative bill?

Des Pres also notes that certain historians at major American universities have been receiving substantial funding from the
Turkish government to support the "other side of the story" to help
Turkey deny the Genocide. If scholars can be funded by "governments to shore up the official claims of nation-states," Des Pres
writes, "knowledge is no longer the mind's ground of judgment but a
commodity for hire."

Scholars for hire. Careerism and cynicism in the academy. I
now was learning that there existed a small but barbaric paper trail
in academe that involved Turkey's attempt to cover up the Genocide.
It's hard to say exactly where and when it began, but it became evi-
dent at some point in the 1960s, after the well-publicized fiftieth
anniversary of the Armenian Genocide.

In 1962, Bernard Lewis, the well-known historian of Turkey
and longtime professor at Princeton, described in his book *The
Emergence of Modern Turkey* what happened to Armenia as "a holocaust that took the lives of 1.5 million people," but sometime after
that he changed his mind. What happened to Professor Lewis after
1962? Soon thereafter, his Princeton colleague, Norman Itzkowitz,
began berating what he called the "alleged" genocide of the Armenians. What was going on at Princeton? Were there ties between the
Near East Studies Department and the State Department? Had cold
war policies infiltrated the academy this deeply? In the 1970s, Stanford Shaw at UCLA pushed the denial of the Armenian Genocide to a
new level by writing that "The Armenians were to be protected and
cared for until they returned to their homes after the war."

The paper trail of denial extends to the present. Most
recently, the case of Heath Lowry has drawn national attention.
Lowry is a man with a Ph.D. in Ottoman studies who went to Turkey
in the 1970s and worked for a research institute in Istanbul and lec-
tured at Bosphorus University. He returned to the United States in
1986 to become the director of the Institute for Turkish Studies in
Washington, D.C., an organization set up by the Turkish government
ostensibly to promote Turkish culture in the United States. Lowry

wrote articles and op-ed columns to deny the Genocide; lobbied in
Congress to defeat successive Armenian Genocide commemoration
bills; organized an advertisement for major newspapers signed by
some Turkish people and some scholars in Turkish studies denying
the Genocide; and published a ninety-page booklet in Istanbul that
attempted to discredit Ambassador Morgenthau's Genocide memoir.
Indeed, Lowry was a man devoted to demonizing the victims and
helping the perpetrator government absolve itself of responsibility.

When Robert Jay Lifton's 1986 book *The Nazi Doctors*
caught his attention, Lowry attacked Lifton's book because he mentioned the Armenian Genocide. Although *Nazi Doctors* is about how
physicians in the Third Reich embraced Hitler's program of mass
murder, Lifton mentions the Armenian Genocide several times, and
in particular, the role of Turkish physicians in the extermination
policy. After reading *The Nazi Doctors,* Lowry wrote a long memorandum to the Turkish ambassador pointing out how dangerous
Lifton's book was:

> Our problem is less with Lifton than it is with the
> works upon which he relies. Lifton is simply the end
> of the chain, that is, from now on we will see all
> works on the genocide of the Jews, including refer-
> ence such as those made by Lifton, on the basis of
> the works of Dadrian, Fein, Kuper, Hovannisian, et
> al. Though this point has been repeatedly stressed
> both in writing and verbally to Ankara, we have not
> yet seen as much as a single article by any scholar
> responding to *D A D R I A N*.... On the chance that
> you still wish to respond in writing to Lifton, I have
> drafted the following letter.

The Turkish ambassador sent the letter, ghost-written by
Lowry, to Professor Lifton. However, when Robert Lifton opened the
envelope from the Turkish Embassy he found a surprise. It contained not only the letter signed by the Turkish ambassador attempting to intimidate Lifton for referring to the Armenian Genocide, but

also inadvertently enclosed were Lowry's long memorandum to the Turkish ambassador and Lowry's ghost-written letter for the ambassador to send to Lifton.

And the plot thickened. By 1994, Lowry had been given the Ataturk Chair in Turkish Studies at Princeton, one of several new Turkish studies chairs funded by the Turkish government at major American universities–chairs that the Institute of Turkish Studies had been involved in setting up. Could a man who never held a full-time academic teaching job attain a chair at Princeton? A man who hadn't written one scholarly book published by a mainstream trade or university press?

In the meantime, Lifton and genocide scholars Roger Smith and Eric Markusen were at work on an article entitled "Professional Ethics and the Denial of the Armenian Genocide." The article appeared in the *Journal of Holocaust and Genocide Studies* in the spring of 1995, with facsimile reproductions of the Lowry–Turkish ambassador documents, and exposed and analyzed Turkey's denial, Lowry's role, and the ethical issues involved with Princeton and other universities that might take such funding from Turkey.

Evil as it is that the perpetrator government cannot come to terms with the Genocide, it is unthinkable that it could come to the United States and corrupt American institutions on a moral issue like this one. The story of the Turkish government's attack on Lifton's scholarship and Princeton's role as a colluder has given genocide and Holocaust denial a new and awful meaning. When I read "Professional Ethics and the Denial of the Armenian Genocide" that spring, it was as if the obscenity of eight decades of Turkish denial had come full circle. I thought that from this unveiling of corruption, something meaningful could come. I felt that Lifton's courage and moral vigilance was a civic statement about the dimensions of corrupt foreign power in American higher education. He had addressed the anguish that Armenians had lived with for decades, and it hit me where I had been living since the rally at Times Square.

In the weeks that followed I drafted a petition called "Taking a Stand Against the Turkish Government's Denial of the Armenian

Genocide and Scholarly Corruption in the Academy," a plain-lan-
guage document that outlined the Turkish government's denial campaign, including the Lowry episode, and called for an end to that
government's coercion and corruption, especially in American insti-
tutions. Within a month the petition had been signed by over a hundred distinguished writers and scholars, including Susan Sontag,
Norman Mailer, Arthur Miller, William Styron, Raul Hilberg, Yehuda
Bauer, David Brion Davis, David Riesman, and Deborah Lipstadt.
The *Chronicle of Higher Education* ran a prominent article, "Critics
Accuse Turkish Government of Manipulating Scholarship," and the
New York Times ran a half-page story, "Princeton Accused of
Fronting for the Turkish Government." The story had become public,
the process of news coverage had begun, and the petition had
become a document of conscience and witness in its own way. I was
happy, too, that Auntie Anna was calling with suggestions of potential petition signers.

THE OPEN WOUND

Wʜᴀᴛ ᴅᴏᴇꜱ ɪᴛ ᴍᴇᴀɴ ᴛᴏ ʙᴇ ᴀɴ Aʀᴍᴇɴɪᴀɴ Aᴍᴇʀɪᴄᴀɴ ᴏꜰ ᴛʜᴇ ᴅɪᴀꜱᴘᴏʀᴀ? A privileged American? The events of the past decade have added to the harsh century that this small, ancient culture has endured. In 1988, one of the most destructive earthquakes in recent history hit the northwest section of Armenia, killing over 50,000 people and leaving thousands maimed and homeless. The experts agreed that substandard building materials, the result of corruption during the Khrushchev and Brezhnev years, had been responsible for such a high casualty rate, including thousands of children killed in the collapse of their schools. On the heels of this disaster, the Nagorno–Karabagh crisis erupted. Armenians demanded the liberation of the mountainous region of Karabagh, part of historic Armenia, with a modern population that was close to ninety percent Armenian. In 1923, Ataturk had convinced the new Bolshevik government to give Karabagh to the Turkic republic of Azerbaijan, because he hoped to create a Turkic corridor from Turkey into central Asia.

By 1991, Armenia was an independent republic for the second time since 1375, and although free from Soviet rule, it was without

Soviet protection. As the Karabagh crisis grew into a war between the Karabagh Armenians and the Azeris, Turkey and Azerbaijan imposed a blockade that cut petroleum and natural gas lines to the new Republic of Armenia and blocked humanitarian and medical supplies. As the blockade made food and fuel scarce, Armenians sat in frozen apartments lit by candles or kerosene lamps, and ate rations of bread and tea if they were lucky. Hospitals became cold, dark places where surgeons operated with the aid of flashlights and often without anesthesia. Morgues were unable to keep up with the piles of the dead, mostly babies and the elderly, and coffins began to accumulate on the sidewalks of cities and towns. As wood became precious fuel, trees were cut everywhere, and Armenia began turning into a land of stumps.

I look on from America. I send money, clothes—whatever I can—to Armenia. I look vainly for news in the paper. I keep thinking about Turkey helping the Azeris blockade Armenia. Turkey refusing to allow planes with humanitarian aid to Armenia fly in Turkish airspace. I read in the paper that the former president of Turkey, Turgut Ozal, has made jokes to the press about dropping a bomb on Armenia. I see the connection between the Turkish government's genocide of 1915 and this ongoing assault against Armenians. I see how the cycle of hating the victims unfolds. I feel growing helplessness, frustration, rage, and I ask: Are Armenians forever to be stalked by the perpetrator government?

I return to the Genocide and its long aftermath. How is an Armenian to live with the predicament of Turkish denial? How is one to heal? Will genocide denial implode the victims, and the descendants of the victims? Can any victim consummate his relationship with the past without the perpetrator's confirmation of wrongdoing? Can there be forgiveness without apology, without some acts or gestures toward justice? The flurry of Armenian terrorist attacks on Turkish diplomats in the '70s and early '80s revealed what perpetrator denial sometimes can provoke. When the past remains unacknowledged, some people will vent their madness in wanton violence, and resolve nothing.

Scholars have noted that the Turkish denial of the Armenian Genocide is singular. No other nation in the modern age has engaged in such a massive cover-up campaign about such a crime. Richard Falk, Milbank Professor of International Law at Princeton, writes that the Turkish denial is "a major, proactive, deliberate government effort to use every possible instrument of persuasion at its disposal to keep the truth about the Armenian genocide from general acknowledgment, especially by elites in the United States and Western Europe."

Criminal behavior always is defined by the perpetrator's compulsion to "promote forgetting," writes Judith Herman in *Trauma and Recovery.* "Secrecy and silence are the perpetrator's first line of defense." If that fails, "the perpetrator attacks the credibility of his victim." And if he cannot silence his victim, "he tries to make sure that no one listens," by either blatantly denying or rationalizing his crime.

> After every atrocity one can expect to hear the same predictable apologies: it never happened; the victim lies; the victim exaggerates; the victim brought it upon herself; and in any case it is time to forget the past and move on. The more powerful the perpetrator, the greater is his prerogative to name and define reality, and the more completely his arguments prevail.

Bound up in the pathology of denial is the blaming of the victim. In denying the crime of genocide and blaming the victim, the perpetrator culture continues to create a false reality through which it attempts to rehabilitate itself. As Charrey and Lipstadt have written, the denial of genocide is the final stage of genocide; the first killing followed by a killing of the memory of the killing. The perpetrator's quest for impunity by denying continues to abuse the victim group by preventing the process of healing for the survivors and the inheritors of the survivors. In denying the crime, the perpetrator seeks to rob the victim of a moral order. Clearly, denying genocide paves the way for future genocide, for it suggests to the world that governments can commit mass murder with impunity. Hitler in 1939 was inspired by the collective absence of memory of the Armenian Genocide.

Commemoration is an essential process for the bereaved and for the inheritors of the legacy of genocide. It is a process of making meaning out of unthinkable horror and loss. Because the dead have not been literally or emotionally buried in the wake of genocide, commemoration is also a ritual of burying the dead—that first act of civilization. Because genocide seeks to negate all meaning, to unmake the world, the survivors and their children must find a way back to civilization. Commemoration, then, publicly legitimizes the victim culture's grief. The burden of bereavement can be alleviated if shared and witnessed by a larger community. Only then can redemption, hope, and community be achieved.

What then, if you are Armenian? True forgiveness can be granted only after the perpetrator has sought and earned it through confession, repentance, and restitution. If the perpetrator government stalks the victims in an effort to prevent the victims' acts of commemoration, there can be no full healing. The victim culture is held hostage in a wilderness of grief and rage, and is shut out of its moral place in history.

Denial strategy is built on a rhetoric of forceful distraction. Armenian Genocide deniers, like Holocaust deniers, claim that all documents are forgeries. They would have you believe that if the Turkish archives, opened in 1989, are thoroughly scoured eight decades after the event, some answers might be found that will surely vindicate them. The deniers want all third parties to ignore the abundance of official records of Turkey's wartime allies, the post-Genocide Turkish military tribunal, and of American diplomats, reports of missionaries, and survivors. But the victims and all moral witnesses ask scholars and academics to be responsible citizens and not be manipulated by the gimmick of "academic" debate. Academics must make moral and qualitative distinctions between genuine scholarly debate and the sinister tactics motivated by the political agenda of helping a perpetrator government absolve itself of responsibility.

The pseudo-scholarship of genocide denial is not, as Deborah Lipstadt notes, a free speech issue; "free speech does not guarantee the deniers the right to be treated as the other side of a

legitimate debate when there is no other side." Nor does free speech
guarantee privileged forums for disseminating morally reprehensi-
ble ideas; free speech should not be confused with the right to teach
at universities or publish books. The competition for professorships,
for space in magazines and newspapers, and for publishing books is
always stiff and exclusionary. The deniers are free to think whatever
they wish, but the rest of us must have the intelligence and courage
to deny the deniers social and cultural affirmation.

When a group of scholars and writers, including Deborah
Lipstadt, William Styron, Susan Sontag, David Reisman, and Yehuda
Bauer, wrote in the *Princeton Alumni Weekly* in April 1996 that
"Genocide denial is an insidious form of intellectual and moral
degradation and a violation of what a university represents," they
were asking Princeton to be an ethical citizen. When the European
Parliament rejected Turkey's request for admission to the European
Community, in part owing to its refusal to acknowledge the Armenian Genocide, it acted as a moral institution. When the House of
Representatives in May 1996 voted to cut aid to Turkey owing to
denial of the Armenian Genocide, it made an act of moral commitment. The United States government, as well as our country's press,
media, and educational institutions, can no longer allow themselves
to be coerced by the Turkish government. The time has come for the
closing of the wound. As one brave Turkish citizen, living in the U.S.,
wrote on the eighty-first anniversary of the Genocide, "History is
waiting for that honest Turkish leader who will acknowledge his
ancestors' biggest crime ever, who will apologize to the Armenian
people, and who will do his best to indemnify them, materially and
morally, in the eyes of the world."

· · · · ·

I come back to the case of my grandmother. She had been uncannily
sharp in her immediate response to the events of death, torture, and
genocide through which she had lived. In Aleppo, where she was
living in the death-filled refugee quarter, she sought some small
emblem of justice. She made a testimony that was both private and

public, spiritual as well as political. Making a claim to U.S. citizenship through her husband's naturalized American status, she began
the legal process of filing a suit against the Turkish government for
the losses endured: family members murdered, property stolen and
destroyed, a microcosm of the murder of a nation. It was an act of
courage and self-possession in a time of chaos and nightmare. She
entreated the court of law that she regarded as a hope for human liberty and justice. The court, she believed, had *meaning* in the West,
unlike the courts of Turkey, which had been places of oppression
and injustice for all Christians and other minorities.

Her claim translates her experience into something more
than merely personal; it casts her story into the international arena
of human rights. She did this in an age before there was a United
Nations, in a time before governments were required, by law, to protect the "inherent dignity of the human person," and were prohibited
from subjecting anyone to "torture or to cruel, inhuman or degrad-
ing treatment."

My grandmother made a modern statement before modernity caught up with what happened to her and to Armenia. In the
closing of her suit filed against the Turkish government in 1919, she
wrote: *I assert that the Turkish government is responsible for the
losses and injuries, because I am a human being and under the support of international law.* A twenty-nine-year-old mother of two
young girls. Orphaned, widowed, stripped of family, possessions,
homeland, nation, her voice was clear and strong and dignified.

I try to picture her in the dusty streets of Aleppo in 1915. Her
daughters yapping at her side like ordinary toddlers. I try to picture
her knocking on doors, standing in lines, walking around to find old
neighbors, friends, the priest Yessayan, so that she could compile the
facts and statements to make the affidavits for her lawsuit. She began
filing the suit in Aleppo and finished it in Newark, New Jersey,
immediately after her arrival. She carried the voice of her witness
from the old world to the new.

When it was finally filed at the law offices of Joseph J. Durna
in Newark, New Jersey, bearing the rubric United States Department
of State, what happened? Did my grandmother have high hopes that

some reparation might be made? Did she feel a moment of consummated rage? Did she walk down the streets of Newark with shopping bags and get on a bus?

The fact remains that there was no one then to listen. There was no social movement or political context in which she and other survivors could be heard. Her fate was the fate of Armenia in the first part of the century. I imagine that when she came to acknowledge that there would be no justice, no condolence, no reparation, that there would be nothing but silence, my grandmother must have been leaden with rage and unfathomable grief. But there in New Jersey a new life was already beginning, and so too a new silence. It was 1920, and she had given her testimony for another age to heed.

THE FACT OF A HOUSE

The ordering response to atrocities is to banish them from consciousness. This is the meaning of the word unspeakable.

— JUDITH HERMAN, *Trauma and Recovery*

As I come to think on the strange sweetness of our life in suburbia, I think of how easily we joined mainstream America. Perhaps our utter assimilation was best symbolized by our country club membership. While we seemed to be oblivious to most suburban badges of material status, and while my parents weren't immersed in suburban social life, we had joined this country club, my father said, so we could swim all summer a few blocks from home. Yet, it was a country club like most gentile country clubs and it did not permit Jews or blacks into its fold or, for that matter, onto its real estate. This fact was made clear to me as a kid when a club member who was hosting a ten-year-old boy from Harlem through the Fresh

Air Fund was turned away by the club management when she arrived one afternoon with the boy to take a swim. "It breaks my heart," my mother said. My father shook his head with disgust. But we didn't protest. We said nothing.

One evening when I was home from college, my father mentioned at dinner that Dr. Reyhadi, one of the most gifted surgeons at Englewood Hospital, had been denied admission to our country club. Dr. Reyhadi was fresh in my memory because he recently had removed a small cyst from my back. A conservative-looking surgeon in a dark suit, he was courteous, soft-spoken, dignified. My father said, "He's got magic hands, don't worry."

I sat at the dinner table, my self-righteous indignation welling up. "What's his background?" I asked, for Dr. Reyhadi had one of those complexions that was ambiguously dark and suggested an origin east of the Pyrenees.

"Persian," my father said.

"He's Christian?" I asked, because even though Jews never came up for nomination, I thought if he were Parsee or Muslim that perhaps the club's policy on those denominations hadn't been tested yet.

"Yup," my father said, as he gulped his *tahn.*

"No skeletons in his closet?"

My father was adamant about Dr. Reyhadi's good character; he had known him for fifteen years.

"Why, then?"

"There was a feeling," my father said, and then hesitated as if he were embarrassed, "that he was too dark."

"*Dark.*" I repeated it. "*Dark?* And we're not? We're octoroon to his quadroon?" I glanced over at my mother, whose skin was Irish-fair with freckles, then back at my father, who was olive-toned. "I can't believe we belong to that kind of place." I was shouting now. "We have to resign. And now."

My father pursed his lips as if to agree, and then he clicked his tongue, as if to say, let's not talk about it anymore, as if to say, what can we do? I asked my father to cancel my name from our family membership, and he said he would. And then everyone looked down at their plates and continued eating.

. . . . .

In the labyrinth of upper-middle-class suburbia, the Balakians always seemed to fit in. We were Christian, professional, apparently white enough. Law-abiding, hard-working, and, yes, American, as far back as 1903, when my grandfather Bedros Aroosian arrived in New Jersey. We weren't vacationing with the Rockefellers on Fisher's Island, but we were welcomed into the fold of upper-middle-class America, and our papers seemed to be in order. I've come to see our assimilation as inseparable from how seamlessly, *most of the time*, my family transformed Armenian culture into manageable codes and stable, civilizing rituals that dovetailed quite well with Protestant, middle-class virtues. Being Armenian informed a sense of ritual and decorum inside our house, on Sundays at church, or with extended family, and regardless of how those codes were connected to the Genocide, the fact remained that the brutalities of the political catastrophe that lay only a historical membrane from my parents' life had been rendered largely invisible.

Except for those infrequent and awkward moments when my father made some kind of gesture that was directed at the meaning of the Genocide, no one in my family considered the events of Armenia's recent nightmare a reality suitable for conversation or knowledge. The scalding facts of the Genocide had been buried, consigned to a deeper layer of consciousness, only to erupt in certain odd moments, as when my grandmother told me a story or a dream. What my parents did, often in unconscious and instinctual ways, was to make sure that my brother and sisters and I were Americans first. Free. Unhampered, unhaunted, unscarred by the unspeakable cruelties of Armenian history. Perhaps that was how it should have been. Perhaps that was a gift my parents gave us. A gift that enabled me to discover the past for myself from the secure vantage of my upper-middle-class American life, where in some sense, too, the small bit of Armenianness I understood gave me a feeling of having a slightly more substantial sense of identity than many of my peers.

If my parents were so capable of freeing us from the past, it seemed to me that they were able to do that because their parents had done their best to close the stone door on their own pasts. My grandmother Nafina Aroosian had witnessed mass murder and endured a death march into the desert with her two babies, the death of her first husband, and the disease-filled refugee quarter of Aleppo. At the age of twenty-five she lost her nation, her home, her family. And my grandfather Diran Balakian had tended the massacred and the dead in Adana, witnessing "one of the most savage bloodbaths of human history." My paternal grandparents had seen their friends disappear at the hands of Turkish executioners in April 1915. They had watched from Constantinople as Armenia was destroyed, and then became nationless refugees.

How did they all survive such catastrophe without some form of confession, release, therapeutic unburdening? Psychologists, psychiatrists, and those who study trauma agree about the importance of coming to terms with loss and grief in order to regain health; did each of my grandparents live close to disintegration, collapse, and breakdown? Outwardly, they carried out productive, humanly engaged lives. They enjoyed their work, raised families with gusto, and found life in America good.

In the case of my grandmother, Nafina, I'll never know of her inner life in the years following the Genocide. Perhaps no one did. After the Genocide, she was silent for more than two decades until the dam broke and she had a breakdown in the wake of the Japanese attack on Pearl Harbor in 1941. The U.S. entry into World War II triggered genocide flashbacks. But after the electroshock treatment worked, she returned to silence. Her friends and family concur that she was quite a pragmatic, level-headed woman, interested in people, popular culture, the stock market, the family business, always focused on the potential of the future. Was there a space behind the space from which she saw you, a space where no one was permitted? Did she ever go there? If my grandmother did not often go to that inner place of the deep wound, it may have been in good part because she lived in a state of numbness. Numbing, Robert Lifton suggests, is a process by which the self distances itself from traumatic experience. It is not repression, which excludes and denies the past, because in numbing one still has the potential for insight and some reclamation of the nightmarish past.

I've come to see my grandmother's numbed response to the Armenian Genocide as a necessary way of survival. What did it mean to be a survivor in an era before the Holocaust and the civil rights movement gave rise to a human rights movement in the United States? What was it like to be a survivor before there was a popular culture of psychology and therapy, whose goal was to help victims achieve a voice and the courage to affirm the moral significance of their wound and trauma? Without social and political movements there can be no public meaning. The word *genocide* didn't exist until Raphael Lemkin coined it in 1943 and the UN made it a crime against humanity in 1948. In the 1920s, '30s, and '40s, if you were Armenian, you had been torn from your home and land and plunked down in some country in which you landed. Most likely you came home to an Armenian family in which there was a common understanding of the unspeakable secret. But for the most part, you came home to silence. From there you started life over again.

In a cultural climate that did not recognize or articulate the moral significance of genocide, my grandmother was forced to turn inward, like those shell-shocked soldiers of World War I who came home, bit their tongues, or bit them off, and went on with their lives. In such a world, my grandmother must have felt that emotional economy was a necessity. She seems not to have dwelled on the past, but became, as the more fortunate survivors do, socially anchored. I think of my grandmother's fastidious kitchen, her vigorous walks to the store every day in rain or snow, her rituals of *choereg* baking, her devotion to the stock market and baseball.

Can one repress such a past, truly? The past did intrude, for trauma is perceived not as it occurs but in the aftermath, often after a long latency period. In my grandmother's case, my boyhood had intersected with her aftermath. I had been the listener, the audience for my grandmother's remembrance and mourning in the stories, dreams, flashbacks she told to me.

When I think of my parents and their second-generation silence, I think of a place of safety. I think of Teaneck, New Jersey. 1950. My parents buying their first house in a quiet suburb. Buying couches and chairs and beds and dressers and one Kashan—twelve by sixteen, with fine wool, intricate floral designs, and subtle rich colors. Then 1960: Crabtree Lane, Tenafly, New Jersey, with its new-age appliances and green lawns. I see those houses not as symbols of American material comfort or upward mobility, but as emblems of peace and refuge from a world of horror and death. It would have been impossible for me as a child to have understood that. It was impossible for my parents to tell me, and they may not have acknowledged it to themselves, but those houses stood against a backdrop of genocidal destruction, deportation, and exile. The Balakian house in Constantinople laced with kerosene and burned down by Turks. The Shekerlemedjian house in Diarbekir—from which my grandmother's family was taken and murdered—pillaged and taken over by Turks.

Safety and numbing were inseparable in my family's pathology. The United States was a free place, that is, a place where Armenians with their ancient culture in a suitcase were free from bodily harm. Free to worship, practice business, raise families, make art. Free to hide from a past that was—in those decades immediately following the Genocide—unutterable. My mother and father in different ways were amnesiac about the past, caught in some twilight of half acknowledgments. At some place in their minds my parents must have found the real issues of being Armenian too hard, too painful, too absurd. As my aunt Gladys had put it, "It was a pill too bitter to swallow, a pain too bad to feel." In affirming the American present, my parents had done their best to put an end to exile. In the suburbs of New Jersey, they found rootedness, home, belonging. Yet, the past was a shadow that cast its own darkness on us all. *The old country.* I realize now that it was an encoded phrase, not meant for children. Spoken by numbed Armenians of the silent generation. It meant lost world, a place left to smolder in its ashes.

But the old mind would not smolder in ashes. Once on safe ground, the old mind would reemerge with new vitality. The old mind would reclaim the facts and circumstances of its civilization of three millennia. And now Armenian Americans might even see the old world in ways that would be dynamic and ground-breaking, in the ways that Arshile Gorky, William Saroyan, Alan Hovaness, Marjorie Housepian Dobkin, Michael Arlen, Ruben Nakian, and many other artists in the diaspora already had—and in ways that would astonish their oppressors, who may have believed that after 1915 no one would hear from Armenians again.

How did my grandmother give credence to the old mind of the old world?

When I think of the stories she slipped to me in the odd moments of her daily routines, or the dreams, folktales, and half-repressed images I was privy to during the last six years of her life, it seems clear now that they were part of a truncated narrative about what she had gone through as a young woman. I was her companion, her captive audience, her beloved witness. Her bits of memory and encoded stories were tips of ice spiles from the frozen sea within, a sea that thawed a bit at the end of her life. In odd, isolated moments—moments that seemed to be out of time—I had been privy to some of her intense sensory images, to her telescopic memory, to genocide flashbacks. This was how she told me about her past. The Armenian invocation, *Djamangeen gar oo chagar*—there was and there wasn't—was like the intrusive past, which seemed to appear out of time, like lyric memory that had been activated. I'm not sure it was calculated to have a great effect on me. I think it was the only way she knew to speak to me about something she wanted to say, but couldn't say in any other language to a young boy, her eldest grandson.

ACKNOWLEDGMENTS

Support and helpful conversation came from a number of friends and colleagues along the way: John Naughton, Bruce Smith, Jack Wheatcroft, Marcie Hershman, Frederick Busch, Ida Giragossian, Wendy Ranan, Christopher Noel, Michael Arlen, and many members of my family. Aram Arkun at the Zorhab Information Center of the Diocese of the Armenian Church was an invaluable source of knowledge at crucial moments. Without Alan Brown, the Colgate Research Council, and the men and women at Colgate's printing shop, this book would have been more difficult to complete. Several stays at Yaddo were immensely important at crucial times. I am indebted to my agent, Carolyn Krupp, to my editor, Gail Winston, and to Christopher Tilghman and Robert Jay Lifton for their wise insights. My wife Helen's critical eye and affirmation were steadfast and sustaining. My debt to Marjorie Housepian Dobkin is profound.

SOURCES

Bryce, James, Viscount. *The Treatment of the Armenians in the Ottoman Empire, 1915–16*, London, Parliamentary Blue Book, 1916 (New York, NY: reprinted, JC&AL Fawcett, Inc. Publishers, 1990).

The Case of Soghomon Tehlirian. Translated by Vartkes Yeghiayan, Los Angeles: A.R.F. Varantian Gomideh, 1985.

Dadrian, Vahakn. *The History of The Armenian Genocide,* Providence, RI/Oxford, UK, Berghahn Books, 1995.

——. "The Armenian Genocide in Official Turkish Records," *Journal of Political and Military Sociology,* Vol. 22 No.1, Spring 1995, pp. 59–61.

——. "The Naim-Andonian Documents on the World War I Destruction of Ottoman Armenians: The Anatomy of a Genocide," *International Journal of Middle East Studies,* Cambridge University Press, Vol. 18, No. 4, November 1991, pp. 313–359.

Davis, Leslie A. *The Slaughterhouse Province: An American Diplomat's Report on the Armenian Genocide,* New Rochelle, NY: A.D. Caratzas, 1989.

Des Pres, Terrence. "On Governing Narratives: The Turkish-Armenian Case," in *Writing Into the World,* New York: Viking Press, 1992.

Morganthau, Henry. *Ambassador Morganthau's Story.* Garden City, NY: Doubleday, Page, 1919 (re-issue, Plandome, NY: New Age Publishers, 1975).

Sarafian, Ara, ed. *United States Official Documents on the Armenian Genocide,* Vols. 1&2, Watertown, MA: Armenian Review Press, 1993.

Smith, Roger, Eric Markusen, Robert Jay Lifton. "Professional Ethics and the Denial of the Armenian Genocide," in *Journal of Holocaust and Genocide Studies,* Vol. 9, No. 1, Spring 1995, pp. 1–22.

Siamanto. *Bloody News from My Friend* (poems), translated by Balakian and Yaghlian, with an introduction by Balakian, Detroit: Wayne State University Press, 1996.

Toynbee, Arnold J. *Armenian Atrocities: The Murder of a Nation,* London: Hodder & Stoughton, 1917 (re-issue, New York: Tankian Publishing, 1975).